The
Greatest Game
Ever Pitched

*Juan Marichal, Warren Spahn,
and the Pitching Duel of the Century*

Jim Kaplan

TRIUMPH
BOOKS

Library of Congress Cataloging-in-Publication Data

Kaplan, Jim.
    The greatest game ever pitched : Juan Marichal, Warren Spahn, and the pitching duel of the century / Jim Kaplan.
        p. cm.
    Includes bibliographical references and index.
    ISBN 978-1-60078-341-8
    1. Pitchers (Baseball)—United States—Biography. 2. Baseball players—United States—Biography. 3. Marichal, Juan. 4. Spahn, Warren, 1921-2003 I. Title.
    GV865.A1K354 2011
    796.357092'2—dc22
    [B]
                                    2010047675

This book is available in quantity at special discounts for your group or organization. For further information, contact:

Triumph Books
542 South Dearborn Street
Suite 750
Chicago, Illinois 60605
(312) 939-3330
Fax (312) 663-3557
www.triumphbooks.com

Printed in U.S.A.
ISBN: 978-1-60078-821-5
Design by Patricia Frey

To my father, Benjamin Kaplan (1911–2010),
whose life had many an extra inning

"Old ballplayers never die—they just finish games."

—Former Braves shortstop Johnny Logan

CONTENTS

FOREWORD

I was fortunate enough to witness the "Greatest Game Ever Pitched" in person. Juan Marichal and my father, Warren Spahn, hooked up in a pitching duel of epic proportions back on July 2, 1963. The 15,921 of us watching at San Francisco's Candlestick Park will treasure the memory forever and not just because of the pure competition. It was an era in which pride and professionalism trumped monetary motivation. We were able to follow baseball without the distractions of strikes, lockouts, mascots, endless announcements, and loud music. Attending a ballgame was an unexpurgated joy.

My father loved being matched against the best pitchers in the National League. When he was the winningest hurler of the 1950s with 202 victories, he was 6–3 against Robin Roberts, who finished second with 199. Even when Dad turned 40 and compiled just three strong late-career seasons in 1960–65, he went 5–5 against Don Drysdale, 3–3 against Bob Gibson, and 2–4 against Sandy Koufax. Among prominent pitchers, only Juan Marichal, who beat Dad six times and lost just once, dominated him. I am proud to say that through the magic of the Baseball Hall of Fame our families became great friends with a mutual respect that reflects the outstanding careers of these two men among men.

I had one last, poignant memory of my father on a ballfield. He returned to his longtime home park at Milwaukee's County Stadium on September 28, 2000, the day the final game was played there. Warren was reunited with Del Crandall, his catcher in the Greatest Game, for a parting first pitch. Seventy-nine and frail, Dad limped toward the mound, stopped after about 30 feet, and threw a two-hopper to Crandall. "It's like the curtain's falling," my father said, and he could have been speaking about his own life as well as the stadium's. "The party's over."

Thanks to this book we can celebrate again.

—Greg Spahn

ACKNOWLEDGMENTS

"Writing a book is a horrible, exhausting struggle, like a long bout of some painful illness," George Orwell complained in his essay, "Why I Write." Happily, I had many sources to doctor both my copy and my soul.

My thanks to Mark Kram of the *Philadelphia Daily News* for suggesting the project. Ira Berkow, John Bowman, Duke Goldman, and my wife, Brooks Robards, gave the book a careful reading. Mike Del Nagro did his routinely superb job of copy editing, and fact checker Bill Deane saved me much embarrassment with his thoroughness. Berkow, Bowman, Rich Westcott, Bob Rosen of the Elias Sports Bureau, and Gabriel Schechter, a research associate at the National Baseball Hall of Fame and Library, were great people to bounce ideas off—and invariably give me reality checks when my logic strayed.

HOF librarians Freddy Berowski and Tim Wiles went to the mat for me. When I journeyed on to Buffalo, Mike Billoni drove me to Warren Spahn's old neighborhood and high school, while brothers Paul and Lou Motyka helped me dig out some of the truths behind the Spahn legend. Reporter Budd Bailey led me to executive sports editor Steve Jones, who led me to David (Fernando) Valenzuela at the *Buffalo News* Library. Archivist Daniel DiLandro opened the Buffalo State College *Courier-Express* collection to me.

Saul Wisnia and Bob Brady supplied valuable background on the old Boston Braves, and Bob Buege convinced me that he's the historian par excellence of the old Milwaukee Braves. Lisa Tuite of the *Boston Globe* library completed my knowledge of the only franchise to win the World Series in three different cities. Garry Brown and Jim Gleason of the *Springfield* (MA) *Republican* had insightful material about Juan Marichal's minor league career. When I reached the City by the Bay, Bill van Niekerken gave me access to clips from the *Chronicle* library, and the San Francisco Public Library staff was helpful and courteous. Jim Moorehead and Mario Alioto of the Giants organization helped me understand the club's West Coast history.

Larry Harrison shared his Dominican Republic expertise from his experience there as a foreign service officer; Cathy Shapleigh and Sandy Shapleigh taught me about Dominican culture; Antonio Rodriguez Mansfield briefed me on current affairs in the island nation; Bob Ruck was among several authors especially helpful with Dominican baseball history; and Paul Laliberte translated Spanish-language documents. Bernardo Vega helped me reach *el gran lanzador*. After my wife and I arrived in Santo Domingo, Juan Marichal found time in his busy schedule to give us a two-hour interview; his world-class daughter, Yvette, answered innumerable follow-up questions by email. Morgan Fouch-Roseboro and Roger Guenveur Smith helped me understand how Marichal and onetime mortal enemy John Roseboro became friends.

Among many helpful members of the Society for American Baseball Research (SABR), Crash and Sheila Parr opened up Spahn's Oklahoma years while hosting my visit to Tulsa, Rockne Skybyrg sent me thick files on Spahn and Marichal, and Neal Mackertich gave me a revealing glimpse of Spahn at the Hall. Howard Nenner told me a useful baseball joke, injecting levity into a subject that lends itself as much to humor as to pontification.

Lastly, some worthies without whom the book would have been nothing but an idea: my agent Karen Johnson; Tom Bast, Michael Emmerich, Adam Motin, and Karen O'Brien of Triumph Books; and Spahn's son, Greg, a veritable fount of enlightenment.

Appropriately for a baseball book, this was a team effort.

INTRODUCTION

It would have been enough just to write about the game. For years friends like Mark Kram of the *Philadelphia Daily News* and the late Ron Fimrite of *Sports Illustrated* told me rapturous stories about the 16-inning duel in 1963 between pitchers Juan Marichal and Warren Spahn. After writing about the contest in *The National Pastime*, an annual publication of the Society for American Baseball Research (SABR), I looked around for other assignments.

But I couldn't stop thinking about the game, and most of all, its protagonists. Spahn and Marichal are marvelous, downright mythic fixtures in baseball history. Visualized in action, they resemble nothing so much as bookends, Spahn kicking high with his right foot, Marichal with his left. They are Hall of Famers but underrated immortals, if you can get your mind around the idea. Their importance extends beyond baseball. A veteran of the Battle of the Bulge and the fight over the Bridge at Remagen, Spahn was one of the most decorated ballplayers in World War II. Everyone in the Dominican Republic knows about Marichal, the first of their countrymen enshrined in Cooperstown, a confidant of Dominican presidents, a philanthropist, a national symbol of pride. In *The Brief Wondrous Life of Oscar Wao* (2007), a Pulitzer Prize–winning novel, Junot Díaz wrote, "Marichal is only the beginning, he said, of a *reconquista* [reconquest]." Díaz doesn't need to introduce Marichal, or even use his first name. In the D.R., everyone knows.

So a book took shape consisting of a dual biography, with the magical game that links these greats woven through the text like a river flowing through time. I hope you enjoy reading *The Greatest Game Ever Pitched* as much as I've relished producing it. The subjects inspired me to borrow numerous

Shakespearean references. As the Bard himself wrote—not about Spahn and Marichal and their stroll through history, to be sure, but eminently applicable to the two remarkable pitchers:

> *How shall I live and work*
> *To match thy goodness?*
> ("King Lear," Act IV, Scene VII, lines 1-2)

Jim Kaplan
Oak Bluffs, Massachusetts
September 27, 2010

~ Chapter 1 ~

HIGH-KICKING
TO GLORY

"A high kick is often the pitcher's individual solution to a universal problem of throwing: how to synchronize the top and bottom halves of the body. Typically, the bottom half moves a little faster, and some pitchers must find a way to slow it down and reset the timing of the delivery. In the history of pitching, two men—the Braves' Warren Spahn and Juan Marichal of the Giants—made the kick into a Hall of Fame art form."

—Kevin Kerrane, *The Hurlers*

For four hours, 10 minutes, and 16 innings, all through the night of July 2, 1963, and into July 3, Warren Spahn and Juan Marichal slugged it out like a veteran boxer and a young contender. Spahn, 42, played an old Archie Moore in flannels, defending his turf with wits, tenacity, and memory. Marichal (pronounced MAHR-ee-chal), 25, embodied a young Muhammad Ali: strong, quick, and confident. By the time the game ended after midnight with a single run, they had completed an epic battle of the ages. It is arguably the best-pitched game in baseball history.

The stars and their stars were perfectly aligned for such a classic duel. Entering the season, the strike zone had been expanded from "top of the knees to the armpits" to "bottom of the knees to top of the shoulder," a rules change that would account for 1,019 fewer hits by National League batters than in 1962. NL home runs were down 16 percent, runs 15 percent (from

1

4.5 per game to 3.9), and batting averages 16 points. As Bill James wrote in his *Historical Baseball Abstract*, "The second dead-ball era had begun."

When the Braves' Spahn and the Giants' Marichal faced off in San Francisco's Candlestick Park, the future Hall of Fame pitchers stood at the peak of their powers. Normally a slow starter, Spahn, 11–3 with a 3.12 ERA and five straight wins, had already set a left-hander's record with his career 328th victory. He had just beaten the Giants and shut out the Dodgers, and he hadn't allowed a walk in his previous 18⅓ innings. Moreover, he was facing precisely the same eight position players he had no-hit in 1961. Marichal, who had won 13 games in his first full season and 18 the following year, held out until March 13, reporting six pounds overweight. But he ran off the excess weight and was already 12–3 with a 2.38 ERA, coming into this game off eight straight wins. A bargain at the reported $24,000 he eventually signed for that year, Marichal had no-hit Houston 1–0 in a tidy one hour and 41 minutes just 17 days earlier, getting 16 infield outs and throwing only 89 pitches despite two walks.

"The idea of Spahn pitching always riveted you anyway," the late Ron Fimrite, then a *San Francisco Chronicle* news-side reporter in the stands as a paying spectator and later a *Sports Illustrated* great, told the *Chronicle*'s Dave Bush. "And the age-youth thing just added to it."

Marichal and Spahn could not have asked for a better locale. Candlestick Park, now used for football, was a pitcher's paradise. Named after San Francisco Bay's Candlestick Point, which itself was named after a nearly extinct wader called the candlestick bird as well as the nearby jagged rocks and trees that resembled candlesticks, the Stick was invariably chilly because the wind came off the waters of San Francisco Bay. Balls don't carry as far in cold weather as they do when it's humid. Nor do hitters fare as well when their hands are cold.

The place could be a mess, where trucks with rubber plows pushed water off the parking lot. After downtown merchants opposed a park in their area, the Giants had innocently settled on the location at Candlestick Point. There was no question the city had to build a new field because Seals Stadium, where the Giants played in 1958–59, seated about 23,500 customers, and Giants owner Horace Stoneham wanted a place twice as big. The club could have expanded Seals to 33,000 seats with a second deck, but the uncompromising Stoneham felt the parking was inadequate.

When the Giants' late general manager, Chub Feeney, visited the Candlestick construction site one morning, he remarked to a worker, "This is going to be ideal." The worker replied, "The wind doesn't come up until around 1:00 in the afternoon."[1] Gulp.

Because it was constructed entirely of reinforced concrete, Candlestick opened on April 12, 1960, as the first modern baseball stadium. Special guest Richard Nixon called it "the finest ballpark in America," and fans filled almost every one of the 42,500 curved, comfortable seats. The $850,000 lighting system was without peer. Unfortunately, the ballyhooed radiant heating system didn't function properly, and the Giants had to pay off lawyer Melvin Belli, who sued them because his six-seat, $1,600 box was freezing cold. Stu Miller wasn't blown off the mound, as later reported, during the first 1961 All-Star Game, but he did get knocked off-balance by a gust and was charged with a balk. Two years later, wind blew the batting cage 60 feet to the pitcher's mound.

After averaging 16,968 and 18,729 fans in their two seasons at Seals, the Giants averaged 23,623 fans in their first year at Candlestick, a figure they wouldn't reach again until 1987. Meanwhile, the Stick became a national joke. "The only difference between Candlestick and San Quentin is that at Candlestick they let you go home at night," outfielder Jim Wohlford said. Jim Murray, the late *Los Angeles Times* wisecracker, wrote, "Candlestick Park is kind of perfect for San Francisco—foggy[2], wind wracked, an outcast from baseball society. Only a place that calls an earthquake a fire could call Candlestick a ballpark."

In perhaps the most devastating critique of the place, former pitcher Jim Brosnan wrote in *Pennant Race*: "Candlestick Park is the gross error in the history of major league baseball. Designed at a corner table in Lefty O'Doul's, a Frisco saloon, by two politicians and an itinerant ditch digger, the ballpark slants toward the bay—in fact, it *slides* toward the bay and before long will be under water, which is the best place for it."

When Mark Twain wrote, "The coldest winter I ever spent was a summer in San Francisco," he could have been referring to Candlestick Point. What visiting team would want to play at Candlestick, where the visiting dugout was down the third-base line and the clubhouse out in right field? Technically, Candlestick gave an advantage to Giants fielders who knew the wind currents— Willie Mays learned that the best way to gauge a fly was to initially stand still, count to three and observe which way the ball was being blown—as long as they could bear 81 games a year there. "How do you catch a ball in that wind," Roberto Clemente, the nonpareil defensive right fielder, said, "unless you're

Willie Mays?" For their part, most pitchers held their tongues and counted their blessings. The irrepressible Marichal couldn't. "I like the cool weather here," he said at one point. "I wouldn't trade San Francisco's weather for any in the world."

By Candlestick standards, July 2, 1963, was by no means finger-numbingly cold. Nonetheless, it was cool with the usual west-to-east wind rippling across from left to right field that presented a major obstacle for right-handed batters—Mays said it cost him 150 homers—and usually helped lefties but sometimes sent shots into foul territory. Radio broadcaster Lon Simmons remembered the following conversation between Mays and pitcher Don Newcombe, who was playing for the Reds late in his career:

Newcombe: "I understand balls don't go out [of the park] to left field."
Mays: "Not usually."

The Say Hey Kid had to adopt an inside-out swing for Candlestick, figuring that if he went to center, the ball would be blown to right-center and might carry out. But there was no consistent pattern with the wind. Ken Aspromonte, a Braves reserve player in 1962, said the wind created another obstacle for hitters by swirling around the plate. All in all, July 2 was a pitcher's night at a pitcher's park. Not that Spahn and Marichal, both off-season golfers, faced a chip shot of opposition. Indeed, rarely if ever have two Hall of Famers matched up for such an extended game, with each facing a lineup of fellow Cooperstownians and other fine players. In addition to Spahn and Marichal, Mays, Willie McCovey, and Orlando Cepeda of the Giants and Hank Aaron and Eddie Mathews of the Braves were headed for induction. (A young Giants pitcher named Gaylord Perry was also bound for the Hall.) Other substantial hitters included left fielder Lee Maye (who had been sizzling all June) of the Braves, plus left fielder/third baseman Harvey Kuenn, and right fielder Felipe Alou of the Giants. For that matter, Spahn, who would lead all National League pitchers with 35 career homers, and Marichal, who would bat .522 with men in scoring position three years later, wielded potentially mean bats themselves.

San Francisco reliever Don Larsen, who knew a thing or two about greatness, called the 1962 Giants as good a team as he'd ever seen. It was still largely intact a year later, another power-packed lineup that would again lead the league in homers, this time by a whopping 58 more than second-place

Milwaukee. At game time the 44–34 Giants were just 1½ games behind league-leading St. Louis. Heading for a sixth-place finish, the 38–38 Braves, 6½ back, were starting to shed players from the 1956–59 teams that first contended to the season's last weekend, then won a World Series, then won a pennant, and finally lost a pennant playoff, respectively. On June 15, they had traded Lou[3] Burdette, MVP of the 1957 Series. But they still had, among others, Aaron and Mathews. In 1963, Aaron would narrowly miss winning the Triple Crown.

The 15,921 brave souls in attendance that cool evening in July had to be rubbing their hands together—not just to stay warm but to anticipate what the worthies on the mound had to offer. Marichal and Spahn, Juan and Warren, Manito and Meatnose, they would never be mistaken for twins. An American who had fought in the Battle of the Bulge and was a remnant of baseball's all-white past (though no racist himself), the left-handed Spahn had a receding hairline and a conspicuous nose that accentuated his long face and earned him several nicknames, Hooks being the most, well, prominent. A Dominican with *café-au-lait* skin, a full head of hair, and a round face with a proportionate nose, the right-handed Marichal had cheeks so full that teammate Eddie Bressoud dubbed him Popeye. He also was called Laughing Boy and, because of his light blue and cream-colored outfits, the Dominican Dandy—nicknames that forecast a more emotive, multinational pastime.

Yet they had much in common. They were an inch or two taller than most pitchers of their time, and two or three inches smaller than today's dominant moundsmen: Spahn at 6' and 172 pounds, Marichal at 6' and 180 pounds. Because both had near-death experiences—Spahn while fighting in World War II, Marichal while enduring a seven-day coma as a youngster—both viewed every day of life as a gift. Each man exhibited a smile that people compared to a clown's because the ends of their mouths curled upward in merriment. Neither had overpowering speed—Marichal's 5.91 strikeouts per nine innings were only 240th best in baseball history, while Spahn's 4.43 were actually below the league average of 4.68—but both had excellent control.[4] Each was the winningest pitcher in a decade—Spahn won 202 in the fifties, and Marichal would win 191 in the sixties. Both used signature high-kicking deliveries that made their release points hard to pick up, threw an impressive variety of pitches, and extended their careers by mastering the screwball. They were constantly linked. "Marichal was the complete pitcher, a right-handed Spahn with his high-kicking delivery," Fred Stein and Nick Peters wrote in *Giants Diary: A*

Century of Giants Baseball in New York and San Francisco. No wonder they both earned statues outside their teams' current parks showing them high-kicking.

The differences in their styles were subtle but significant. Spahn's son Greg, a real-estate executive who was born the day before the 1948 World Series, hit .524 as a high school senior, but had to give up baseball when shoulder problems sidelined him at the University of Oklahoma, remembered eloquent word pictures of his father's skills. As Braves catcher Del Crandall once explained to Greg, the older Spahn showed the batter three things: the sole of his right shoe, the back of his glove, and finally the ball. Spahn leaned forward in an almost courtly bow to the hitters, arms high behind him, then rocked back, his right leg raised above his head in what *The Sporting News*' Dave Kindred called a five-minutes-to-six position, followed by an overhand delivery that was as smooth and regular as a dipping oil-field pumping jack back home in Oklahoma. His pitching hand finished the delivery almost touching the ground. Since every pitch was thrown with the same motion, the batter had no idea what to expect. "Sometimes the motion deceived me, and I was the catcher," Crandall told Greg Spahn.

Trained as a first baseman before he pitched, Spahn followed through in perfect fielding position. And there was something else. Because of an old separated shoulder that two opponents landed on when he was an end on his high school football team, Spahn couldn't raise his right hand higher than his shoulder. As he moved toward the plate, his glove rose slowly then descended quickly through the hitter's line of vision. "People kept telling me that the motion of the glove really bothered hitters," Spahn told Kindred. "So I kept doing it. Whatever bothered hitters, I was for."

"He was a machine," Giants catcher Ed Bailey said. In fact, when the Dodgers installed a steel-armed pitching machine that threw overhand strikes during 1949 spring training, they called it the Warren Spahn. By contrast, Marichal was a one-man *merengue* band. He'd throw an overhand fastball (pound the *tambora* drum), a sidearm curve (scrape the *guayano*), and a three-quarters slider (saxes go wild), while sometimes throwing a change-up/curve and always mixing speeds. Most pitchers wore toeplates on their trailing shoe because it scraped against the dirt. Marichal didn't need one because his trailing foot followed his lead foot well off the mound. *The New Yorker*'s Roger Angell wrote that Marichal threw "like some enormous and dangerous farm implement." As

Kevin Kerrane described in *The Hurlers*, Marichal kicked higher and whirled to the side more than Spahn, showing the No. 27 on the back of his uniform and leaving the batters "to locate a ball that seemed to come from somewhere between Marichal's left knee and the sky." He extended his right arm fully, and his follow-through propelled him almost helter-skelter toward the first-base line. This was the only flaw in his delivery because it left him out of position to field and in jeopardy from line drives.

No one was sure what they'd seen. Dick Allen thought Marichal threw five different pitches, Joe Torre said seven, Billy Williams 12, and Lou Brock 16. At his Hall of Fame induction, Marichal said he had five pitches: "Fastball, slider, curve, screwball, and change-up." He paused and added, "Overhand, sidearm, underhand, three-quarter speed, full speed." If every speed and angle were used for every pitch, the total would be 25![5]

"People were intrigued by his motion, but he was as much ball [movement] as motion," Bailey said. "Juan was not a pattern-type pitcher. He was unorthodox." So unorthodox that he wanted his catchers moving their mitts around even after he began his windup. That kind of movement would upset many a pitcher. In Marichal's case, it upset many a hitter.

There was no predictable pattern to his pitches. According to Orlando Cepeda, Marichal would deliberately fall behind on the count against top hitters, convincing them they could expect a fastball. In one celebrated case, the Cardinals' Curt Flood was facing Marichal in the ninth with the tying run on base and a 3–2 count. The catcher called for an overhand fastball, the kind of safe pitch normally thrown in such instances. Marichal shook him off and gambled on a sidearm, crossfire curve. A miss would have put the winning run on base. The pitch flicked over the outside corner for strike three.

Marichal felt preparation was the key to his success. He would do some running, throwing, stretching, and luxuriating in hot-water baths and showers in the days between starts, covering his shoulder and elbow with a towel while absorbing the heat. He never had a sore arm. Before leaving his $40,000 San Francisco home, his tropical plants in the greenhouse, and his music maybe 2½ hours before game time and driving his Pontiac at a stately pace for about six minutes to Candlestick Park, Marichal placed the medal of San Rafael and the cross of Altagracia around his neck and a picture of Blessed Martin the Peacemaker in his pocket. Morning and night, Juan read three passages from the Book of Psalms, one of which, the 121ˢᵗ, seems especially appropriate for a pitcher:

I will lift up mine eyes unto the hills, from whence cometh thy help.
My help cometh from the Lord, which made heaven and earth.
He will not suffer thy foot to be moved; he that keepeth Israel shall neither slumber nor sleep.
The Lord is thy keeper; the Lord is thy shade upon thy right hand.
The sun shall not smite thee by day, nor the moon by night.
The Lord shall preserve thee from all evil; he shall preserve thy soul.
The Lord shall preserve thy going out and coming in from this time forth, and even for evermore.

His feet, hands, and eyes blessed, Marichal took his warm-up pitches from the bullpen mound rather than on the sideline because it was closer in height to the one on the diamond. In competition, he toed the inside of the rubber closest to first base to improve the angle for pitching away from left-handed hitters and to give his slider more room to break away from right-handers. "When we had a meeting before the game, it was only Mays, Bailey, and myself," Marichal said. "When Willie told you to pitch a guy one way, and you threw a different pitch and the guy pulled it, Willie would let you know. Having Willie behind me made my position easier." Marichal had no way of knowing how prophetic those words would be on July 2, 1963.

Spahn prepared for the game the way no other pitcher did. For one thing, he watched the opposing team's batting practice like a ranger with night-vision goggles. "It's important to know hitters as well as yourself. I used to make a study of it," Spahn said. "A hitter will show you what he can't hit [by what he does hit]. A lot of Polish hitters hit high fastballs. Lou Novikoff—they called him the Mad Russian—hit one that I threw over his head between my legs! Don't pitch these guys high!"

Even if you cringe at his ethnic generalizations, verboten today but common in his time, Spahn had a mental book on hitters almost as sophisticated as today's hitting charts. It included factors like home and away, day and night, big parks and small, headwinds, crosswinds, and tailwinds, with the bases loaded or empty, with a lead or trailing. He also had, shall we say, a relaxed mien on game

The Babe Was Some Pitcher

In another extra-inning classic, Babe Ruth of the Red Sox and Sherry Smith of the Brooklyn Robins hooked up for 14 innings at Braves Field in Game 2 of the 1916 World Series. Having gone 18–8 and 23–12 in his first two full seasons, Ruth was quickly establishing himself as the best left-hander in baseball. He would face Walter Johnson 10 times and go 6–2 against him, with two no-decisions. Smith had gone 14–8 and 14–10 in his first two full seasons but would finish his career well short of immortality at 114–118. Much depended on him when the 1916 game began on October 9 because Ernie Shore had defeated the Robins' Rube Marquard 6–5 two days earlier.

Brooklyn scored in the first when Hy Myers's two-out drive to right-center fell safely, both right fielder Harry Hooper and center fielder Tilly Walker fell down chasing it, and Myers scampered home for an inside-the-park homer. Boston tied the score in the third on Everett Scott's triple and Ruth's RBI ground out. The Babe, who went 0-for-5, had homered just three times in 1916.

Afterward, goose eggs spread across the scoreboard, and defensive wizardry helped send the game into extra innings. Smith struck out Ruth with a man on third to end the fifth. Myers robbed Hooper of a hit with a shoestring, somersaulting catch in the sixth and threw out Hal Janvrin at home in the ninth. In the 10th, the Red Sox got Everett Scott to second on a single and a sacrifice, but he was thrown out rounding third on Hooper's infield single when third baseman Mike Mowrey threw to shortstop Ivy Olson. In the 13th, Boston left fielder Duffy Lewis made a great running two-out catch to keep Mowrey from scoring. Boston catcher Pinch Thomas nabbed two runners trying to steal, Brooklyn catcher Otto Miller picked a runner off first, Ruth contributed two putouts and four assists, and Scott added one putout and eight assists.

Finally, in the home 14th, Boston's Dick Hoblitzel worked Smith for Hoblitzel's fourth walk, and Duffy Lewis sacrificed him to second. Mike McNally was sent in to run for Hoblitzel. In his World Series debut, McNally scored the game-winning run on a timely single over Mowrey's head by pinch hitter Del Gainer. Under a headline that read, "Greatest Game Ever Staged in Any World's Series," the *Bismarck (North Dakota) Daily Tribune* reported that "a pinch hitter and a pinch runner won for Boston just as twilight threw its mantle of semi-darkness over the field."

Boston 2, Brooklyn 1. There was no relief from the tension, and no relievers, either. Ruth allowed six hits and three walks while fanning four. Smith yielded seven hits and six walks with two strikeouts. In a thriller that took only 2:32, 47,373 fans got enough entertainment for two postseason games. Authors Richard M. Cohen and David S. Neft called it "the most tenacious pitching duel in Series history."

The Red Sox went on to win the Fall Classic four games to one.

day. Pitching turn or not, he invariably whacked a teammate upside the head or stuffed bubblegum in someone's glove or placed a live mouse in his pocket or otherwise made mischief. "If you took everything in life too seriously," he told biographer Al Silverman, "you'd go nuts. When I'm kidding, I'm actually relaxing. It's my way of coping with pressure."

Spahn would pick on anyone anytime. When Bobby Thomson was lying on the trainer's table after breaking an ankle in 1954, Spahn ragged him so relentlessly that Thomson threw him in a whirlpool. The next day Spahn returned, resumed the patter, and threw *himself* in the whirlpool.

Spahn's warm-ups, this day as every day, seemed perfunctory. "He used to drive me crazy," Spahn's son, Greg, said. "He'd throw five pitches on the sideline, then talk to someone, throw another five and then talk."

There was method to Spahn's apparent madness. The joking kept him loose. The pitches had purpose. "He'd throw five fastballs, five screwballs, five curves, five change-ups," Greg continued, "and see what was working."

"When he got to the mound, he threw eight pitches as hard as he'd throw all day," said Bailey, who caught Marichal in '63 and Spahn in '64. "Then he'd nibble around the corners and change speeds."

"If he had trouble, it was usually in the first or second inning," Greg Spahn said. "Then he'd figure out what to do."

As the national anthem was played before the scheduled 8:20 PM start of that fateful 1963 duel, Spahn, as he did before every one of his starts, said a wordless prayer of thanks that he lived in the United States and had the ability to compete in Major League Baseball.

As it happens, the game that was about to be played this July evening was on the 30th anniversary of another great performance by a Giants pitcher—Carl Hubbell. On July 2, 1933, Hubbell outpitched two Cardinals, striking out 12 and walking none to win a complete game in 18 innings, 1–0. Thirty years later and now the Giants' director of minor league scouting, Hubbell was watching when Marichal went to the mound. In the stands, someone with a suspicion of more history approaching must have asked of the age-and-youth pair, as the fictionalized Butch Cassidy would a few years later, "Who *are* those guys?"

~ Chapter 2 ~

SEARCHING FOR JUAN IN COOPERSTOWN

"No somos estadounidenses, somos differentes. Talvez ésa es la razón por que podemos sobrevivir."

"We are not Americans, we are different. Maybe that is why we are able to survive."

—Felipe Alou, June 1993, as quoted in the Hall of Fame's *¡Viva Baseball!* exhibit that opened in 2009

Before we get to the legendary game, let's introduce Juan Marichal, who springs from a long tradition of superb baseball players from the Dominican Republic. I finally met him at a grand occasion celebrating that very tradition.

The locale was the National Baseball Hall of Fame in Cooperstown, New York, a place that epitomizes the word "shrine." In its self-imposed solemnity, no food, drink, or gum are allowed within the premises except on special occasions. Fans are forbidden from asking for autographs from visiting immortals. Scholars in the Giamatti Research Center don white gloves to comb through aged documents. And even the yappiest of children grow calm and respectful upon entering the marble-columned plaque gallery. No sporting temple in this country commands the same exalted status as Cooperstown. Say "Hall of Fame" in Tierra del Fuego, and any other vagrant American should know you mean baseball.

When Marichal and I converged in Cooperstown on May 23, 2009, we arrived for the unveiling of ¡Viva Baseball!, a bi-lingual, multimedia Latin American exhibit. Despite some spelling mistakes (I've edited the Alou quote for accuracy) and lurches into political correctness, the display and related material in the Hall properly honor Hispanic stars and baseball in the Spanish-speaking countries of the Caribbean Basin without minimizing the obstacles they faced in language, culture, stereotyping, racism, and exploitation. Among the exhibits is a 1964 Sport article titled "Latin American Players Need a Bill of Rights" by the distinguished former player and manager Felipe Alou, who himself deserves a plaque. Latinos have come so far since the article that they now dominate the major leagues, not only in ever-increasing numbers but also in excellence. In 2010, 27 percent of the players on Opening Day rosters were Latinos. The best everyday player was the Cardinals' Albert Pujols (Dominican Republic). The most productive pitcher by the 2010 All-Star Game was the Rockies' Ubaldo Jiménez (Dominican Republic).

What accounts for Latino excellence? As Alou illustrates in the quotation at the beginning of the chapter, it's in part because of their differences. "They knew that they had to try harder," Milton Jamail, Coordinator of Latin American Cultural and Education Programs for the Tampa Bay Rays, told me at the Hall. "They were aware that people would treat them differently because they were black and foreign. As a result, they had to overachieve. They really get in the game, they're excited, and everything else falls by the wayside."

An even bigger reason might be that some Latino players who have had little education realize that baseball offers them a real opportunity for success.

Sooner or later, the conversation always shifts to the prime source of Latino players, the Dominican Republic. Consider the picture caption by José Luis Villegas in a splendid exhibit of photographs elsewhere in the Hall:

"For a century, the Dominican Republic has lived in the shadow of the United States, endured two occupations by U.S. Marines, and seen its prized sugar and fruit resources co-opted by American conglomerates. Destitute even by Latin American standards, the people of the Dominican Republic got one thing in return—the American pastime of baseball."

The first Marines who intervened in 1916–24 built roads, created a national guard, and funded health care and education while admittedly lording over the population; the sugar resources were largely stolen by dictator Rafael Trujillo;

the U.S. owned only one sugar conglomerate when it invaded the country in 1965; and the Dominican Republic was more representative of Latin America than destitute (see Haiti). But we can all agree that baseball was a major gift well exploited.

Cuba got baseball first. In 1864, two Havana-bred students, Ernesto and Nemesio Guilló, brought bats and balls home from Alabama's Springhill College and introduced baseball to their country.

In 1866, U.S. sailors and Cuban longshoremen played perhaps the first game in Cuba with locals, most of them dockworkers. Eight years later *El Club Habana* beat *Matanzas* 51–9 in the inaugural contest between Cuban teams. In 1871, Estéban Bellán became the first Hispanic to compete professionally in the U.S. in Troy, New York. He played several seasons for the Troy Haymakers and New York Mutuals. Three years later, the first Cuban ballpark opened in Matanzas. In 1878, Cuba started league play: Habana vs. Matanzas.

The driving force behind the *Liga de Béisbol Profesional* was Emilio Sabourín, who ended his days in a Spanish prison after advocating for Cuban independence. Escaping the Ten Years War (1868–78), Cubans took the game with them to the Dominican Republic, where they earned themselves the nickname "apostles of baseball." Two Cuban ironworkers, the brothers Ignacio and Ubaldo Alomá, moved to Santo Domingo and formed the first two Dominican clubs, which were composed of Cuban immigrants, some Dominicans and Americans, and even a German restaurateur. In the interior, another Cuban, Dr. Samuel Mendoza y Ponce de León, formed two clubs in 1893 called the *Azules* (Blues) and *Rojas* (Reds). Santo Domingo's *Licey*, later the first of six professional teams, began play in 1907, and its archrival, *Escogido*, took root in 1921. Spirited play between Dominicans and American sailors and Marines during the 1916–24 occupation provided the natives with a national consciousness to go with mixed feelings about the occupiers. A win in a close game with the Marines three months after the occupation began constituted repudiation of *Yanqui* rule. Estéban (Tetelo) Vargas y Marcano, who won a batting title when he was almost 50, was the best Dominican player in the early years, before they swamped the major leagues. Eventually, the Dominicans became the No. 1 source of Spanish-speaking major leaguers. There are several reasons for this phenomenon.

After a plane carrying the national champion *Caballeros* from Santiago crashed in the *Rio Verde*, a substitute Dominican team won the 1948 *Mundial* (world amateur) tournament, fueling an emotional rebirth of the sport that has never subsided.

In 1962, Fidel Castro forbade Cubans from playing professionally, and scouts eventually concentrated most of their efforts in the Dominican Republic.

The country's *Dirección General de Deportes*, a government body modeled after the Cuban prototype, organized local and national competitions often in concert with the armed forces and local companies.

Sugarcane mill towns in the republic's southeast and banana companies in the northwest cultivated teams that produced professionals. The six-month *tiempo muerto*, or dead season, in which cane needed little work, gave opportunities for play to idle men. Immigrants from the British West Indies arrived in the mills and cane fields when their own industries failed, forsaking cricket to take up baseball. That's why the country produces major leaguers with names like Carty, Offerman, Duncan, and Bell. Players especially congregated in the sugarcane center, San Pedro de Macorís, a coastal city of about 300,000 that has recently produced the most major leaguers in the world.

Baseball fit the national psyche. "Baseball is a part of the life of the Dominican village," Dr. Tirso Valdéz wrote in his *Notas Acerca del Beisbol*. "Through it the village experiences moments of happiness, when its team realizes its desires and wins, or passing moments of dejection, if a defeat becomes a rout…but above all, the village experiences the hope that always prevails in baseball of coming from behind or winning the next game."

Because the Spanish had been brutal governors before they were ejected in 1821 (they reoccupied the country in 1861–65, then left for good), Spanish sports like *jai alai* and *pelota basca* were never popular. Nor did *fútbol* (soccer) have a chance, possibly because the hated Haitians played it in the D.R. during their occupation of 1822–44. Since the native Taíno Indians had been decimated by then, virtually every ballplayer would be white, mulatto, or a descendant of black African slaves who first arrived in 1503.

Baseball spread elsewhere in the Spanish-speaking Caribbean Basin, including Venezuela, Puerto Rico, Colombia, Panama, Mexico, and Nicaragua in particular. The U.S. consul started a team in Managua, Nicaragua. Marines, oil and sugar companies, rum distilleries, and tobacco manufacturers used workplace teams to keep their employees occupied and friendly. In a region noted for political instability, baseball provided opportunities for individual skill, group identity, and national pride.

Starting with Colombia's Luis "Jud" Castro, who joined the Philadelphia Athletics in 1902, Latinos made their presence felt in modern American baseball. In 1911, Cincinnati manager Clark Griffith signed Cuban outfielder Armando Marsans and infielder Rafael Almeida, earning his team the sobriquet *el querido Cinci* (the beloved Cincinnati). Griffith later took over the Washington Senators and established a pipeline to Havana using scout Joe Cambria, an Italian-born minor league owner who signed more than 400 Cubans, including prominent pitchers Luis Tiant and Camilo Pascual, three-time batting champion Tony Oliva, and 1965 MVP Zoilo Versalles, between the mid 1930s and his death in 1962. Cuba's Adolfo "Dolf" Luque threw five scoreless innings in the 1919 World Series with the Reds and went 27–8 while leading the league in wins, winning percentage (.771), shutouts (6), ERA (1.93), and opponents' batting average (.235) in 1923. Luque was celebrated after the season as if he led a nation of three million people to victory over a country of 110 million. And he wasn't through. Luque won 194 victories in 20 seasons and pitched the last 4⅓ innings to win the finale of the 1933 Series for the New York Giants. Americans called him the Pride of Havana and the Havana Perfecto; back home, even though he was white, he was called Papá Montero after a famous Afro-Cuban rhumba dancer and pimp. Compatriots respected him on a par with two other Cuban gamesmen, chess grandmaster Raúl Capablanca and world fencing champion Ramón Frost.

Alas, the stereotyping began with Luque. In *The Pride of Havana: A History of Cuban Baseball*, Roberto González Echevarría described Luque as "a snarling, vulgar, cursing, aggressive pug, who though small at 5'7", was always ready to fight," and went into opposing dugouts to take on hecklers. Understandably, he took offense when he was called a "Cuban nigger," but he overreacted by attacking offenders, throwing beanballs, and threatening people with a gun.

In the winter 1998 edition of *Elysian Fields Quarterly*, Peter C. Bjarkman wrote, "The first great Latin pitcher, Dolf Luque of the Cincinnati Reds, had authored the lasting stereotype when he charged from the mound in 1922 to hit Casey Stengel on the New York Giants bench in old Crosley Field. It had taken a host of helmeted officers to subdue the enraged bat-wielding Luque once he charged back upon the diamond after an initial ejection from the field of play." Bjarkman went on to cite Rubén Gómez of the Giants, who starred in the beanball wars of the 1950s and infamously fled the field when confronted by beanball victim Joe Adcock, whom he'd hit on the arm. Gómez reappeared in the dugout with a switchblade or an ice pick, depending on your source. The stereotype would die hard, if at all.

* * *

At 11:00 AM on May 23, 2009, Hall of Famers Juan Marichal and Orlando Cepeda, along with other Latino worthies like Roberto Clemente Jr., son of the late HOF rightfielder, gathered for a press conference and ribbon cutting to open the ¡Viva Baseball! exhibit on the Hall of Fame's second floor. Once in front of a microphone, Cepeda spoke seriously and mentioned "some obstacles" he endured. Marichal, natty in a blue suit, blue shirt, and striped tie, smiled and seemed to compliment everyone in sight. (He is notably absent from an audio in the exhibit in which players answer the question, "What obstacles did you encounter in the United States?") His gray hair still reasonably full, his mustache expertly clipped, his stance upright, his bearing regal, his walk just a little stiff from years of back trouble, Marichal looked at least 15 years younger than his 71 and resembled less a one-time Dominican farm kid than a Spanish grandee. "Could you take my hand?" he asked someone. "I'm in heaven."

In Spanish, Marichal expressed his gratitude for Dominican baseball then referred to it as a boy's dream.

"*En mi país, es un país donde el béisbol es número uno.*" ("In my country, baseball is number one.")

"*Cada día es un sueño del niño.*" ("Every day is a boy's dream.")

"I met Juan Marichal when he was at the museum to film something," said Gabriel Schechter, a Hall of Fame research associate. "He had some friends with him. I introduced myself to him, he introduced me to his friends, and we talked for about 10 minutes. He made me feel that it was an honor for him to meet me."

"I don't know of anyone as sweet as Juan," said Rob Ruck, author of *The Tropic of Baseball*.

Two hours after Marichal, Cepeda, and Clemente cut the ribbon, they took their seats in the Grandstand Theater, which is lined by paintings depicting fans as well as ersatz railings and a scoreboard. When asked how he learned baseball, Marichal said, "Those were very good times," and proceded to explain.

Juan Antonio Marichal Sánchez (in Latino countries, the mother's surname comes last, but the father's is used on second reference) was born on October 20, 1937, in Laguna Verde, a farming village—"rice, bananas, *plátanos*," as he described it—about 15 miles from the Haitian border, or *La Línea*. The land was irrigated by diversions from the country's longest river, the *Yaque del Norte*. Nearby Monte Cristi was a prime port until the August 4, 1946, earthquake destroyed the docks and sea walls and shifted the export market to Santo Domingo. Juan grew up in a six-room *bohío*, or farmhouse, made of palm-bark walls and a roof thatched with banana leaves. The name Marichal comes from the French surname Maréchal, which means Marshall; Juan's ancestors were French settlers who migrated to the Canary Islands where his paternal grandfather was born.

The youngest of four children, he has no memory of his father, Francisco, who drank heavily and died when Juan was three and whose absence caused him some grief in the presence of two-parent families (his mother never remarried). Juan's mother, who was known as Doña Natividad and Mamá Tibico, dressed in black for years and never wore lipstick or earrings after her husband's death. Nonetheless, Marichal speaks of a generally joyous boyhood living in a house with indoor plumbing, water tanks for bathing, bottled gas for cooking since there was no electricity, and hand-pumped gasogene lamps. He loved listening to games on a battery-powered radio, hunting with slingshots, fishing, swimming, and diving (he once pulled 40 lobsters out of the water without using an aqualung). His mother, who gave her children plenty of chores and Catholicism, ran the 60-acre *parcela* where a herd of 150–200 goats, plus a few horses and donkeys, roamed. In a distinct departure from the Latin American model of indulged boys, Juan worked the farm in the morning and walked 8 km to school in *El Duro* in the afternoon. He liked math and reading. There was no church locally, but Juan studied catechism from monks who came to town. "We didn't have much money, but we had a lot of food," Marichal said.

In 1947, nine-year-old Juan almost died. Farming was a communal activity, with families helping families at harvest time. "We called it a *junta*, inviting many people to work and then eat," Marichal said. "They'd bring their kids and feed them first, so there were no kids round when the adults ate. After we kids ate, we went back to swimming in the irrigation ditch. I was near my grandmother, who was in a rice field where they were digging weeds out from between the plants. I told her, '*Vieja*, [old lady, meant affectionately] I'm dreaming that I'm digging gold out of that plant.' Then I passed out."

The youngster had suffered cramps from eating and swimming and he had gone into a coma. "They had to put me across a horse and take me to my home

4 kilometers away from there. Then they took me in a car to Monte Cristi to see a doctor. The doctor told them to give me hot-water baths continuously and see what happens. On the sixth day, he said that if I didn't wake up by midnight, I was gone. At about 11:45 I woke up with a cry."

Wonder no more about the joy he carries with him. Juan awakened to especially good news. Jackie Robinson had broken the color barrier, giving Dominicans renewed hope. Before Robinson, about 100 light-skinned Latinos, mostly Cubans, played in the majors, and roughly twice as many Afro-Latinos competed in the Negro Leagues. There was spirited competition for talent between the Negro and Caribbean Basin Latino leagues. Explaining his decision to forsake the Newark Eagles for Vera Cruz in 1939, Willie Wells wrote Wendell Smith of the *Pittsburgh Courier*, "I am not faced with the racial problem.... I've found freedom and democracy here, something I never found in the United States.... Here, in Mexico, I am a man."

The best *pelotero* to dominate both Negro and Latino League competition, Cuba's Martín Dihigo, won a reported 256 games, threw no-hitters in Mexico, Puerto Rico, and Venezuela, copped three home-run titles playing for the Homestead Grays, and made the halls of fame in Mexico, Venezuela, Cuba, the Dominican Republic, and the U.S. "For versatility on the baseball diamond, Martín Dihigo was in a class by himself," the Cooperstown plaque reports. His bust in Havana's *Estadio Latinoamericano* reads, "*El Inmortal.*"

In 1948, there was only one Latino playing even semi-regularly in the majors—light-skinned Cuban catcher Mike Guerra of the Philadelphia A's. Minnie Miñoso (pronounced without the ñ by his American fans), also Cuban, became the first black Latino in the majors when he joined the Indians in 1949. In his autobiography, *Baby Bull*, Cepeda described Miñoso "to Latin ballplayers what Jackie Robinson is to black ballplayers. As much as I loved Roberto Clemente and cherish his memory, Minnie is the one who made it possible for all us Latins. Before Roberto Clemente, before Vic Power, before Orlando Cepeda, there was Minnie Miñoso. Younger players should know this and offer their thanks. He was the first Latin player to become a superstar."

"I never let the world hurt me," Miñoso told Tim Wendel, author of *Far from Home: Latino Baseball Players in America*. "The world didn't break me. They used to call me terrible things, but I let it go in one ear and out the other. None of it stayed with me. I never wanted them to know my feelings on the inside. On the outside I just gave them my smile. Smile all the time." Miñoso would smile more on the inside if baseball accorded him the same Hall of Fame designation it gave fellow pioneers Robinson and Clemente.

In some sense, it's a greater hurdle for Latinos to succeed in their home country than America. "Pressure? What pressure?" the former big league slugger Sammy Sosa once said. "Pressure was when I was a child and I didn't know where my next meal was coming from. Pressure was shining shoes for a living. This is baseball. I love baseball."

In 1956, Ozzie Virgil of the Giants became the first Dominican to be called up to the majors. Most Dominican youngsters probably envisioned a future in the National League. Though scout Joe Cambria of the American League's Washington Senators, which later became the Minnesota Twins, had been signing Cubans for years, he often made them sign blank contracts he later filled in himself. The parent club was every bit as exploitative when Latinos reached the majors. Though the Indians and White Sox were active in the Caribbean Basin, the shadow of the racist Yankees hung over the Junior Circuit. It's known that the Yankees encumbered the entire American League by refusing to integrate until Elston Howard appeared in 1955. What's less appreciated is whom they deliberately passed on. Vic Power, an Afro–Puerto Rican with a social conscience and an exceptional person to those who knew him, was eminently qualified. Yankees general manager George Weiss, leery of Power's propensity for stylish play, clubhouse jokes, snazzy cars, and white girlfriends, said he wasn't the "right kind" of black pioneer and told the media that "the first Negro to appear in a Yankee uniform must be worth having waited for."

"The black Puerto Rican ran counter to the genteel black southerner or the corporate player who abided by the rules," Adrian Burgos Jr. wrote in *Playing America's Game: Baseball, Latinos and the Color Line*. Power languished in the Yankees farm system, batting better than .300 and becoming a *cause célèbre* for organized labor and civil rights activists, while Yankees officials refused to promote him and produced a phony scouting report that described him as "a good hitter but a poor fielder."

After the Yankees traded the International League batting champion to the Philadelphia Athletics, first baseman Power won seven Gold Gloves and pioneered the one-handed catch that today is *de rigueur*. "If the guy who invented baseball wanted us to catch with two hands, he would have invented two gloves," Power once explained.

As an indication of how he swatted away problems, Power was denied service at an Arkansas restaurant when he was in the minor leagues. "We don't serve colored people," the proprietor said.

"That's all right," Power said. "I don't like to eat them."

As far back as Juan Marichal can remember, he looked for inspiration from baseball players. "When I was a kid, one of my idols was Duke Snider," he told Joan Culkin in the December 1983 *Baseball Digest*. "Since the Dodgers trained in the Dominican Republic in 1948, they became very popular in my country. They used to call [Snider] the Duke of Destruction."

Baseball has been referred to as the D.R.'s second religion. It was the only sport discussed in Laguna Verde. Starting from the time he was nine, Juan and his friends made bats from the smoothed, dried, and trimmed branches of *vasima* trees, which are like large apple trees; balls from the insides of golf balls snatched from a nearby course, wrapped in a nylon stocking with tape and sewed into a leather cover for 50 cents by the local shoemaker; and gloves of burlap folded around cardboard and sewed up with fishing line. Even before he became a pitcher, Juan had good control from hunting birds with slingshots and throwing rocks at trees to dislodge coconuts.

Juan first played for Laguna Verde's youth team when he was 15. The boys competed in uniforms produced from flour bags. According to author Hector J. Cruz in *Juan Marichal: La Historia de Su Vida* (The Story of His Life), Juan would wear his uniform to sleep the night before games. The next morning, he'd rise, wash his face, eat breakfast, and promptly head off to play baseball. "We played all day, every day, whenever we were not in school or working," Marichal told Rob Ruck. "We played on a field that we made ourselves…. Laguna Verde had a team for the boys that would play [other] youth teams…. We traveled to those towns on horseback or in the back of a dump truck, or they would come to Laguna Verde, every Sunday. If they came to Laguna Verde, we would have a meal for them after the game, with goat meat, *enchiladas,* rice, and beans. Sometimes we would go from house to house, asking for contributions so that we could feed the other team. Often Ramón Villalona, who was a bit better off and helped coach us, would give us money so that we could have a little *fiesta* after the game."

Baseball leagues go back almost a century in "the Dominican" (no English speaker in baseball says the Dominican Republic). *El Benefactor,* dictator Rafael Leonidas Trujillo Molina, who ruled from 1930 until he was assassinated in

1961, strengthened his power base by having his minions consolidate the *Licey* and *Escogido* teams from his capital city, *Ciudad Trujillo* (Santo Domingo), into the *Dragones* for one season in 1937 and import black Americans to play for it.[6] While there had been no Dominican major leaguers at the time of Juan's birth, one of the greatest player pools in sport was about to open with the integration of the national pastime.

Juan got spikes, gloves, bats, and balls from his brother, Gonzalo, who was seven years older and the closest thing the sometimes-lonely boy had to a father. Juan would ride a horse to Monte Cristi, a larger town six miles away, to watch Gonzalo play for the local team, then ride behind with Gonzalo on the horse, quizzing him about baseball as they returned to Laguna Verde for another game. Among Gonzalo's insights: 2–2 is a great pitcher's count, because the pitcher can still waste a pitch while the batter can't afford to take anything close. "He played every position but catcher," Marichal said. "One day the catcher got hurt, and I felt so proud when I saw him in catcher's gear."

Mostly Gonzalo played shortstop. Hero-worshipping his brother, who he swears was a better ballplayer than he, Juan naturally dreamed about growing up to be a big-league shortstop. That changed when he was 9 or 10 and attended a game with his brother-in-law Próspero Villalona, his older sister Maria Alta Garcia's husband. They saw Bombo Ramos, a pitcher who later died in the 1948 crash that took the lives of everyone on the national team but the one player who stayed home. Like Luis Tiant, Ramos turned his back to the plate on his windup, then came at batters with a blinding sidearm delivery. He also talked to the hitters, saying things like, "You better hit this one because if you don't you won't even see the next one," as Marichal later reported to Ira Berkow, then of the Newspaper Enterprise Association, later a Pulitzer Prize–winning writer and columnist for the *New York Times*. Juan ran home and announced to friends that he'd be a Bombonian hurler.

Gonzalo had already showed him a sinker and a curve. In fact, contemporaries say Juan, who had strengthened his arm through farm work, could throw the curve at age nine. Realizing he was destined to play baseball, he quit school at age 15 against his mother's wishes and moved to the capital city, Santo Domingo, where Gonzalo was running a fleet of dump trucks. With Gonzalo's help, Juan joined the Esso Company team that played games on Saturday or Sunday. After returning to Laguna Verde in 1955, Juan played for Monte Cristi's *Las Flores* team sponsored by the Bermúdez Rum Company, and he helped his team win an island-wide zonal tournament in Monte Cristi. Then he led an All-Star team to victory in a central zone regional in Santiago and won two games to help Monte Cristi win the national amateur tournament in Santo Domingo. Playing mostly for expenses, he would drive tractors all Saturday night for five pesos, clean up, and hitch a ride to his Sunday game.

His pitching reputation awarded Marichal a promotion to a Massacre River port called Manzanillo and a team owned by the United Fruit Company's local affiliate, the Grenada Company, which offered meals, housing, laundry, bus travel, and part-time work picking mashed bananas off the docks or driving a tractor-lawnmower for $12 a week. If there were no ships to load, Juan would water trees and flowers. If it was too wet, he'd cut the grass on the nine-hole *Club de Golf de Manzanillo*. Often, he just played baseball. "The people who owned the team were very nice to us," Marichal said.

At 5'11" and 170 pounds, Juan had filled out by the time he was 18. There's often a dramatic turning point in an athlete's life. For Marichal, it came when he pitched Manzanillo to a 2–1 victory over *Aviación*, the Dominican Air Force team, in the 1956 national amateur tournament.

Back at the Hall of Fame, leaning forward slightly as he spoke into the microphone, Marichal told a good story that the crowd ate up. "At eight o'clock the next morning, a lieutenant knocks at the door [of my bungalow] with a telegram that reads, '*Reportase de inmediato al Equipo de la Fuerza Aérea.*' ('Report immediately to the Air Force team.') I was being drafted! I told them they'd have to ask my mother."

The officer and his draftee headed to Laguna Verde, where they met a stern Doña Natividad who doubted he belonged in the Air Force. "I got over to her house around 11:00," Marichal said. "She was walking all over the place, back and forth." At 4:00 PM, another telegram arrived wondering if Juan had left for *Ciudad Trujillo*. It was signed, like the first one, by Rafael (Ramfis) Leonides Trujillo Martínez *hijo* (son), the dictator's offspring. "*Bueno,*" said Doña Natividad, a realist above all. "You don't say no to the Trujillos." Their directives, after all, were known as "summons from God."

Within 24 hours, Marichal arrived at the San Isidro base and was welcomed by General Fernando Sánchez, Ramfis' assistant. As Marichal was leaving the room, the general presented him with 100 pesos, a huge sum for the time, amounting to about $100. His first assignment was to head for *Estadio La Normal* to try out for a youth tournament in Mexico. Juan actually lived in the clubhouse under the stands for more than a week before making a team that included future major leaguers Manuel Mota and Mateo Alou. Taking his first plane trip, to Mexico, Juan won one game and saved another against Puerto Rico to advance to the finals against the home team. There he and his teammates encountered fans with knives and guns sitting directly on top of their dugout. "When we went to the bullpen, they showed us the guns," he said. "We were so scared, we couldn't handle the pressure." The Mexicans won. The Dominicans escaped.

Back at San Isidro, Juan got a shaved head; a heavy, ill-fitting, long-sleeved khaki uniform—and 57.50 pesos a month, plus a 30-peso bonus, or more than twice the salary for the other recruits. (Memory is a cruel mistress. At other times, Marichal has also said he made 52.50. In either case, he was way ahead of other draftees.) He sent part of his salary to his mother and his brother Gonzalo. He was also eating what the officers ate: rice, beans, meat, salad, milk, fruit. He had one job: play ball.

Every day there would be an intrasquad game and a practice session. On Sundays the team would host an opponent or go off-base to play one. Marichal got plenty of vitamin supplements and also plenty of visits to Gonzalo's house, where he'd stay until 5:00 AM and then get a truck ride to the base. Despite his growing reputation, Marichal didn't impress his coach Francisco Pichardo, who was called Viruta. "He had never encountered an instructor as harsh and exacting as Viruta," Cruz wrote.

"There are many things I have never seen you do," Viruta said in a conversation from Marichal's autobiography *A Pitcher's Life*, written with Charles Einstein.

"Such as?" Marichal asked.

"Such as running."

"Running?"

"Yes."

"Do you run in order to be able to pitch?"

"Yes."

"Who says so?"

"I do."

"Where do you run? A pitching mound is a small place."

"Then we will find a bigger place. You will run from the left-field foul line to the right-field foul line."

"Then what?"

"Then you will turn around and run from the right-field foul line to the left-field foul line."

"I will get tired."

"Then we will get you a medical discharge."

Marichal's veteran teammates called him *niño de faldas*, or mama's boy, and *cobarde*, or coward, because he didn't want to drink *romo*, which means rum literally and booze generically. Marichal finally yielded to the ritual custom of downing a glass and then turning it over on the table. When Viruta heard the news, he worked Marichal harder than ever.

"Why do you work me?" Marichal asked Viruta.

"Because you drank."

"The guys wanted me to."

"Fine. Stay with those guys and their habits, and you'll be one of them. *Romo* is no good for you."

If Marichal's control was good, Viruta made it better. "In rainouts, he would take everybody to the bullpen," Marichal told me. "He didn't throw hard, but he had perfect control. He told us anyone with control can succeed in any league.

"He also told us to get down and bring up dirt when you follow through. When you touch the ground many times, you create a habit." And here's the payoff: "When you have control, you can pitch many complete games, because you don't need many pitches."

Marichal listened to Viruta and followed his pitching advice about emphasizing control while moving the ball up and down, inside and outside. After he'd spent a year in the Air Force, *Aviación* traveled to Manzanillo to play a doubleheader against Juan's old buddies. Marichal lost the opener 1–0, and another pitcher lost the nightcap.

Ramfis Trujillo was incensed, and he was not a man to be trifled with. The son of the elder Trujillo and his mistress, Maria Martínez, Ramfis Trujillo became a full-fledged colonel at age four and a brigadier general at nine. The handsome playboy, polo player, and degenerate ordered an investigation into the inconceivable twin killing and concluded the players had been drinking. Actually, Marichal said, they were sickened by stale water. No excuses! Most of the coaches and managers were given a 30-day jail sentence, Viruta got 10 days, and the players got five days incarceration and a $2 fine.

"You can see how seriously we take baseball in the Dominican Republic," Marichal said to the audience's laughter at the Hall of Fame.

Marichal then talked about his jail experience. "The jail was on a military base and wasn't too bad. But we felt we shouldn't lose two games. Losing two games was bad. Going in jail was worse."

They never lost another doubleheader on Marichal's watch. Easily the best team in the country, Aviacion won regularly in Cuba, Puerto Rico, and Panama as well as the D.R. In 1957, Washington Senators scout Carlos "Patato" Pascual, brother of major league star Camilo Pascual, approached Marichal after a 16-strikeout effort in Aruba but never followed up. A Yankees scout was interested but wanted Marichal to play for *Licey*, which drew *Escogito fanático* Ramfis' ire. Juan also caught the eye of the Dodgers, Pirates, and the Giants' bilingual director of Caribbean/Latin American scouting Alejandro "Alex" Pompez, former owner of the New York Cubans of Negro League fame. Back when the Dodgers brought up Jackie Robinson and took the lead in minority recruiting, Jack Schwarz, the Giants' minor league director, turned to Pompez, whose team shared the Polo Grounds with the Giants. His Afro-Latino network landed Marichal, Cepeda, McCovey, Mota, Monte Irvin, and the Alou brothers, opened the spigot on Dominican talent and made the Giants the *gigantes* of the Caribbean Basin. Pompez's former shortstop, now his Dominican bird dog, or unofficial scout paid on commission, Horacio "Rabbit" Martínez, had become good friends with Gonzalo and alerted Pompez about him. Pompez's scouting report said, "He is devout. He reads the Bible constantly. He has a beautiful delivery. Nobody taught him anything."

A delicate negotiation followed. After Martínez spoke with Gonzalo and Gonzalo spoke with Juan, the three of them got permission from Ramfis Trujillo. On the afternoon of September 16, 1957, Juan and Gonzalo took a Lincoln Continental to Santo Domingo's exclusive Hainamosa neighborhood and the home of dictator Trujillo's brother-in-law and *Escogido* president Francisco Martínez "Paquito" Alba, who signed him to play winter ball for the *Leónes de Escogido*. A day later, by pre-agreement, Juan signed with *Escogido*'s parent company, the New York (soon to be San Francisco) Giants for a bonus of $500. Normally, Martínez was restricted to $200 bonuses, so the figure he insisted on made the Giants take notice.

That night Juan watched an exhibition between a Dominican team and the Willie Mays All-Stars that he never forgot. The following day he gave the good news of his signing to Doña Natividad, who had softened toward his career aspirations. From the $500 bonus, he bought her clothes, gave some money to Gonzalo, and kept the rest. Juan was a month short of his 19th birthday and psyched. What once seemed remote and distant to him—*¡las ligas grandes!*— now loomed as a dream within reach.

Late in the Hall of Fame event, Marichal addressed the evening session of the *¡Viva Baseball!* opening. Despite an exhausting day, he stood ramrod-straight and smiled through the introductions, some of which duplicated earlier remarks. When it was his turn to speak, he stepped forward in slacks, shirt, and a zip-up jacket. The Cooperstown High School jazz band played in another room, and its sweet sounds drifted into the plaque gallery where Marichal stood. He took in the scene and thanked the people who helped him through the years. "What a time, what a day," he concluded. "For that reason, I say nothing is impossible."

~ Chapter 3 ~

SEARCHING FOR SPAHN IN BUFFALO

"For me, personally, I like the sense of tradition that's still left in Buffalo. There's a feeling that you feel from the people about pride in their city—that means a lot to me. I was driving over the Skyway Bridge the other day. It was a very clear day, and I looked out because the wind had blown all the storm clouds across the water, and I saw all those steeples that just dotted the horizon. It was just beautiful, and I thought that Buffalo was really something…. The people here were great. I liked their friendliness and their openness. They really got behind us and were supportive and enthusiastic. That means a lot to me, and the people who helped us are very much a part of this film."

—Robert Redford, about shooting *The Natural* in Buffalo

There's every good reason to visit Buffalo in search of Warren Spahn's past, and not just for the nice people you'll meet. Anyone who becomes famous inspires tales, and some of them are bound to be taller than others. It was fun to investigate Spahn lore and separate truth from myth. According to numerous clips that fanned the legend, here are the details of young Warren's life that people have believed for years.

- Born on April 23, 1921, the fifth of six children and the first of two boys to Mabel and Edward Spahn.
- Named Warren Edward Spahn after President Harding and Spahn's father.

- Grew up in South Buffalo, in a multi-family house with a tavern on the ground floor at 189 Roberts Avenue.
- Moved from first base to pitcher because Billy Benzerman, who later became pro wrestler Killer Kowalski, was an all-scholastic first baseman and teammate of Spahn's at South Park High School.
- Led South Park to championships his junior and senior seasons.
- Threw a no-hitter in his senior season and signed with the Braves after scout Billy Myers quit the Red Sox when he didn't like the deal they offered Sibby Sisti, who was also from Buffalo.

But what if some of these details are apocryphal, or just false?

Through Buffalo native and former *Sports Illustrated* writer Mike Del Nagro, Michael J. Billoni provided the facts on Spahn's home city. As close to a Mr. Buffalo as there can be, Billoni learned the streets on delivery runs for his father's dry cleaning business, Colvin Cleaners; he worked the phones as an award-winning newspaperman getting reluctant people to talk; he convinced former New York Governor Mario Cuomo to introduce mandatory bicycle-helmet legislation after nearly dying in a bicycle accident; and he channeled P.T. Barnum[7] when he six times inspired million-fan seasons as vice president and general manager of the Buffalo Bisons minor league baseball team. Now Billoni is marketing and public relations director of the Food Bank of Western New York, a perfect job for such a people-guy.

Billoni arranged a lunch with Spahn *cognoscenti* at Pettibones Grille on the second floor of the Bisons' Coca-Cola Field, a splendid downtown park that Anthony Violanti, author of *Miracle in Buffalo: How the Dream of Baseball Revived a City*, credited with "neoclassical design, simmering emerald grass, and nostalgic ambience," and Hank Aaron said it reminded him of Wrigley Field. Opened in 1988 and originally named Pilot Field, it indeed revived the downtown, at least on home-game dates. In attendance at the lunch were Budd Bailey, a sportswriter for the *Buffalo News*; Bob Miske, a longtime baseball scout; and Don Colpoys, another former Bisons G.M., Cardinal farmhand, scout, and baseball coach at Canisius College in Buffalo.

Colpoys gave me two priceless photos of schoolboy Spahn sporting a long nose, prominent ears, and shy expression. For good measure, Colpoys added a clip of a six-inning no-hitter Spahn pitched for a summer-league team in which he fanned 16 batters. One guy reached on a walk. Spahn probably picked him off. Miske informed me about something I'll check on later, that Spahn made more money as a celebrity rep for Borden's than he ever did pitching. Bailey said that when an inaccuracy appears in print, it gets a life of its own and reappears so often it becomes a truth. Will Bailey's remark prove to be prophetic?

After lunch, Billoni and I climbed into Billoni's maroon Hyundai for a trip around town. A 6'3", 210-pound guy with a full head of dark hair, wearing glasses, slacks, and a golf shirt, Mike Billoni is the living embodiment of the regular guy everyone respects. Often he's asked, "Do I know you?" He replies quietly, "I was general manager of the Bisons." Working the cell phone that appears to be attached to his left ear, he searched for people who may have known Spahn. We stopped at Wiechec's Bar in a Polish neighborhood called Kaisertown that was once German. A specialty is "beef on weck," a roast beef sandwich on a kummelweck roll that is peculiar to Buffalo. We found an old fellow who played ball with someone who played with Spahn. Alas, the teammate is long dead and the old-timer had no stories. Undeterred, Billoni drove to what he was told is Spahn's old Schiller Park neighborhood, which is on the East Side, not in South Buffalo. The area has gone from solidly German to largely African American, but Scharf's German-American restaurant still holds family parties and funeral breakfasts. Generally well-kept two-story, wood-and-shingle houses with six steps up to their front porches and plenty of wrought-iron railings line what we're both sure is Spahn's old street, Sprenger Avenue. The eight Spahns rented the ground floor of a two-story house. "I remember sewing up baseballs because we didn't have one [new ball]," Spahn once recalled.

As you might expect, the Schiller Park neighborhood contains a Schiller Park and borders Sprenger Avenue. A huge space with plenty of room for fields, we suspected that Schiller Park was where Spahn must have begun playing baseball.

Whoops! Later we learned that Spahn grew up not in South Buffalo but in Kaisertown. I asked Paul Motyka, whose family lived in the neighborhood and who is active in the Society for American Baseball Research (SABR), to investigate the claim of 189 Roberts Avenue. "My brother Lou drove down Roberts and looked for 189 Roberts," he reported. "He said the numbers only go to 131. Roberts is only one block long and ends at Clinton Street. If there was a 189, it would have been on the other side of Clinton, which is now a section of the New York Thruway and was the bed for a major railroad line before that. To his knowledge no street existed on the land across Clinton Street."

Why is this information significant? Because Motyka's family lived in a house at 114 Kelburn Street that abutted the actual Spahn residence at 105 Roberts, a two-story house in an industrial neighborhood plainly less threadbare than the 189 Roberts Avenue apartment of legend, although they probably shared it with another family. Lou said his father, Lou Sr., used to see young Spahn playing catch on the street, probably in 1925–29. Two blocks to the east and behind an elementary school is Houghton Park, where the Spahns practiced baseball. In this especially close-knit community, Mabel's sister was married to Edward's brother.

* * *

Little noted or remembered by outsiders, Buffalo has both a distinguished history and an eminent baseball tradition. The western terminus of the Erie Canal, an Underground Railroad stop, and a major railroad hub, Buffalo was the nation's eighth largest city in 1900, the largest inland port, host of the 1901 Pan-American Exposition where President McKinley was assassinated and, yes, the birthplace of Buffalo chicken wings. Getting cheap electricity from the Niagara River and Falls, the Queen City of the Great Lakes at one point had the country's largest grain-milling center and the world's largest steel-making operation. A man could get a job in a factory and have guaranteed lifetime employment, or so it seemed. Best known today for its snowy winters, vanished steel mills and auto plants, and declining population/industrial base, Buffalo in 2009 nonetheless retained the NHL's Sabres, the NFL's Bills, the Triple A Buffalo Bisons, a downtown ballpark and arena, plus hope for the future through its rising economic development and shift from an industrial to service-based economy.

Buffalo fielded its first pro baseball team in 1877 and the next year joined the game's first minor league, the International League. Already called the Buffalo Bisons, the team joined the National League in 1879 and for its seven years in the association suited up Hall of Famers Pud Galvin, Orator Jim O'Rourke, and Dan Brouthers. There were Buffalo entries in the Players League (1890) and the Federal League (1914–15). The Buffalo Bisons bred other immortals among players and managers, such as Ray Schalk, Joe Tinker, Joe McCarthy, Bill Dickey, Gabby Hartnett, Lou Boudreau, Johnny Bench, Eddie Collins, Old Hoss Charley Radbourn, Herb Pennock, Bucky Harris, Jim Bunning,

A Double No-Hitter

On May 2, 1917, right-hander Fred Toney of the Reds and left-hander Hippo Vaughn of the Cubs entertained Wrigley Field regulars with nine innings of no-hit ball, the only time that has happened in major league history. Winning 178 games over his 13-year career, James Leslie Vaughn, called "Hippo" because he was 6'4" and weighed 215 pounds, was a 20-game winner five times, and he led the National League with 22 victories, eight shutouts, 148 strikeouts, 290⅓ innings, 33 complete games, and a 1.74 ERA in 1918. Toney went just 139–102 during 12 seasons, but he was in the zone on May 2 en route to a 24-win season.

The game was scoreless through nine, each pitcher allowing two walks, Vaughn recording 10 strikeouts and Toney three. There was one close call, but Cubs center fielder Cy Williams made a fine running catch of Greasy Neale's blooper in the first. With one out in the 10th, Reds shortstop Larry Kopf, a .255 hitter for the year, singled to right-center, and the Chicago crowd moaned. Vaughn's no-hitter was lost, but not the game. Vaughn got a second out. Alas, Williams dropped Hal Chase's fly, putting runners on first and third.

Then who should step up but Jim Thorpe, triple gold medal winner in the 1912 Olympics, All-American football player, and the best-known athlete of his era. Thorpe laid a fine bunt down the third base line, and Vaughn instantly knew he had no play at first. But when he fielded the ball cleanly and threw to catcher Art Wilson, the out-to-lunch backstop allowed the ball to bounce off his chest and Kopf scored. When Chase tried to score all the way from first, Wilson had the presence of mind to tag him.

Now the shutout was gone, too. Toney sped through the 10th to win his no-hitter 1-0. According to Vaughn, "Wilson cried like a baby after the game. He grabbed my hand and said, 'I just went out on you. Jim—I just went tight.'"

and John Montgomery Ward, not to mention that Buffalo was the hometown of Warren Spahn. Buffalo-born Buddy Rosar, a catcher for the Philadelphia Athletics, played in the 1947 All-Star Game, as did Spahn.

There were dozens of youth leagues when Spahn was growing up during the Depression. Though the following testimony occurs years after Spahn's youth, it underscores how seriously families raised their sons on Buffalo baseball and how long the tradition persevered. "I used to play three times a day two or three days a week for various teams from the *Buffalo Evening News*-Police Athletic League (BEN-PAL), the Cheektowaga League, the All-American Amateur Baseball Association (AAABA), and the American Legion," said Kevin

Lester, athletic director at Williamsville South High School, official scorer at the Bisons' game I attended and the catcher for Roy Hobbs' New York Knights in *The Natural* when it was filmed at Buffalo's War Memorial Stadium. "When we weren't doing that, we'd play games like Three Flies, where you got to bat after fielding three flies, with three grounders counting as one fly."

Maybe their father made only $27 a week, maybe there was meat on the table only one day a week, maybe Warren (the second, not the fifth child), his four sisters, and his brother Eddie had to use newspapers to plug up holes in their shoes, but life was pig heaven for a kid in love with the national pastime.

How many American boys have said, "My best coach was my father?" A good bowler and semipro ballplayer but small at 5'7" and somewhere between 135 and 150 pounds (accounts differ) and not as talented as Wee Willie Keeler to dream of a big-league baseball career, Edward Peter Spahn realized his dreams only though Warren. Otherwise, he struggled to make a living. At 21, Edward registered for the draft in 1918 but did not fight in World War I. He was a packer for an ice cream company in 1920 and living at 67 Mulberry Street with a family consisting of himself, his Canadian-born mother Christine, his five siblings, and two other families, according to census data. Edward's first child, Gertrude, was born to him and Mabel Marring in 1919 or 1920. On March 17, 1921, Edward and Mabel received a marriage license. Thirty-seven days later—on April 23, 1921—Warren was born.

"His mom told him that he looked like a frog when he was born," Warren's son, Greg, said. "He used to kid her about that: 'What mother would say her kid looked like a frog!'"

Three more girls and another boy followed. By 1930, Edward was either a shipping clerk (Census) or a salesman (city directory) for the Syracuse Wall Paper and Paint Company and living with his wife and six children at 109 Baitz Avenue, where the eight Spahns shared a house with the eight-member Wisntewski family. Edward held the same job when the family relocated to 105 Roberts Avenue in 1932–36. In 1937 the Spahns moved to 131 Roberts, and Edward was listed as a clerk for Lutz Wallpaper Company. He returned to the Syracuse company in 1938, but as a clerk. By 1941, he and Mabel were listed as the only residents living at 53 Juniata Place in South Buffalo across Buffalo Creek from Kaisertown. In 1942, only Mabel Spahn was listed at that address. "I think they separated," Greg Spahn said. "I don't know if they got divorced."

"He was a great guy," Warren's first cousin, Ken Spahn, said of Edward Spahn. "We used to talk sports a lot."

Edward Spahn didn't own a car, but he did have that dream. Edward obsessively taught baseball to Warren, the most promising athlete in the family, in the backyard. Father was playing catch with son when the kid was six years old. "We didn't have a left-handed glove," Warren recalled, "so I played with a glove that had the thumb hole right here [at his right pinkie, the way he held it]. I may have become a better fielder than other guys from using it."

"I noticed then," Edward told Al Silverman, an early Spahn biographer, "that he could throw with control and didn't have any jerk in his motion. I know this may sound like bragging, but he seemed to shine right off the bat, and I was sure he'd someday be a baseball player."

Edward knew there were only so many positions open for a left-hander. Just in case Warren couldn't hit well enough to play first, Edward taught him exhaustively how to throw fastballs and curves from a mound he built in the backyard. "Control...control...control," Warren told author Robert Cutter. "'If you're going to throw a baseball,' he used to say to me, 'aim it at some target, don't just throw it. And throw it overhand...follow through...nice and smooth and easy.' He was absolutely right, of course. Throwing sidearm or some other unnatural way just ruins young arms."

"He insisted that I throw with a fluid motion, and the high leg kick was part of the deception to the hitter," Warren told the *Daily Oklahoman* in 1998. "Hitters said the ball seemed to come out of my uniform."

"He taught me how to follow through with my shoulder and body, how to throw without any strain, how to get the most out of my pitch and out of my weight even when I was a skinny kid," Spahn explained to sportswriter Bob Broeg. "He taught me how to roll a curve ball, how to let it go off my fingers at the last moment. He taught me how to pass my knee by my right elbow.

"I thought it was a lot of drudgery. It was lots more fun just to pick up the ball and throw, but Dad wouldn't let me play catch unless I did it correctly."

"You ask about my smooth motion, my high leg kick?" Spahn told a Buffalo reporter. "Well, my father taught me that.... I am delighted he lived to see this great thing happen." He presumably was referencing his entire baseball career, because Spahn's father died in 1976.

Perhaps most importantly, Edward told Warren he could make a mistake once, but not twice. "Don't pop off too much. The guy who is noisy, always blowing off, is the guy who has an inferiority complex. Be yourself, be polite, respect other people's feelings, and treat them with deference."

Starting when Warren was eight, Edward and Warren would go to Buffalo Bisons games at Offermann Stadium on Buffalo's East Side. Warren admired slugger Ollie Carnegie and first baseman Big Bill Kelly, a former major leaguer (A's 1920, Phillies 1928) who had played semipro ball with Edward and hit 149 homers for the Bisons in 1922–30. Edward also instructed Warren to watch Bisons pitcher Charlie "Lefty" Perkins (A's 1930, Dodgers 1934). "Now, if you want to be a pitcher, watch every move Charlie Perkins makes," Edward told his son. "If you want to be a first baseman, watch Bill Kelly."

Because of his father's connections playing with the Bisons in earlier leagues, Warren got to shag balls in practice. When he couldn't remember names, he called all the players Kelly, and they called him Kelly Spahn. "After those Bison games my dad gave me the option of an ice cream cone or a streetcar ride home," Spahn told the *Tulsa Daily World*'s John Ferguson. "Many times we took the ice cream and rehashed the game walking home."

Noticing his son's attachment to Kelly, Edward bought Warren a first baseman's glove for his ninth birthday. Plainly, the kid wanted to be like his hero Lou Gehrig, whom he listened to on Yankees radio broadcasts and imagined was a dead ringer for Tarzan. All other sports at the time genuflected to baseball. With his sights set on first base, Spahn learned to be a good fielder and a dangerous hitter. When he was still nine, Warren donned a uniform for the Lake City Social Club midgets and played with them for three years.

But pitching had its place in his mind, too. "Warren came into the house one day and asked if I thought he could throw as well as Norbert Goehle, a youngster who lived near us on Bates Avenue," Edward Spahn told sportswriter Jack Horrigan in 1958.

"I told him he could. That was all he needed. He was about 10 at the time and pitched his first game for the Lake City Social Club."

The kid got support everywhere he could have hoped. "His mom really looked at Warren as the special child of the family," Ken Spahn said. "She traveled with him [to away games] more than his father did." Playing several different positions, Spahn competed in the *Buffalo Evening News*' Midget Leagues (10–12, 13–14), followed by the *Evening News*–American Legion play for the Louis J. Boland and South Buffalo posts. "I loved to play catch and play ball, and I played every chance I got on street teams and in the Buffalo Twilight

League, the American Legion, and in the City Municipal League," Spahn told Roger Kahn in *The Head Game.* "I was always playing ball and always thinking about playing ball."

Eventually, Warren was playing for three local teams six days a week. In a dream sequence on the Lake City Athletic Club team, the 13-year-old son played first base with his 37-year-old father and handled Edward's hard throws from third, some of which he thought would knock him into the bleachers. "You'd think he was going to throw it right through me," Spahn told the *Christian Science Monitor*'s Ed Rumill. "I weighed only about 110 pounds in those days. But he was teaching me to play hard, and it did a lot of good."

Spahn told another interviewer, "I gave him heck for making bad throws, and he gave me heck for not catching them."

Cazenovia Park, where Warren played in leagues, and South Park High School, which he attended, were a healthy bike ride from his home. When Warren arrived at South Park, he discovered an All-Scholastic player named Billy Benzerman, who later became a professional wrestler (though not Killer Kowalski), occupying first base, and another good one, Bill Klas, on deck. Spahn spent a year as an outfielder and then pitched. But the presence of two good first basemen doesn't fully explain why Spahn became a pitcher, according to biographer Silverman. He had the right stuff to pitch, and when his father wasn't warming him up, Spahn's sisters Eleanor, Marjorie, June, and Gertrude were—especially Eleanor, a good athlete who played softball. (Warren's only living sibling Eddie, a retired steelworker, declined to be interviewed for this book. "I'm not a baseball fan," he said.) Warren's high leg kick gave him tremendous momentum.

When South Park coach Joe "Chief" Shoemaker—whose name was also sometimes spelled Schumaker in the papers—asked Warren if he had a favorite uniform number, the ever-contrary Spahn said 13. "Thirteen, eh? Not the superstitious kind, I see." "Uh-huh," Spahn replied. "Thirteen has always been good luck for me."

In Spahn's two years as a pitcher, South Park terrorized the other 11 Buffalo high schools and won two Cornell Cups for city championships. In a 1939 game against Technical High, teammates made a couple of errors behind Spahn, loading the bases. After motioning the infielders to the mound, he reportedly said, "Relax, fellas. I'm going to throw nine pitches, and we'll walk to the bench." And then, the story goes, he struck out the side on nine pitches, *à la* Lefty Grove pitching an exhibition against minor leaguers.

In the championship game against Bennett High, Spahn loaded the bases in the first inning but fielded a squeeze bunt and fired to the plate in time. He struck out the next two batters, and South Park won 6–0. In 1940, he no-hit East High on 17 strikeouts and would have no-hit Masten High as well if he and his catcher hadn't gotten tied up on a bunt that went for a single. Spahn averaged 14 Ks a game in his final season.

"Warren was a quiet boy but still one of the crowd," Shoemaker told Silverman. "He did what he was told. He never got discouraged. I only had to relieve him once or twice, he was that good, and then he went to the outfield." Though he already had a great schoolboy curve, Shoemaker underscored Spahn's control over all his other pitching assets.

* * *

Still looking for Spahn history, Billoni and I headed over to South Park High School, which is indeed on the South side. Though temporarily closed for a state-of-the-art renovation when we arrived in 2009, the four-story brick building remained a substantial sight with long corridors, a large auditorium, an imposing natatorium, and Greek statues in the foyer. "It's an important school because of its graduates," project co-manager Kevin Maxwell said. "A lot of the fellows remember this place as fondly as kindergarten. There must have been some great teachers."

Billoni looked for old trophies and records, but we were told they were all in storage. Then he got on the phone to the Buffalo Academy for Visual and Performing Arts (BAVPA), where South Park was holding classes. Billoni reached unofficial SPHS historian Peggy Hannon, who invited us over. As we left South Park, Maxwell turned to his co-manager Luis Rodriguez. "You would have liked playing with that guy," Maxwell said of Spahn. "I hear he was a hell of a player."

"I know," said Rodriguez, who is solidly built, like a major league second baseman who can take a hit in the pivot.

We drove to BAVPA and met Hannon, who directed us to her stored copies of *The Dial*, the South Park yearbook. I went right to the 1940 book because Spahn signed with the Braves (then called the Bees) that spring. One face among many in the all-white pantheon—Buffalo schools were peacefully integrated in the seventies—Spahn is pictured with the baseball team, but he's not listed among the seniors. Billoni opened the 1941 book. No Spahn. I went back to the 1940 book and found Warren listed as a junior in the same class as his sister, Marjorie.

Billoni and I stared at each other as our eyes widened. Warren Spahn never graduated from South Park High School![8] He was a 19-year-old junior. Two years earlier he had been classified as a sophomore, so he either repeated his sophomore or junior year, as well as another year earlier in his education. In any case, the records show that Spahn hit .487 as an All-Scholastic outfielder in his sophomore year, then he pitched South Park to city titles in his next two years on varsity.

With nothing left to prove and no draft at the time to keep him in school, the kid turned pro in 1940. He was too skinny at 6' and 140 pounds to impress most scouts, but one of them liked his control and reported that his curve dropped off a table. That came from a disgruntled former Red Sox scout named Billy Meyers, not Myers as is so often represented. A part-time scout when he wasn't selling tickets for the New York Central Railroad, Meyers was peeved by the Sox' pathetic offer to Sibby Sisti, so much so that Meyers jumped ship and signed Sisti to a contract with the Boston Bees, who would resume being called the Braves a year later. Sisti played 11 seasons for the club in Boston and two in Milwaukee, missing three more for service in World War II, and later he was the Pittsburgh Pirates manager in *The Natural*. If the Sox had satisfied Meyers about Sisti, he presumably would have signed Spahn for them, as well. That makes Spahn, Willie Mays, and Jackie Robinson the three most prominent players the Sox passed on. Robinson never heard from the Sox again after they gave him a faux tryout ("I still remember how I hit the ball that day, good to all fields," Robinson said years later) at Fenway Park in 1945. Mays had to look elsewhere in 1948, when he was playing for the Birmingham Black Barons. He was recommended by Boston's Deep South scout and its manager of the all-white Birmingham Barons, a Red Sox farm club, but Mays was spurned by the racist brass in Boston. Spahn was lost to the Sox after they disregarded the Sibby Sisti recommendation from the scout who would have signed Spahn and did sign him to the other Boston team for $80 a month. (Spahn's father said the contract included a $150 bonus and two suits of clothes.)

Spahn listened to Yankees games on the radio but had never attended a major league game. "I never thought I'd be a professional," he said in an interview filmed for the Hall of Fame. "Guys were making $15-$17 a week in steel mills, and I was making $20. I was in heaven."

"After that," he continued, "I had an inquisition [sic] from the Yankees, but I had already signed, and it would have been tough to make the Yankees." Spahn supposedly had a partial scholarship offer from Cornell that would have left his parents with too many expenses. As Spahn was fond of saying, things always work out for the best.

"It was like all those dreams I had as a kid came true," Spahn told author Violanti. "It was such a wonderful thing to make money by playing baseball.

"For me, it all started in Buffalo. That's where I learned about caring and sharing. I grew up playing for neighborhood teams. We didn't play for money; we played because we loved the game, and you busted your butt, and you hated losing. I carried those traits on to pro ball, and I carried on what my father and my family taught me."

* * *

By now the school's principal, Pat Thomas, was in the office. The four of us beamed at our newly discovered knowledge. As we left, Billoni, back in his food-bank mode, turned to the women and said, "Don't forget to put food on your front doorstep tomorrow for the postal drive. Saturday is Stamp Out Hunger Day."

~ Chapter 4 ~

BIG LEAGUE IN
THE BUSH LEAGUES

"[Marichal] had such a good delivery that he did not need the slightest changing.

"Most kids imitate some established favorite in their formative years, but Juan didn't look as if he had copied anybody. And he had very good control from the start.

"It took me a few years in the minors to acquire it, but Marichal could get the ball over the first day he reported to us in Sanford, Florida."

**—Hall of Fame pitcher Carl Hubbell,
director of the Giants' farm system, December 7, 1963**

"He's only 20 years old and needs work. If nothing happens to that boy, he's going to be one of the best pitchers in the business. He has an easy motion, and every time he throws the ball it does something."

—Casey Stengel on Spahn, 1942

Marichal and Spahn sailed through the first three innings of the July 2, 1963, game, with Marichal yielding one hit, Spahn yielding one hit, Marichal throwing all his pitches but eventually getting the most mileage out of his fastball, Spahn learning quickly that his screwball flummoxed right-handed hitters while his curve curbed lefties.

When he looked washed up back in 1953, Spahn began experimenting with the screwball. He adopted it for good three years later and started crossing up bewildered right-handed hitters. The screwball extended his career. Spahn also perfected the slider in 1958.

When asked about his pitching philosophy, Marichal said, "Relaxation and confidence. When you relax, you can do it better. If you're tense, you can't work with your body. When you have confidence, you can relax. It's an important point in pitching."

But where does this confidence come from? "It's not wrong to think you're the best. I wanted to be a pitcher so hard, I worked very hard. When you work hard, most of the time you'll be successful."

Against left-handed power hitters like Eddie Mathews, Marichal went to his own screwball frequently. Facing pesky Punch-and-Judy hitters in the Braves lineup like Frank Bolling, Roy McMillan, and Don Dillard (who entered the game in the 14th inning as a pinch-hitter), Marichal tried not to be too fine and fall behind on the count. "You try not to let them get on base. If you let a little guy get on base, when the big guy comes up…" Marichal's strategy against Hank Aaron was universal: "Throw the ball and close your eyes!"

Above all, Marichal respected whatever virtue each hitter possessed. "Our philosophy was to stay away from the power alley of each batter," he said. The Braves' leadoff hitter, Lee Maye, had a much more interesting life than the scattered stats of his 13-year baseball career as an unfulfilled power prospect who sometimes fought with teammates and coaches. Under his full name, Arthur Lee Maye, he spent 40 years singing rhythm and blues and then soul. He had a social conscience, complained about racism, and never got a post-career job in baseball. But Marichal's knowledge of Maye was understandably limited and focused. He knew that Maye's power alley was belt-high from the middle in, so he pitched around that zone in the first inning and got him to pop up to first. Second baseman Frank Bolling singled, but Marichal got Aaron on a foul to first and struck out Mathews. Note who got the hit—a pattern may be forming.

"The first pitch of the game and the first out [were] always important," Spahn told the *Buffalo Evening News*. "Once you're ahead of the batter, you take away the options of the other team to run and steal and play aggressive baseball.

"I always started a game with the idea that the game revolves so much around the first strike and the first out, which means that you must have control."

"Home plate is 17 inches wide," Spahn famously said. "I give the batter the middle 13 inches. That belongs to him. But the 2 outside inches on either side belong to me. That's where I throw the ball." He also said there were two places to pitch a hitter: "Low and outside, where he can't see the ball very well, and up close on the handle of the bat at the belt, where he can't get the bat around."

But control, he told the *Evening News* writer, may consist of throwing pitches just outside the strike zone. "You throw the real strikes only when you must. I won because I could induce a batter to go after a bad pitch, to chase a slow curve, or swing at something not in the strike zone."

Hitters usually need to succeed against excellent pitchers early in a game, before the pitchers find what works for them and establish their rhythm. "The mound in the bullpen and the mound on the field are different," Spahn said. "You have to get acclimated. Get the first out, then the second, then the third. If I get the first three guys out, the No. 4 man leads off the second inning, which is not what his manager intended."

Leading off against Spahn, Harvey Kuenn played shortstop and outfield, was Rookie of the Year, an eight-time All-Star, and the 1959 batting champion with the Detroit Tigers. The convivial tobacco chewer married and divorced a Miss Wisconsin, owned a bar, and managed the 1982 Milwaukee Brewers (aka "Harvey's Wallbangers") to a pennant. Although on the downside of his playing career in 1963, Kuenn was still an excellent contact hitter who struck out just 38 times that season. Above all, he was a keen (pun intended) student of baseball. As recently as 1960, Yankees manager Casey Stengel had said of him, "If the guy was hurt, his team might be hurt, but the pitching all over the league will improve." Spahn got Kuenn on a pop fly to short.

That brought up Mays, who had tormented Spahn ever since he came out of Birmingham, Alabama, in 1951. In fact, Mays' first career hit was a homer off Spahn. "For the first 60 feet, it was a hell of a pitch," Spahn said. He later concluded, "He was something like 0-for-21 [actually 0-for-12] the first time I saw him. His first major league hit was a home run off me—and I'll never forgive myself. We might have gotten rid of Willie forever if I'd only struck him out." Mays would homer against Spahn more often (18 times) than any other hitter. But this time Warren got Willie on a called strike three. Willie McCovey grounded out meekly to first. Four future Hall of Famers had batted, and none had hit a ball out of the infield.

In the top of the second, Marichal got first baseman Norm Larker on a grounder to third and center fielder Mack Jones on a strikeout. Marichal seemed to get a break in facing Spahn's personal catcher, Del Crandall (.201 in 1963), rather than the promising youngster Torre (.293, 14 homers, 71 RBI). But there would be no easy outs, no pit stops in this game. Crandall (who would be heard from again later) reached second base when Kuenn, getting a start at third as manager Alvin Dark tried to put more heft in the lineup, picked up his grounder but threw it away.

Did a man in scoring position with two outs constitute a threat against Marichal? Gaylord Perry, then a young pitcher watching from the Giants dugout, was learning a lot about pitching from observing Juan and speaking with him. Perry had already learned that a situation like that facing Marichal was little to worry about. "I used to win a minor bet in the clubhouse by betting that a run couldn't score from third with no outs against Juan," he said. Sure enough, Marichal got Roy McMillan on a lazy fly to center.

In the Giants half, Felipe Alou flied to left. Then Orlando Cepeda singled to center and stole a base that must have infuriated Spahn even after he survived the inning by getting Ed Bailey to fly to center and José Pagan to foul out. Spahn had the best pickoff throw in baseball, one so subtle and sure that he picked off Jackie Robinson twice in one game. Spahn's motion to first and home were identical, and base runners swore that he eyed them until the very instant he released the ball to the plate. Through 1955, one sportswriter claimed, the Dodgers' Pee Wee Reese was the only runner to steal second off him. The writer erred by a small handful, but his mistake underscores the widespread respect for Spahn's pickoff move.

By the third inning, both pitchers had established their mastery. For the Braves, Spahn grounded out pitcher to first base, Maye flied to center, and Bolling grounded to third. For the Giants, Chuck Hiller grounded to second, Marichal flied to center, and Kuenn grounded to center. Six up, six down.

Looking out at the two pitchers, Perry saw virtual mirror images. "They had so many great pitches. They weren't overpowering, but they had great control and a high kick that made them hard to pick up."

In retrospect, this kind of dominance seemed all but preordained, even if Marichal and Spahn had to overcome many a roadblock on their way to the game of July 2, 1963. The 42-year-old Spahn probably faced more obstacles than the 25-year-old Marichal because his journey covered 17 more years of life and 15 more seasons in the majors.

* * *

The first two batters Marichal faced with the *Escogido* team in the Dominican league back in 1957, big league veterans Harry Chiti and Dick Stuart, went down swinging. Manager Salty Parker, who also coached third for the Giants, was less impressed when Juan grooved too many pitches in his second outing and relieved him in the third inning. But attention had to be paid to his potential.

Though Alejandro Pompez, the Giants' director of Caribbean Basin scouting, met the 20-year-old Marichal and his countrymen Manuel Mota, Mateo Alou, Danilo Rivas, Julio César Imbert, and René Marté when they arrived at 1958 spring training in Sanford, Florida, Marichal underwent the culture shock familiar to his antecedents: learning a new language from scratch, understanding different coaching, shivering in cold weather, living with a black family in the black part of town and rarely leaving it except to go to the ballpark, staying on the bus while white teammates ate at a segregated restaurant and brought him unfamiliar food. "I went through many depressions," Marichal said. "Thank God I survived."

"Like the other Latin players, I had problems with the food and got homesick," Marichal told Rob Ruck in *The Tropic of Baseball: Baseball in the Dominican Republic*. "There was a group of us…that would play *merengue* after practice. But that made me so sad that I finally took my records and broke them one by one and stopped listening to any Dominican music at all."

At the park, though, Marichal broadcast a different image. "He acted as if he'd been a pro for 10 years," said Hubbell, the Giants' farm system chief and Marichal's biggest fan.

Richie Klaus, manager of the Giants' Class C team in St. Cloud, Minnesota, wasn't impressed with Marichal's sidearm deliveries and thought he'd break down. Buddy Kerr, who was managing the Giants' Class D team in Michigan City, Indiana, was happy to take on the kid at a salary of $250 a month. After riding buses north for two days and having food from segregated restaurants brought to them, Marichal and fellow Latinos René Marté, José Tartabull, and Julio Santana gaped at the sight of bare trees in the early spring—that's the standard response Marichal makes when asked about his introduction to the minors—and they gagged when some people sneered at them on the street and refused them service in town and on the road. However, plenty of other residents, it should be added, were welcoming.

"I'll never forget the manager there, Buddy Kerr, he was very good to me," Marichal told the *Boston Globe's* Leigh Montville in 1974. "I'd never been anyplace where everybody couldn't eat in the same restaurant.

"Buddy Kerr was very good. He never went to the restaurant that served only the white players. He came with the black players to make sure we were eating right."

"I didn't speak any English at all then," Marichal told Ruck. "I used to eat a lot of fried chicken because a restaurant [owner] there gave a meal of fried chicken to the pitchers for every game they won. They only gave us $2.50 for meal money, and I won lots of games that year. Sometimes I would see what someone else was eating and point to his plate."

The only time Marichal spent time with his white teammates was at the ballpark, and that stung worse than anything. The thought persisted: *Show my mother I can play baseball.* "I used to love to talk baseball all the time and learn, but I only had four or five players to talk to," he said.

In his May 5, 1958, minor league debut before about 50 shivering fans with the temperature in the 30s, Marichal gave up eight hits, three earned runs, and three walks, striking out six in 7⅓ innings of a 10–6 loss. Five days later he shut out Dubuque on seven hits, fanning 11, and he was off to the races. Completing 24-of-28 starts, recording more strikeouts than innings pitched (246–245) and walking just 50 batters, Marichal led the White Caps to a first-half championship and a second-place overall finish as MVP while leading the Midwest League in wins (21), strikeouts, innings, and ERA (1.87), and he won twice more in the championship series.

Hubbell had put out the word: don't mess with this guy's approach. "I found this out late in the season because nobody came up to me," Marichal said.

"He was kind of an eccentric guy," Don Hood, the team's business manager at the time, told Tom Wyatt of the local *News-Dispatch* in 1998. "We'd be ready to start the game, and he'd either not been down to the bullpen or he was down in the bullpen and everybody was waiting for him to come out and start the game. Most pitchers warm up, come down and sit in the dugout, stand for the national anthem and out they go. Not him."

The following winter, Marichal won eight games for *Escogido*, then he jumped to Class A Springfield, Massachusetts, in 1959 and his salary increased to $450 a month. Despite its name, Class A was considered a high-level minor league, and Springfield was a much friendlier place for Marichal than Michigan City had been. He completed 23-of-32 starts, walked 47 batters in 271 innings, led the Eastern League in wins (18), innings (271), ERA (2.39), and strikeouts (208) and won two playoff games in another MVP season, so impressing Hubbell that he said he had never seen a youngster with so much poise. Rooming with Mota and Mateo Alou, Marichal even learned to cook.

When the Springfield club played in Albany, New York, Marichal and some teammates visited the Hall of Fame an hour away, never dreaming that one of them would be enshrined there. Marichal's manager in Springfield, Andy Gilbert, began to pave the way. Though Hubbell had told him not to change Marichal's style, Gilbert asked the side-arming youngster, "Why do you pitch like that?"

"That's how I learned."

"You would be more effective against left-handed hitters if you didn't throw sidearm."

So Marichal pitched overhand as well and realized something interesting: "I couldn't do that unless I kicked my leg high," he said. He also asked Gilbert how to throw a screwball. "I don't know—I think you have to turn your hand backward," Marichal reported Gilbert as saying. So Juan began experimenting with a screwball in impromptu games of catch with teammates. "The only problem with [pitching overhand] was it took two or three years off my career because it took so much out of my arm," Marichal told sportswriter Rich Westcott. (Note the contrast to Spahn, whose father told him he'd ruin his arm pitching sidearm.)

Gilbert taught Juan the change-up and slider, which he mastered at once, and then Gilbert gave him something more. "Andy Gilbert always wanted me to stay in and finish," Marichal explained to Garry Brown of the *Springfield Union*. "I learned a lot from him. I learned to have courage and not to fear any hitter. He always told me I could get anybody out."

Gilbert also trusted Marichal to go long. In a game that was sure to be referenced later, he lost 1–0 in 17 innings to the Reading Indians and left-hander Julius "Swampwater" Grant, brother of the major league pitcher James "Mudcat" Grant, at Springfield's Pynchon Park on July 29. All of 1,684 lucky fans watched Grant allow 13 hits while walking 10 and fanning nine. Marichal allowed 11 hits, struck out 17, and walked three. The game lasted 4:24 and ended after midnight.

"We could see that Juan would make a great major leaguer," said Eric Fuller, who attended the game with his brother, David, while both were on summer vacation from Milton Academy in the Boston area. "Around the 13th inning, Walt Bond [who later played six years in the majors] came up to bat for the Indians. I think the poor guy had already struck out three or four times. 'We see you coming, Walter,' a drunk behind us yelled. 'We know what you can do!'"

In each of the two seasons, Marichal had thrown 200+ innings and at least another 100 in winter ball for *Escogido*, where he was 8–1 and 4–2. Giants manager Bill Rigney wanted Marichal to pitch exhibitions in 1960 spring training, but the injury jinx reared its ugly head. "In those days they didn't use a screen when you throw batting practice," Marichal said. "They had me pitching it every day. Then one day the pitching coach, Larry Jansen, told me I wouldn't have to that day. I had a rash from my cup so I said, 'Good, I won't have to wear it.' Then Larry came up and said, 'Alvin [manager Alvin Dark] wants you to pitch B.P. I was afraid to tell him that I had to put the support on, so I went ahead and pitched without it. I got hit by a line drive in the right testicle!

"Let me tell you, I couldn't believe it. They took me to the hospital. I was lying on my back for four days. After the fifth, I got a plane ticket to take me from Phoenix to Sanford, Florida, to practice with the Tacoma team. I got there and couldn't practice without pain. I finally got well and started pitching."

After Marichal recovered and began the season at Triple A Tacoma, Washington, where Hubbell ordered Marichal's salary raised to $700 a month, manager Red Davis told Hubbell that Marichal wasn't hiding his pitches and batters could tell when a fastball or curve was coming. "Leave him alone until he gets to the big leagues," Hubbell replied.

Marichal began winning regularly and earned the nickname "Laughing Boy" for his constant smiling and gripe-free attitude. After he won his first five decisions with 41 strikeouts in 44 innings, Tacoma general manager Rosy Ryan told Ed Honeywell of the local *News Tribune*, "Sure, he's a major league prospect. He has the poise of a veteran and is a smart student of pitching. Nothing bothers him, and he has a knack of saving his best stuff for emergencies.

"It should be remembered, though, that he's only 21 [actually 22] and has only two seasons of experience. He needs another season in the minors to acquire his polish to be a winner in the majors." In May, a scouting report said, "Potential major league material, should make the parent club in two years." But two months later Marichal was 11–5, with a 3.11 ERA, 11 complete games in 18 appearances, and 121 strikeouts and 34 walks in 139 innings. Despite some hip trouble, he was promoted to the Giants on July 19 with a telegram that thrilled him much more than the one from Ramfis Trujillo. During his 2½ seasons in the minors, Marichal went 50–26, with a 2.35 ERA, 575 strikeouts (he was called "*El Rey de Ponche*," or "King of the Strikeout," back home) and only 131 (1.80 per game) walks in 655 innings. Those control numbers are staggering for a minor leaguer.

* * *

Minor league rookie Warren Spahn had one advantage over Marichal: he spoke the language. But he was almost as bewildered. Back in 1940, Spahn got off the train in Bradford, Pennsylvania, scared and excited and weighing all of 150 pounds with no idea how to find the local ballpark. "It was 80 miles away [from home in Buffalo]," he said. "It could have been 9,000. I bought a meal ticket from a diner and rented a room."

He joined the PONY (Pennsylvania-Ontario-New York) League's Bradford (Pennsylvania) Bees, managed by Jack Onslow. The *Olean Times-Herald* referred to "Lefty Spahn, a Buffalo high school product rated as one of the best schoolboy hurlers in these parts," and an AP story in the *Bradford Era* quoted Spahn's high school coach, Joe Shoemaker, saying, "If he's developed properly, he'll be a big league pitcher. I've never seen a pitcher as natural as Spahn in my life."

When Spahn asked for No. 13, Onslow muttered, "Just what I need, a screwball lefty." Then to Spahn, he said, "Fella, we don't carry any No. 13s. A guy's liable to run into enough tough luck around here without wearing any No. 13 on his back."

After Spahn's first game, a win, *Era* sports editor Johnny Nelson wrote, "Young Warren 'Lefty' Spahn failed to last the route against the Batavia Clippers the other night but was on the mound long enough to prove he has a future in baseball. Spahn whiffed 10 batters in seven frames." Spahn followed that with a 4–3 win over the London (Ontario) Pirates on July 18 when he struck out 12 before 1,500 hometown fans at Community Park—where box seats cost 65 cents, grandstand seats were 44 cents for men and 28 cents for women, and bleacher seats were 28 cents for men and 25 cents for women. You might say the fans got their money's worth.

The Longest Day(s)

A pitching duel involving more than two hurlers surely deserves mention. The Pawtucket Red Sox and the Rochester Red Wings (then a Baltimore farm club) began playing a game on April 18, 1981, and completed it on June 23, 1981. Okay, they weren't playing the entire time.

They did, however, set U.S. professional baseball records of 33 innings and 8:25 for time elapsed (not counting a 30-minute power delay at the start). Started on the cold, windy Saturday night of April 18 at Pawtucket's McCoy Stadium, the game was suspended with the score 2–2 after 32 innings at 4:09 AM on April 19. It continued before a scheduled game the next time Rochester was due in Pawtucket. The conclusion took only 18 minutes before Dave Koza singled home Marty Barrett to give the Red Sox a 3–2 win in the 33rd. Future Hall of Famers Cal Ripken Jr. of Rochester (2-for-13) and Wade Boggs of Pawtucket (4-for-12) combined to go 6-for-25.

The real heroes were the 14 pitchers, especially Rochester reliever Jim Umbarger, who threw 10 shutout innings, allowing four hits and no walks while striking out nine. In fact, if he had been allowed to continue pitching at the game's resumption, they might still be playing.

Everything from kismet to comedy went into the making of history. The Red Wings almost scored a run in the 11th, but Boggs made a game-saving stop at third base to prevent a double into the left-field corner. A few innings later, Pawtucket's Sam Bowen hit a towering fly to left that seemed certain to go out. "It was gone.... But it came back in [due to a stiff wind], and I caught it," said Rochester left fielder Dallas Williams.

In the top of the 21st, Red Wings catcher Dave Huppert doubled home a run to put Rochester ahead, 2–1. Not to be outdone, Boggs doubled home a run to tie the score in the bottom of the inning. "A lot of people were saying, 'Yeah, yeah, we tied it, we tied it!'" Boggs said. "And then they said, 'Oh, no, what did you do? We could have gone home!'"

According to the revised International League rulebook, the game was supposed to be suspended at 1:00 AM, but home plate umpire Dennis Cregg didn't have the updated version including that proviso and play continued. At 2:00 AM, Luis Aponte of the Red Sox, having pitched the last four innings, got permission to leave the park. When he returned home, his wife Xiomara barked, "Where have you been?" According to Baseball-reference.com, Aponte replied, "At the ballpark." "Like hell you have!" she retorted. Aponte assumed the game would be reported in the Sunday papers, but it was still going at press time. Not a word in print. Reportedly, Aponte spent the rest of the night on the couch.

When Pawtucket general manager Mike Tamburro finally reached International League president Harold Cooper around 3:00 AM, Cooper ruled that the game should be suspended at the end of the inning. It actually wasn't stopped until 4:09 AM with 19 fans in the stands. All were given lifetime passes to McCoy Stadium by team owner Ben Mondor.

Play resumed on June 23, attended by a sellout crowd of 5,746, as well as 140 writers from around the world and four networks, all of them eager to cover any baseball during the major league strike.

Pawtucket's Bob Ojeda, one of the game's 25 players who would reach the majors, took the mound as designated "starting reliever." Ojeda retired Dallas Williams, whose 0-for-13 performance set a single-game record for most at-bats without a hit, surrendered a single to Ripken, struck out Floyd Rayford, and got John Valle on a fly to left. In the bottom of the 33rd, Steve Grilli hit Marty Barrett with his first pitch. Chico Walker singled Barrett to third. Russ Laribee was intentionally passed, and Cliff Speck relieved Grilli. On a 2–2 curveball, Koza singled to left to score Barrett with the walk-off run. Final score: Pawtucket 3, Rochester 2. The game's leading hitter, Koza, went 5-for-14.

Remembering the April 19–20 start, Ripken said, "It's the only time I ever remember our postgame meal being breakfast."

In retrospect, even hitless wonder Dallas Williams got a kick out of the event. "It sank in the next day," he said. "Man, we just played 32 innings of baseball. We joked about it. We had smiles on our faces. I was thankful I was a baseball player and on the field that night. As time went by, I appreciated it more."

Every participant could tell his grandchildren about the game. And why not? It made them all baseball immortals. "Everyone associated with that game is in Cooperstown...and that's the destination of everyone who ever plays this game," said Rochester's Dave Huppert.

The longest major league game in time played (again, delays are not counted) took 8:06 before the Chicago White Sox's Harold Baines hit a walk-off, 25th inning homer to beat the Milwaukee Brewers 7–6 on May 8–9, 1984. The longest major league game in terms of innings occurred on May 1, 1920, when the Dodgers' Leon Cadore and the Braves' Joe Oeschger pitched 26 innings before the game was called after 3:50 due to darkness with the score 1–1.

Though Spahn lost to Jamestown 4–3 on July 21, he beat Batavia 9–2 on July 24 and smiled up to the press box where Onslow was sitting while on leave because of illness. Then it was Spahn's turn to take a leave of absence.

Experimenting with a new delivery for an overhand curve early in an 11–2 loss to Hamilton on July 30, Spahn, now listed as 168 pounds, snapped the pitch too sharply and tore several ligaments in his left shoulder. Billy Meyers, who had scouted and signed Spahn, took him to a chiropractor who advised rest. Spahn went home with his arm in a sling. When the youngster returned to Pennsylvania two weeks later, he beat London 6–1 on one hit in a five-inning game then lost to Olean 7–3 on August 22. At some point during his second stay at Bradford, he reportedly threw a hard pitch and tumbled off the mound clutching his shoulder. The Bees sent him home on August 23. "They said I was throwing too much with my elbow," Spahn told his old high school teammate Bill Klas. "I don't know what the arm's going to be like from now on."

The Bradford trainer said Spahn would need a year off if he was lucky, and Onslow (recovered from his illness) muttered, "You know, maybe I should have given that fella No. 13 after all." Back home, Edward Spahn went into a depression and was hospitalized. Warren spent the remainder of the summer, the fall, and the winter checking baggage at the Buffalo railroad terminal and wondering about his future.

With a 5–4 record, 62 strikeouts, only 24 walks and 53 hits in 66 innings, and a 2.73 ERA in his brief stay, however, Spahn was named a league Honorable Mention All-Star and showed enough promise to be invited to the Boston Braves (they had just junked the name Bees after five seasons) 1941 spring training camp in San Antonio. His arm had recovered by then, and so had his father's health. After throwing half a dozen pitches at full speed, Spahn said, "My arm's all right. Feels perfect. I won't let Dad down now." But Spahn suffered a broken and permanently disfigured nose courtesy of a teammate's errant throw, and he got some nicknames he didn't appreciate, such as Hooks, the Nose, and the Great Profile. Even his father called him Meatnose.

"When Dad's nose was broken, [St. Louis Browns infielder] John Berardino's nose was also broken the same day," Spahn's son, Greg, recalled. "They sent John to a specialist to have it fixed. They called Dad in and told him, 'Warren, we would send you to a specialist to have your nose fixed, but most people that have that done end up with sinus problems, and you're not a very good-looking guy.' The ballclub didn't want to spend the money on Dad's nose. John Berardino, being an actor, was a different story." As an actor who later became a soap opera star, John usually used the name Beradino.

Braves manager Casey Stengel thought the world of Spahn's potential. "That fella can wear No. 13 on his socks, for all I care," Stengel said. "If a kid ever looked like a pitcher, this fella's it." Playing at $125 a month for a Braves farm club, Evansville, Indiana, of the Class B Three-I (Indiana-Illinois-Iowa) League, Spahn played under manager Bob Coleman, who helped him develop a smooth motion and was "an excellent teacher" in Spahn's estimation. "He once paid me the greatest compliment I've ever had," Spahn told writer Al Hirshberg. "When I was at Evansville, he bawled me out for something I did in a game that we won, 2–1. 'You've made the same mistake before. I allow two mistakes per ordinary ballplayer. I only allow you one, because you're not an ordinary ballplayer.'" It was shades of Edward Spahn speaking to young Warren!

Spahn led the league in wins (19), winning percentage (.760), shutouts (7), and ERA (1.83) while striking out 193 batters in 212 innings. With Spahn throwing 42 consecutive scoreless innings and three one-hitters, Evansville won the pennant. Coleman adjusted Spahn's delivery to put less pressure on his elbow (he never again had trouble with it), and Spahn's roommate, pitcher Willard Donovan, helped him perfect the pickoff move an old coach, Johnny Cooney, had taught him in spring training.

"I spent a good deal of time perfecting the motion—more so than the average pitcher, I would think. I used to go in the outfield with a catcher and just practice all the time. When I wanted to throw to first, I'd throw at the outfield wall. I tried to coordinate my head and leg movements until it became almost automatic. If I ever learned more in one year than any other, that was the year."

Spahn's smooth, overhand delivery and flawless follow-though won raves at 1942 spring training in Sanford, Florida. Cincinnati pitcher Bucky Walters said, "I don't know whether he's a two-bit pitcher or not, but he's got a $100,000 delivery." When Spahn's Boston teammate Johnny Sain told him, "I wish I had your form," Spahn replied, "I'll swap it for your curve."

The old Hall of Fame catcher Ernie Lombardi warmed Spahn up. When he threw one of his best fastballs, Lombardi reportedly caught it barehanded, spat tobacco juice on it, and threw it back harder. Turning his back to rub off the juice, Spahn recalled, "Right then and there I decided to start learning as many pitches as I could because maybe my fastball wasn't all it was cracked up to be."

Spahn made the club. He even had a short-term, future Hall of Fame roommate, Paul "Big Poison" Waner. "I got up the first morning and Waner reached under the bed and brought up a bottle of whiskey," Spahn told Cy Kritzer of the *Buffalo Evening News*. "He said he always drank the stuff, and he saw two baseballs. He always hit the bottom one."

In his second big-league outing, Spahn hit rock-bottom when he failed to obey Stengel's order to throw at Pee Wee Reese, who had been hospitalized by an earlier beanball. Spahn did throw three straight inside pitches,[9] but Stengel stalked to the mound and growled, "After your shower, pick up your railroad ticket to Hartford." He also added, "Young man, you've got no guts." Later, after Stengel calmed down, he said Spahn had star potential.

Spahn reported to Hartford for twice his 1941 salary and wowed the Eastern League with a 17–12 record and a 1.96 ERA. "He struck out a dozen of us," Danny Carnevale, who played for Scranton and had faced Spahn in Buffalo schoolboy games, told the *Buffalo Evening News'* Robert J. Summers. "He had one of the greatest curveballs ever." His minor league totals over the course of three seasons included a 41–22 record with 355 hits, 396 strikeouts, and 244 walks in 526 innings. Batters weren't putting much wood on Spahn's pitches, and once his control improved they wouldn't have much success reaching base against him at all.

Spahn was later recalled to pitch twice more for the seventh-place Braves. He had no wins but did get credit for a complete game on September 26, when Polo Grounds kids who had been admitted for working in a wartime scrap-metal drive swarmed the field and forced the Giants to forfeit a game in which they were beating Spahn 5–2. (No pitcher gets a win in a forfeit, unless he's already qualified for one by a usual route such as starting and lasting 5+ innings with a lead.)

For his efforts, Spahn—who had a 5.74 ERA in 15⅔ innings for the season—was not assured a place on the Braves. Even so, a club official told him, "We hope you'll be back with us next season, because you'll probably stick. If not, we'll be waiting for you after the war."

Uncle Sam made the question moot. Spahn enlisted on December 3, 1942, and was listed at 5'10" and 150 pounds, numbers that may be challenged since the enlistment record also said he had four years of college. He was also listed as single with dependents. Spahn joined the Army as a buck private and was sent to Fort Niagara for basic training. "Then we were put on a train and rode all day and night," Spahn told the *Buffalo Evening News*'s Kritzer. "Somewhere we changed trains and rode a lot more and reached the end of the world—a place called Fort Chafee, Arkansas."

His past followed him when the weather warmed up and his superiors learned of his skills. Pitching on August 5 for the 1850th Service Unit team, whose lineup included future major league pitcher Zeb Eaton, Spahn threw a 15–0 no-hitter against a broadcaster's team in which he struck out 15 batters. Two men reached base—on errors.

Spahn eventually got on a second train and decamped at Camp Gruber, 60 miles southeast of Tulsa, Oklahoma. "I filled out another questionnaire at Camp Gruber, and put down my occupation, professional ballplayer," Spahn told his *Evening News* interviewer. "The sergeant said, 'What can a ballplayer do in this 14th Armored Division?' and I couldn't answer him."

Spahn wound up in the 276th Combat Engineers Battalion, where Buffalo friend Roy Reimann introduced him to his future wife, LoRene Southard, an oil company executive secretary with spectacular business acumen, who would later help to make him rich. Pitching in the summer of 1944 for the Gruber Engineers and with Reimann as his catcher, Spahn won his first 10 games—seven on shutouts—and struck out 186 batters in 80 innings before uncharacteristically committing three throwing errors in a 7–1 loss to the semi-pro Atlas Electrics of Tulsa at Texas League Park on July 30, 1944.

Leaving his last stateside post at Fort Dix, New Jersey, Spahn was shipped to Europe aboard the Queen Mary. As a staff sergeant for the Army's 1159th Engineer Combat Group's 276th Engineer Combat Battalion, he arrived in France in August and survived for about 10 days on peanut butter sandwiches provided by friendly British soldiers. Of his fellow American soldiers, Spahn was quoted as saying in *Baseball in Wartime*, "That was a tough bunch of guys. We had people that were let out of prison to go into the service. So those were the people I went overseas with, and they were tough and rough, and I had to fit that mold."

In December 1944 and January 1945, Spahn fought in Germany's Hürtgen Forest and the frozen Battle of the Bulge. "We were surrounded in the Hürtgen Forest and had to fight our way out of there. Our feet were frozen when we went to sleep, and they were frozen when we woke up. We didn't have a bath or change of clothes for weeks."

"Surviving in combat is a grueling experience," Spahn told writer Bob Obojski. "At one point in 1944, I was on the line for 30 straight days. Toward the end of that point you try like hell not to act like an animal for 30 days, no power, no change of uniform, no nothing. But we did survive on K-rations."

Later, Spahn and his engineer battalion preceded the troops while repairing roads and bridges. Crossing France and Belgium, his U.S. 9th Armored Division arrived at the Rhine River and the Ludendorff railroad bridge at Remagen on March 7, 1945. While retreating, the Nazis had destroyed every intact bridge but the one at Remagen, and the Allies hadn't knocked it off, either. The demolitions were in place, but according to one account, two Polish soldiers who had been forcibly conscripted by the Germans cut off the fuses. "The German demolitions didn't go off," Spahn said at a World War II ceremony. "We shot the people on it, dragged the bodies off."

The bridge's defense was considered crucial to the Allies for delivering men, vehicles, and equipment into the German heartland. On March 9, Sergeant Spahn and the 276th were ordered to the bridge to remove the demolitions, fix the girders, maintain the roadway, and construct a 140' Double Bailey bridge close by. Working furiously to maintain the girders, Spahn and company were bombarded by V–2 rockets while troops, tanks, and trucks crossed above them. Biographer Al Silverman described the scene:

"While the bridge vibrated and twanged like banjo strings, swaying precariously as marching infantrymen tramped across each catwalk, and tanks rumbled across the planked railbed, the units patched holes, bolstered the bridge with heavy supports, repaired damaged flooring, and cratered approaches."

On March 15, Spahn was wounded in his right leg and foot by German bombers. He kept working with shrapnel in it. The next day, Spahn received an assignment at a meeting over the center of the bridge and walked off it to explain to his platoon that they'd be taking over the bridge's security at 4:00 PM. At 3:56, a platoon member shouted, "Look at the back! The bridge is falling down!" Possibly overloaded with repairs to its holes and certainly bombarded, the span slipped into the river with rivets peeling off in a machine-gun staccato, leaving 28 soldiers dead and 93 wounded according to one account. Having crossed the Rhine, however, the Americans were able to protect the Double Bailey bridge and the other pontoon bridges they had built. The shrapnel in

Spahn's leg and foot was removed by surgeons. "Something like that makes you a fatalist," Spahn said of the experience.

For keeping the bridge operational under enemy fire, Spahn was given a battlefield commission and promoted from staff sergeant to second lieutenant on June 1, 1945. In all, he earned a Bronze Star, a Purple Heart, and a battlefield commission, making him one of the most decorated major leaguers in the war. Also highly decorated was future Hall of Famer Bob Feller, who served four years as a gun captain on the USS *Alabama* and received five campaign ribbons and eight battle stars.

Some players who had not yet reached the majors deserve mention. Among them are two more Hall-bound players—Hoyt Wilhelm, who earned a Purple Heart, and Yogi Berra, then 18, who rode in a dangerous LCSS (Landing Craft Support Small) when the allies peppered Omaha Beach and Marseilles. Berra received a Purple Heart, a Distinguished Unit Citation, two battle stars, a Good Conduct medal, and an ETO (European Theatre of Operations) ribbon while being promoted to Seaman First Class. Ralph Houk, later Berra's backup for eight years and the first manager to win pennants in his first three years, fought in the Battle of the Bulge and was at Remagen with Spahn. Houk earned a Purple Heart, Silver Star, Bronze Star, four campaign stars, and clusters. Perhaps the most incredible story belonged to Lou Brissie, who was severely wounded in Italy on December 7, 1944, and nearly had a leg amputated en route to two Purple Hearts and a Bronze Star.[10] Nonetheless, he returned to pitch seven seasons for the A's and Indians with a metal brace on his left leg and even made an All-Star team.

"Bullet nicked me here," Spahn told Lester J. Biederman of the *Pittsburgh Press*, motioning to a scar on his stomach, "and another one grazed me on the back of the neck." (He didn't bother mentioning the shrapnel wounds.) Aged rapidly into a partially bald and fully grown-up veteran, Spahn also built up stamina, concentration, and discipline. "After what I went through overseas, I never thought of anything I was told to do in baseball as hard work," he insisted years later. "You get over feeling like that when you spend days on end sleeping in frozen tank tracks in enemy-threatened territory. The Army taught me something about challenges and about work and what's important and what isn't. Everything I tackle in baseball and in life I take as a challenge rather than work."

Typically, Spahn found humor in the grimmest of situations. Because German spies would wear American uniforms, he said, "Anybody we didn't know, we'd ask, 'Who plays second for the Bums?' If he didn't answer 'Eddie Stanky,' he was dead." Spahn had no use for being labeled a hero. "The guys who died over there were heroes," he told his son Greg. Nor did Spahn cotton to the view of baseball historians who claimed he lost 30 or 40 wins to service time. "I matured a lot in those [war] years," he said. "If I had not had that maturity, I wouldn't have pitched until I was 45." A statement like that says much about character. By contrast, Feller has said that if it weren't for *his* wartime service, "I'd have won more games than Warren Spahn."

Unaware that the war would end quickly after Hiroshima and Nagasaki, Spahn accepted the battlefield promotion—"the dumbest thing I ever did," he joked—which forced him to remain in the service until he was discharged on his 25th birthday, April 23, 1946, thereby missing the start of that season. Instead, he became the hottest pitcher in Germany. Working for the 115th Engineers Group at the University of Heidelberg, he allowed one run on nine hits and struck out 73 batters in four games. After what he'd been through, succeeding as a major league pitcher would not be his biggest challenge.

~ Chapter 5 ~

FROM THE STICKS
TO THE SERIES

"One of the beautiful things about baseball is that every once in a while you come into a situation where you want to, and where you have to, reach down and prove something."

—**Nolan Ryan, Hall of Fame pitcher**

As the game moved into the fourth inning, Juan Marichal and Warren Spahn were keeping the ball down, always a good idea. "A pitcher pitches low instead of high because how often have you seen a 410' ground ball?" Hall of Fame right-hander Jim Bunning once said. In Spahn's words, "When I throw a ground ball, I expect it to be an out—maybe two."

Leading off the top of the fourth, Hank Aaron took his signature walk to the plate, one best described by Lonnie Wheeler in the book he wrote with Aaron, *I Had a Hammer*.

"The Aaron home run became a familiar routine, the way he carried his bat in one hand, his helmet in the other, stopped outside the batter's box, balanced the bat on his thigh, affixed his helmet with two hands, stared at the pitcher, twisted his spikes into the deep part of the box, waved his bat over the plate in two or three loose, rhythmic, rising parabolas, cocked his right arm, took a pitch or two, stepped out, stepped in again, waited, watched, saw something, recoiled, stepped forward, turned his hips, snapped his hands, raised his eyes, dropped his bat, and commenced to circle the bases in that loping, effortless

57

stride, head straight, shoulders back, elbows swinging high beside him, a gait intended to show up nobody and still make the point."

Aaron had built up strong wrists from hitting bottle caps with a broom as a boy, and he also had the capacity to be patient and take full advantage of opportunity. By the time he was 18 he was playing professionally. When a teammate on the Indianapolis Clowns, a leading team in the Negro Leagues, got hurt, Aaron took over at shortstop. After 18 games, he was hitting .467. On June 14, 1952, Braves G.M. John Quinn purchased Aaron's contract for $10,000. Before his promotion to Milwaukee, Hank had some brutal experiences in segregated minor league cities. "I learned in life to be patient and not to show pain," he said later. When Bobby Thomson broke an ankle in 1954 spring training, Aaron made the big club and took his job.

Aaron became so dominant during the next decade that the Dodgers' Jim Lefebvre told writer George Will for the book *Bunts* that in 1965, Lefebvre's rookie season, when the Dodgers discussed how to defend and pitch to the league's top hitters, names like Mays and Mathews drew discussion but the room went silent when Aaron's name came up. "Then someone said, 'When he hits one, make sure nobody's on. Next.'"

Most batters hit with the weight on their back foot, but Aaron hit off his front. Most hitters anticipate a fastball, figuring they can adjust to something slower. Not Aaron. "I looked for the same pitch my whole career, a breaking ball," Aaron said. "All of the time. I never worried about the fastball. They couldn't throw it past me, none of them." When Lou Burdette and Warren examined Aaron's bat after half a season's use, Will goes on, they found a dent massed on the "sweet spot" of the bat. And that wasn't all Aaron could do. In 1963, manager Bobby Bragan said the reason Willie Mays was making $125,000 while Aaron was making $75,000 was that Mays stole bases.[11] Aaron promptly stole 31 in 36 tries to place second in the league. He won Gold Gloves for his fielding in 1958–60. Long respected as a premier power hitter, Aaron was in fact the prototypical five-tool player. In Bragan's autobiography, he called Aaron "the ultimate ballplayer to manage."

Spahn's son, Greg, joined the Braves during his school vacations and became Aaron's buddy. The young man noted that Aaron couldn't stay in segregated hotels and had to eat in the kitchens of segregated restaurants. "This just isn't right," he told his father.

The elder Spahn agreed. Spahn had once told an insensitive joke calling a dead cockroach "Hank"—he meant it as a comment about Aaron's slow gait, not his color—that he later apologized for. A conversation with Aaron changed their relationship. "When Dr. King was leading all the marches," Aaron recalled in *I Had a Hammer*, "Spahn came up to me in the clubhouse one day and said, 'Henry, just what is it that you people want?' I said, 'All we want is the things you've had all along.' We got along fine after that."

According to Greg Spahn, his father became a confidant for Aaron on matters personal and professional. Spahn later contributed to the building of a Hank Aaron statue in Atlanta. For his part, Aaron had to psyche himself up when he faced a 44-year-old Spahn pitching for the Mets in 1965. (It spoke well for Spahn that he and Greg were two of the few whites invited to Willie Mays' 50th birthday party.)

At this point in his career, Aaron was still hitting line drives more often than fly-ball homers; on one famous occasion the shortstop leaped for a ball that carried over the fence. It wasn't until the Braves moved to Atlanta in 1966 that he changed from a line-drive to a high-fly stroke to suit the hotter climate and higher altitude of a new park.

* * *

Aaron always seemed to hit the ball just far enough to clear the fence. In the fourth inning of the game on July 2, 1963, though, nature caught up to him when he flied out deep to left field. "Did you see him hit that ball?" Marichal said after the game. "It was going out of the park, and then that wind caught it. What a break that was!"

Marichal got Eddie Mathews on strikes, but Norm Larker walked and Mack Jones singled him to second. With two out and two on, Crandall hit a sinking liner to center. Mays elected to one-hop it rather than dive, and he quickly set to throw.

If there was a more serviceable villain for Milwaukee fans than Larker, he was hard to find. Playing for the Dodgers in 1959, he had kayoed Braves shortstop Johnny Logan with a body block in the pennant-deciding playoff series won by L.A. Ten days after the memorable Marichal-Spahn game, Larker would be beaten up by Braves teammate Bob Shaw in a dugout fight, and he would be sold to the Giants on August 8. Larker provided at least one moment of mirth in his career—his complaint about Braves pitcher Burdette. Phil Pepe of the *New York Daily News* captured this exchange:

"'C'mon, Frank,' he complained to umpire Secory, 'the guy's throwing spitters.' 'Naah,' Secory replied, 'them were sinkers.' 'Sinkers!' Larker replied. 'My foot! One of them sinkers just splashed me in the right eye!'"

Now Larker, who batted .177 for the Braves and .071 for the Giants in 1963, his last season, was running on contact with two outs and trying to outrace a Mays throw. The indignity! Mays nailed Larker at the plate in "one amazing motion," according to the *San Francisco Chronicle*'s Bob Stevens and on a "100 percent perfect peg," according to Stevens' colleague, Bill Leister.

"Omigod, I was so happy!" Marichal said years later when interviewed at his Santo Domingo home. "He made a perfect throw. We had better throwing than they have today. Most teams don't practice it now. In our day people would come out early to see infield and outfield practice. They loved to see Roberto Clemente throwing from right field to third and home."

That man Mays. He had tormented Spahn with his bat, and now he was burning him with his arm. When Mays returned to the dugout, teammates shook his hand. There were no high fives, low fives, fist bumps, hugs, or anything else. Personal style hadn't taken over the game. Anyone standing at the plate to admire a homer could expect to be knocked down on his next at bat. Everyone was clean-shaven with short hair. There was no diversity in dress—no earrings, bracelets, chains, necklaces, backward caps, or pants drooping around the ankles. Sports jackets and ties were *de rigueur* on planes. "The idea was for everyone to look the same," said Al Stanek, a 19-year-old Giants rookie pitcher who witnessed the historic game.

* * *

In the bottom of the fourth, Denis Menke replaced Mathews, who had missed three games with a right wrist injury and plainly returned too soon. Though Menke batted just .234 in 1963 and hadn't yet attained the skills that made him twice an All-Star in Houston and a mainstay for postseason Cincinnati teams, he already had played 6½ years of pro ball at 23, was in the process of learning to play seven different positions, and was earning the cherished label "hard-nosed." A scrub playing like a star, Menke got two hits and stole a base before the game ended.

In the Giants fourth, Mays grounded out, McCovey singled to right, Alou forced McCovey (short to second), and Cepeda popped to Spahn who, unlike most pitchers, didn't give way to an infielder and fielded the ball himself. After the Braves' Roy McMillian grounded to short and Spahn struck out in the fifth, Lee Maye walked and stole second. This time Marichal owed his man-in-scoring-position escape to Harvey Kuenn, who caught Frank Bolling's liner. When the Giants batted, they were feeble indeed: Ed Bailey grounded to first, José Pagan popped to short, and Chuck Hiller popped to second.

The old man was outpitching the *wunderkind*! And against a tougher lineup! You had to give Spahn credit. All but McCovey, Bailey, and Hiller were right-hander hitters against the left-handed Spahn. A right-handed pitcher has a natural advantage over a left-handed thrower because his pitches break away from the more numerous right-handed batters and out of their power zone. But they break into a left-hander's prime hitting area low and inside. With the odds against them, left-handed pitchers have to be crafty. In baseball mythology, however, they're flaky, unorthodox, and wild. When Spahn came up, some baseball people thought a left-hander's heart was closer to that side of his body than a right-hander's.

Being crafty meant playing against type. "I got to hit against Carl Hubbell [in 1942], and he threw me a screwball that broke more than a right-handed pitcher's curve," Spahn said. "He threw inside to a left-handed batter! That influenced me."

Hitters were always off-balance against Spahn. "Hitting is timing," he used to say. "Pitching is upsetting timing."[12] By using the same motion on all of his pitches, Spahn gave hitters no hint about what was coming. Though he was best known for the fastball, slider, and screwball, Spahn wrote in a 1955 *Collier's* piece, "In my opinion, the change-up is the most valuable pitch in any hurler's repertoire. You can't fool the hitters consistently until you learn how to vary the speed of your pitches."

Spahn often seemed to shake off the catcher when they'd actually agreed on a pitch "He's standing up there figuring, 'Spahn's coming in with this kind of pitch, and I'm going to hit it,'" Spahn said, "and then I shake my head and he stops and thinks, 'Why did he do that?' Then he figures out something else and I shake my head again, and the first thing you know, I got him thinking the way I want him to. Then I've got the confidence and he doesn't. You have to get every psychological advantage you can in this game."

Meanwhile, Milwaukee was probing for a weakness in Marichal's pitching. Though he had a good pickoff motion, he also suffered the right-hander's dilemma of facing third while a runner edged off first. After Aaron popped to the catcher leading off the sixth, Menke singled and stole second. Then, as so often happened in this game, Marichal stiffened. Larker popped to second and Jones to third. For their part, three Giants flied out: Marichal to center, Harvey Kuenn, and Mays to right.

No breaks, no pit stops. Marichal and Spahn worked unimpeded by instructions from the bench, just pitcher and catcher. Through six scoreless innings, Marichal had a four-hitter and Spahn a nifty two-hitter. This had been the pattern since the start of their major league careers.

* * *

Warren Spahn made the Braves roster for good in 1946, and he was tickled pink to be in Boston—or possibly frozen pink because the weather was similar to that back home in Buffalo. He could relate to the Braves' working-class fans and blue-collar history. And Braves Field was made for him.

No need to explain Boston weather, except to say that the wind was coming off the Charles River and in from left and center field—a pitcher's delight. The country's "oldest continuously operated franchise in the league," the Braves were founded in 1871 as the Red Stockings, won four consecutive championships, beat Philadelphia 6–5 in the National League's first game on April 22, 1876, and morphed into the Beaneaters, who won five pennants in the 1890s under manager Frank Selee. With Hall of Famers like Kid Nichols and Hugh Duffy, they were baseball's first dynasty. They adopted the name Braves in 1912 and have kept it except for five years of folly as the Bees from 1936–40. Though they had won just a single pennant in the 20th century, it was a classic—the Miracle Braves pennant and World Series sweep of the mighty Philadelphia Athletics in 1914.

The Braves abandoned their 11,000-seat firetrap, South End Grounds ("an ornate but dilapidated double-decked wooden edifice," according to writer Bob

Brady), and opened Braves Field on August 18, 1915, on the 10-acre site of a golf course in the Allston section of Boston. With smoke from the Albany Railroad yard blowing in with the wind from left and center, the place could be an ordeal for fans and players. Nonetheless, it was a ground-breaking edifice that symbolized the change from wood to concrete that was about to appear all over baseball. With seating that could be expanded to accommodate 43,500 spectators, Braves Field was described as the "Largest Ball Ground in the World" on a contemporary postcard. Christened the "perfect park" by owner James E. Gaffney, it was initially 402' down the lines and 550' to center: a dead-ball haven in deference to the dead-ball era. (The dimensions were later scaled down.) The Red Sox liked Braves Field so much they played the 1915 and 1916 World Series there.

Constructed from 750 tons of steel and 8,200,000 pounds of concrete, the place received excellent reviews from everyone but hitters who confused it with a desert island. Boston columnist Harold Kaese described Ty Cobb, who "stood at home plate one day, shaded his eyes with his hand like an Indian scout looking over the prairie, and said, 'One thing is sure. Nobody is ever going to hit a ball over those fences.'" Nonetheless, Cobb conceded, "This is the only field in the country on which you can play an absolutely fair game of ball without interference of fences."

But as one losing season followed another, only wins would bring people to Braves Field in respectable numbers. A section of the right-field stands with vocal regulars became known as the Jury Box, because a writer swore there were only 12 people in 2,000 available seats there. The Braves couldn't compete with the free-spending Red Sox owner Tom Yawkey. But if they were losers, at least the Braves were lovable losers who let kids join a Knot-Hole Gang, attend games for nickels and dimes, and get instruction from the players. Braves fans were mostly working class and urban—they'd come in via streetcar and subway from neighborhoods like Dorchester—in contrast to the business community and suburbanites who patronized the Red Sox. At Braves Field, moreover, there were amenities like fried clams, an electronic scoreboard, and team yearbooks.

In the mid-1940s, three self-made construction men and sons of immigrants, primary owner Lou Perini and his partners Guido Rugo and Joseph Maney, purchased the club and became known as the Three Little

Steamshovels. Through trades, signing, and player development, they built a contender. Notably, the progressive ownership also began scouting black players—who would in turn bring out black fans—in contrast to the sport's most racist organization down the trolley tracks.

With Spahn due back from the service in 1946 (and still a rookie because he hadn't pitched 60 innings in a season), the win-starved Braves gave him a big buildup. "There is a young left-handed pitcher who is due out of the service in a month or so, who may help us," said new Braves manager Billy Southworth, who had won three pennants in five seasons with the Cardinals, unaware that Spahn had already pitched for the club. "His name is Spahn, Warren Spahn, and our organization has good reports on him from Evansville and Hartford, where he pitched before going into the service."

Spahn hadn't forgotten his fiancée, LoRene Southard. "I met him at the train [after his return], and we didn't recognize each other until the station platform was almost deserted," she said. "He had lost so much hair and looked—well, so much older and so different. My doctor had put me on a special diet, and I had gained a lot of weight."

The Braves promoted Spahn to the majors on June 10, 1946. "This is the first time in years I've reported to anybody without saluting," Spahn told Southworth. He asked G.M. John Quinn to double his $250-a-month salary, and Quinn did.

Spahn appeared in his first postwar game as a reliever in the sixth inning seven days later—Bunker Hill Day in New England—and gave up one run and four hits, struck out two, and walked none in four innings against the Cardinals at Braves Field. "He was all grace," biographer Al Silverman wrote, "kicking his right leg high in the air, his left elbow passing his right knee, just as his dad had taught him, then uncoiling and the ball snapping to the plate out of flapping sleeves and trousers, the ball streaking in and on the batter almost before he could measure it, blazing in like a freight train coming out of the darkness. It was one of the most extravagant and picturesque motions in baseball, but it served a purpose. The big-leg-high-arm-way-back stance gave him maximum body leverage behind the pitch and minimum effect on the arm."

To think that he hadn't pitched against a serious opponent in four years. Spahn considered the wind from the river and the smoke from the railroad yard, and he rubbed his hands together in glee. It was a pitcher's park; that was all that mattered. In his fourth start on July 14, Spahn beat the Pirates 4–1 and allowed just one runner past second base (Frankie Gustine, who homered). Like Lefty Grove, Spahn got his first big-league victory at age 25. Then he beat the Cubs 6–1 on July 19 and the league-leading Cardinals 5–2 on July 27 to the disbelief of a St. Louis broadcaster, Hall of Fame pitcher Dizzy Dean. "Spahn is pitching for the Braves," Dean said. "Who in the world is Spahn?" Spahn was the guy who beat the Cubs 4–1 for his fourth win.

Fearing that an in-season wedding would distract Spahn, Southworth wanted him to wait until the season was over before marrying LoRene—he even offered to be best man and pay for the wedding and honeymoon—but Spahn instead got a day off and married her on August 10 with only family in attendance. After winning a fifth game, he lost two straight. Chuck Dressen, a Dodgers coach, said Spahn was tipping off his pitches. "We can beat Spahn every time he pitches," Dressen crowed. "We know every pitch he throws."

Even so, Spahn, who would correct the flaw the following spring with help from pitching coach Johnny Cooney, went 8–5 with a 2.94 ERA in 24 appearances and completed 8-of-16 starts over the second half of the 1946 season. "Pressure? What pressure?" he said. "If I do badly, what's the worst thing that's going to happen? No one is going to shoot at me!"

Spahn knew life can cut to black in a trice, and he seemed to celebrate daily that it hadn't. "Before the war I didn't have anything that slightly resembled self-confidence," Spahn told the Associated Press in August 1946. "Then I was tight as a drum and worrying about every pitch. But nowadays I just throw them up without the slightest mental pressure."

"I feel like, wow, what a way to make a living," he was quoted as saying in a 1990 *USA Today* story. "If I goof up, there's going to be a relief pitcher come in there. Nobody's going to shoot me."

"When I first reported to the Braves after the war, I didn't know how I'd do it," Spahn said, "so I took a devil-may-care attitude to protect myself. The more pressure I feel, the more I kid [around]. That's my way of relaxing."

Because of his military service, balding pate, and relatively advanced age, Spahn fit in quickly, lost his shyness, and became an instant elder statesman on the Boston club. Soldier that he was, Spahn would give his life for his mates and enjoyed sometimes-rough humor. Foolishness aside, he was a hard man who could deliver a plain message bluntly. "He was born old," a teammate said, and the writers described him as a downright Homeric figure.

In a conversation captured by a Philadelphia sportswriter, Phillies manager Ben Chapman and slugger Del Ennis traded impressions of Spahn with Giants slugger Johnny Mize:

Chapman: "Spahn has one of the greatest overhand curves I've ever seen."

Ennis: "Never mind the curve. What I have to watch for is the change of pace he throws. I swing at it before it is halfway to the plate."

Mize: "The curve and change of pace are all right, but it's that fastball. It does tricks as it reaches the plate."

* * *

Meanwhile, the 1946 Braves were creeping back into respectability. They finished fourth at 81–72 and set a home attendance record of 969,673 (even after 5,000 fans left the opener with fresh green paint on the seats of their pants), while their batters led the league in fewest strikeouts (466) and their pitchers in lowest opponents' on-base percentage (.314). Johnny Sain, who returned from the service to go 20–14, would have had a perfect game but for a you-take-it popup that fell for a hit. Like Spahn, Sain was profoundly influenced as a pitcher by his wartime experience, although it hadn't been the dangerous kind. "He told me that he was a five-inning pitcher before the war, and when he got on an Army team they had one pitcher and he had to learn to pace himself so he'd just aim and throw the first pitch right down the middle," teammate Clint Conatser told author Brent Kelley.

In an act that influenced Bernard Malamud's novel *The Natural* and the movie of the same name, Boston's Bama Rowell homered to shatter the Bulova clock above the scoreboard in Brooklyn's Ebbets Field. It stopped dead at 4:25 PM. The Braves were just coming alive.

They contended in 1947, finishing third and only eight games out with an 86–68 record. Newly acquired Bob Elliott, whom Southworth accommodated with a permanent home at third base after he was shuttled around in Pittsburgh, won the league's MVP Award with a .317 average, 22 homers, and 113 RBIs. Sain won 21 games, and Spahn became a star with his fastball, curve, and suddenly masterful change-up. He had stayed in shape over the winter as a foreman for the Perini Construction Company. In notching a 21-win season— the first of 13 seasons as a 20-game winner—he led the league in ERA (2.33), innings pitched (289⅔), and shutouts (7), while getting just 11 total runs in support in his 10 losses, five of which were shutouts. He might have won nine straight, but Johnny Hopp misjudged a fly by the Cardinals' Red Schoendienst that turned into a triple that led to the only three runs of the game on June 3. "What the hell, Johnny, if we hadn't lost it one way we'd have lost it another," Spahn said. "My curve ball was hanging."

The statistic wasn't kept officially, but Spahn picked off at least 16 base runners. Commenting on Spahn in the November 1947 issue of *Baseball Magazine*, Southworth said, "A good curve, fastball, change of pace, and control of all three. Every ball he throws does something. He simply has good stuff, plus that confidence I just mentioned. That's always a winning combination in any league." Even Dressen, the Dodgers coach who had ridiculed Spahn a season earlier, admitted, "The kid learned fast."

After they added slugger Jeff Heath and Eddie Stanky, an All-Star second baseman, the 1948 Braves were picked to finish second. The Braves Field dimensions—337' to left, 370' to center, 319' to right—were now more homer-friendly if still challenging with a 25' wall stretching from left- to right-center and a 10' barrier in front of the Jury Box. Fan-friendly as well, Braves Field offered box seats for $2.40, reserved grandstand for $1.80, unreserved grandstand for $1.20, pavilions for $0.90, bleacher and boys grandstand for $0.60, and women's seats on Ladies Day for $0.50. Patrons could buy season tickets for $200 (Skyboxes), $150 (box seats), or $100 (grandstand), and a 30-game package of night games in the reserved grandstands cost $54. (The average major league ticket price at the start of the 2010 season was $26.74, according to *Team Marketing Report*.) The Troubadours, a three-piece jazz band exiled from Fenway who were sometimes called the Three Little Earaches, serenaded Tommy Holmes with "Holmes on the Range" while dressing as Bolsheviks when the Reds came to town and Quakers for the Philadelphia Phillies. The musicians were told it was inappropriate to greet the umpires with "Three Blind Mice." Celebrated fan Lolly Hopkins shared her searing opinions through a megaphone. All in all, games at Braves Field were a happening.

Optimistic fans anticipated an all-Hub World Series with the Red Sox rebuilding to their 1946 greatness just 1¼ miles away. Preoccupied by LoRene's difficult pregnancy, which went 10 months, the October 1 birth of their only child, Gregory, and an erratic fastball when he toyed too much with breaking balls, Spahn was only 15–12 with a high 3.71 ERA (he got 25-run support in the 12 defeats). Down the stretch Spahn and Sain pitched the Braves to their first pennant since 1914, prompting the celebrated verse of *Boston Post* sports editor Gerald V. Hern and repeated around the Hub:

First we'll use Spahn / Then we'll use Sain
Then an off day / Followed by rain.
Back will come Spahn / Followed by Sain
And followed / We hope / By two days of rain.

The poem was shortened popularly to "Spahn and Sain and pray for rain," or "Spahn and Sain and two days of rain," and Spahn was reminded of it constantly throughout his life. "We got it [the jingle] because it rhymed," he said later. "But guys like Vern Bickford [11–5, 3.27 ERA] and Nelson Potter [5–2, two saves, 2.33 ERA after joining the team in June following his release by the Athletics] had good years and they're not remembered." Neither were pitchers Bill Voiselle and Bobby Hogue, who helped the Braves get to first and stay there, or position players Tommy Holmes, Alvin Dark, Frank McCormick, Phil Masi, Jeff Heath, and Clint Conatser, all of whom batted better than .300 in September. You had to credit Southworth, too. Before Casey Stengel popularized platooning with the 1949–60 Yankees, the Braves skipper was running players in and out. Only Dark, Holmes, and Elliott could be described as regulars.

But you could understand Hern's emphasis. Spahn and Sain started 74 of the Braves' 154 games. On September 6, Spahn threw a 14-inning 2–1 win over the Dodgers in which he picked off Jackie Robinson twice and allowed only five hits. Probably the best-pitched game by any Brave all season, it thrilled the crowd of 40,000 at Braves Field. Sain won the nightcap, popularly called a "Wigwam dusk-beater," 4–0 to give the Braves a four-game lead over Brooklyn. After two off-days, there were two rainouts. Spahn and Sain both won on September 11, Spahn getting his first big-league homer in a 13–2 laugher. Sain beat the Cubs 10–3 on September 14, and the poem appeared soon after. Spahn beat the Cubs 5–2 on the 15th. One more off day and Sain set down the Pirates 6–2. When Spahn one-hit the Pirates through eight, got out of a ninth-inning jam, and held on to win 2–1 on September 18, the pair had started eight of the team's 10 games over 13 days and won them all. Not only that, but they also had time to teach batboy Charlie Chronopoulos how to throw the curve. Over a critical 26 days in September, the Braves were 17–5 with 10 regular-season games, six doubleheaders, seven days off, and three rainouts. Typically generous toward his teammates, Spahn credited Hogue with spotting a flaw in his follow-through that he corrected late in the season.

When Bickford won the pennant-clincher on Elliott's home run September 26, owner Perini pushed his way through a clubhouse overflowing with champagne and victory dances. "I'm walking on air and tripping over clouds," Perini said.

The Red Sox and Braves drew 3 million spectators combined over the season. The plebeian Braves finished 91–62, a strong 6½ lengths ahead. The high and mighty Red Sox finished in a dead tie with Cleveland at 96–58. Then their future Hall of Fame manager Joe McCarthy started 8–8 Denny Galehouse in place of well-rested Ellis Kinder (10–7) and Mel Parnell (15–8) and lost a one-game playoff to Cleveland 8–3, ruining the dream of a Boston-Boston World Series.

Though no one used overblown terms like "America's Team," the underdog Braves had to have touched America's heart. This was the year Truman beat Dewey; *Gentleman's Agreement*, a movie attacking anti-Semitism, won the Academy Award for best picture; and the Allies flew in supplies when the Soviets staged the Berlin blockade. The civil rights movement was gathering momentum after Jackie Robinson reported to the Dodgers in 1947 and President Truman ordered the armed forces to integrate on July 26, 1948.

It may not have been New York against Chicago, but the Braves-Indians World Series wasn't bad theatre. (The Braves had actually rooted for the Indians over the Red Sox because they'd get larger Series shares playing in Municipal Stadium than Fenway Park.) Like every Series game until 1971, the opener was played in daylight, enabling the very old and very young to hear or watch its conclusion. Sain, whose 24–15 record made it three seasons in a row with 20 wins, won Game 1 1–0 when an umpire blew the call on Bob Feller's pickoff attempt in the eighth inning. Feller nabbed pinch runner Masi off second, but he was ruled safe by National League umpire Bill Stewart. Then Holmes singled home Masi with the game's only run. Pitching in his first World Series after his second full season, Spahn lost his only start 4–1 in Game 2.

"A few inches the other way and a couple of those hits would have been outs," Sain consoled him. "You gave it a good try."

"I pitch to win them all, same as you," Spahn replied.

Spahn, Sain, and the Hall of Fame?

One of my greatest regrets as a baseball writer was failing to accommodate Johnny Sain when he wanted to plead his case for the Hall of Fame.

Baseball people constantly argue that a coach or scout deserves inclusion. Was there ever a pitching coach like Sain (1917–2006), who worked with the Athletics, Yankees, Twins, Tigers, White Sox, and Braves over 18 seasons? Coaching five of the American League's 10 pennant winners in the 1960s and handling 16 pitchers who won at least 20 games, Sain stressed establishing a good fastball and initiated charting pitches the day before you start. Favoring throwing over running for conditioning, he argued, "You don't run the ball up to home plate," and swore an arm would rust out before it wore out. Sain further clashed with his superiors by favoring the four-man rotation and advising pitchers on contract negotiations—hence his nomadic coaching career.

Sain was a great motivator who said, "Anything you can conceive or believe, you can achieve." When he was coaching the Braves, he tutored minor league coach Leo Mazzone, who later replaced Sain and in the nineties became the most successful pitching coach in the majors. "Johnny Sain is the best curveball coach who ever lived," Mazzone told author Roger Kahn.

Sain's own pitching numbers—a 139–116 record with a 3.49 ERA and 51 saves—disguise some striking accomplishments. After missing three seasons during World War II, he won 20 games four times from 1946–50 and went 24–15 while completing 28-of-39 starts for the 1948 National League champion Boston Braves. Sain led the league that year in wins, complete games, starts, and innings pitched (314⅔), won 7-of-9 consecutive complete games in a 29-day span down the stretch, and beat Bob Feller 1-0 in a great World Series duel. (Sain allowed four hits on 95 pitches, Feller two on 85.) Sain was the National League Pitcher of the Year and finished second to Stan Musial in MVP voting.

Considered over the hill, Sain was traded to the Yankees in 1951. As a spot starter and reliever in 1952, he went 11–6 with seven saves and a 3.46 ERA. Showing that his versatility was no fluke, Sain was 14–7 with nine saves, a 3.00 ERA, and an All-Star berth in 1953. The Man of a Thousand Curves,

With the Braves trailing three games to one, Spahn won Game 5 11–5 with 5⅔ innings of one-hit, seven-strikeout, one-walk relief before the largest crowd in World Series history—86,288 strong in Cleveland. Getting stronger by the inning, Spahn struck out five of his last six batters. Cleveland manager Lou Boudreau credited Spahn with "one of the greatest jobs of pitching in the clutch I have ever seen," although Spahn's burden was lightened considerably when the Braves broke open the game with a six-run seventh.

as he was known, pitched exclusively in relief and led the league with 22 saves in 1954. He was 2–2 with a 2.50 ERA in four World Series.

And then there was his hitting. Sain's .245 lifetime average ranks him among the best hitting pitchers. His 101 RBIs in 774 at-bats makes him the earliest to reach 100 RBIs with the exception of Earl Wilson (740). In 1947, Sain realized every pitcher's aspiration to win 20 (22) and bat .300 (.346). He homered in Braves Field, Yankee Stadium, and Forbes Field, all considered nightmarish for right-handed hitters. Perhaps most extraordinary, in his 774 regular-season at-bats, Sain struck out only 20 times. "That's the fewest strikeouts for any hitter—position player or pitcher—with a comparable number of at-bats since batters' strikeouts were first recorded in 1910 in the National League and 1913 in the American League," Jan Finkel wrote in *The Baseball Research Journal.*

Sain never approached Hall of Fame induction in the writers' voting, but he deserves consideration from the Veterans Committee. "The Hall of Fame admits broadcasters, umpires, entrepreneurs, even newspaper writers," Roger Kahn argued on behalf of Sain in *Newsday.* "For goodness sake, let's enshrine a great coach."

Actually, Kahn is wrong. Neither writers nor broadcasters are enshrined in the Hall of Fame. Instead, one of each is given a yearly honor: the Spink Award for "meritorious contributions to baseball writing," and the Frick Award for a broadcaster's "major contributions to the game of baseball." Nor are coaches eligible for enshrinement under the current rules. I would vote for Sain as a pitcher with the tacit understanding that he was also an excellent coach.

[Author's note: In a striking parallel to Warren Spahn, Sain said missing three years from baseball was beneficial. "I think learning to fly an airplane helped me as much as anything," he was quoted as saying in Thomas E. Allen's *If They Hadn't Gone: How World War II Affected Major League Baseball* (Springfield: Southwest Missouri State University). "I was twenty-five years old. Learning to fly helped me to concentrate and restimulated my ability to learn."]

The next day, Southworth asked the weary Spahn if he had anything left, since the manager had to pinch hit for starter Voiselle in his next at bat and the Braves were trailing Game 6 3–1.

"I'll give it all I've got," Spahn said, but he had trouble warming up. When he relieved in the eighth, the Indians scored an insurance run off him with three straight singles to make it 4–1. Spahn ended the inning by stranding Eddie Robinson off first with a pickoff. Thurman Tucker, the runner on third, tried to bail out Robinson by dashing for home, but first baseman Earl Torgeson threw to catcher Bill Salkeld, and Tucker was out in a rundown. The Braves' two-run rally in the bottom of the eighth fell a run short when Tucker made a great catch on Conatser's bases-loaded drive to left-center. Spahn struck out the side in the ninth to record 12 Ks in his 12 Series innings, but the Braves lost 4–3 when Sibby Sisti bunted into a double play. *New York Daily News* columnist Jimmy Powers, never noted for understatement, compared Spahn's bullpen work to Carl Hubbell striking out five consecutive Hall of Famers in the 1934 All-Star Game, calling it "one of the most magnificent relief performances I have ever seen."

In retrospect, the absence of Heath, who broke his ankle on September 29, and hot-hitting outfielder Jim Russell, who developed heart trouble in July and was done for the season, may have doomed the Braves offense, which averaged more than one run in Games 1–4 and 6. If it was any consolation, each Brave received $4,570.73 for his Series share.

Members of the Boston Braves Historical Association sometimes speculate that if Spahn had held the Indians scoreless, the Braves might have rallied to win the game and—with Sain starting Game 7—the Series. Or if the Braves had beaten the Red Sox in a "Streetcar Series," would they have left town so soon? To muse further, after an off-year or two, would they have been given the time to rebuild with Eddie Mathews and other future stars? In short, would they still be in Boston today?

For his part, Spahn was already planning his life out of town. With no guarantee of job security, he was thinking about his post-baseball life. "I was interested in engineering and thought of going to a technical school," he told Cy Kritzer of the *Buffalo Evening News*. "[Braves owner] Lou Perini had contacts going in many places and urged me to take a job with his company and go to Pittsburgh and work on a tunnel. He said there was a great future for me.

"It wasn't what LoRene and I wanted. I was away from home so much and in the public eye for so many months, we decided to invest what money we had and what we could borrow in land around Hartshorne, Oklahoma.

"We wanted the rural life. We bought about 200 acres [and a five-room ranch house] to start." Raising white-faced Hereford cows and bulls, Spahn would eventually have nearly 10 times as many acres on his ranch, which happened to sit in natural gas land. Spahn traded winter's icy grip for the milder climate and endless horizons of the Southwest, and he never looked back.

* * *

If Spahn was already planning for the future, Marichal was understandably focused on the present. Once promoted to the majors, he and Matty Alou were housed next door to Felipe Alou and near Candlestick Park with Blanche Laverne (Mama) Johnson, a stern but well-intentioned elderly black woman who accepted no excuses for anything. "If we didn't pay attention to what she said," Alou told *Time*, "she'd grab her dish mop and give us a swat. She'd tell us, 'You want to make good in this country, you learn to speak English. Nobody makes shaving commercials in Spanish.'" Marichal explained to broadcaster Bob Costas in a 2010 interview, "She told me, 'You have two mothers.' She was awesome—one of the finest human beings I ever met." Juan got over homesickness by once more destroying another collection of his Dominican *merengue* records.

When he entered the Giants clubhouse for the first time, in July 1960, Marichal was transfixed. "Felipe Alou and Orlando Cepeda met me with handshakes and took me to Willie Mays," he told the Hall of Fame audience at the 2009 opening of the *¡Viva Baseball!* exhibit. "I thought that I was in heaven because I dreamed for so many years to be in the major leagues, and I was shaking the hand of the best player in the game. Then they took me to Willie McCovey's locker. They were very happy to introduce me.

"I went to the mound to warm up for my first game," he continued. "When they announced my name, a feeling came out that I cannot describe. I didn't know how I could pitch. I threw seven warm-ups with goose bumps. But when I saw the leadoff hitter, I relaxed. I was a very happy man."

In his first start, against the Phillies on July 19, 1960, the 22-year-old Marichal had a perfect game for 6⅓ innings before allowing base runners on an infielder's error and a walk with no scoring. He still had a no-hitter until there were two outs in the eighth. Before he faced pinch-hitter Clay Dalrymple, Giants manager Tom Sheehan told him to throw a breaking ball rather than the fastball Juan might have preferred. Not wishing to disobey a superior in his first game, Marichal complied, and Dalrymple singled to center.

The pattern of all patience, Marichal turned his back to the plate, grabbed the resin bag, squeezed some white powder out of it, and waited for Mays' throw that would return the ball to the infield. Then Marichal turned to the plate and set down the last four batters to beat pitcher John Buzhardt 2–0 with 12 strikeouts to go with the hit and walk. Only a handful of modern pitchers have matched Marichal's feat of pitching a one-hitter in his first major league game.

Juan already had that big-league swagger. Translating for him in postgame interviews, Cepeda said, "Juan said he expected to win. He always expects to win." Bob Stevens wrote prophetically in the *San Francisco Chronicle*, "Rookie Juan Marichal, a young man with the equipment and the poise of a combat line veteran, broke into the major leagues with a breathtaking one-hitter last night as he fired the Giants to a 2–0 victory over the bedazzled Philadelphia Phillies." Philadelphia manager Gene Mauch said, "He changed speeds tonight better than any pitcher I've seen this year."

Four days later, in a game broadcast back to the Dominican Republic, Marichal beat the championship-bound Pirates and seasoned Harvey Haddix 3–1 on another complete game ("Sensational," wrote Stevens.) Five days after that, he beat the Braves and Spahn 3–2 in 10 innings in spite of Milwaukee manager Chuck Dressen's spurious claim that Marichal was making illegal pitches from the side of the rubber. Pirates catcher Smokey Burgess said Marichal "throws like he's 32 instead of 21," and Hank Aaron said he was "faster than Walter Johnson, I bet."

"Juan used to throw harder," Felipe Alou told the *San Francisco Chronicle*'s Art Rosenbaum. "We played for the same team, *Escogido* in the Dominican winter league, and he burned them in. Every year he learns a little more, he gets a new pitch. Now he's more clever with curves and sliders to go with his fastball."

By this time, Coach Wes Westrum had taught Marichal to hide the grip on his pitches. Insisting he never learned how to pitch other than picking up pointers from his catchers, Juan finished the year 6–2 with a 2.66 ERA despite missing most of a month with a back injury. Sheehan believed Marichal when he said he was in pain and took him to doctors everywhere the Giants set down. (He finally had surgery in 1972.) "I pitched my whole career with a back problem," Marichal said years later.

At the time, though, he couldn't have been much happier. He had joined a storied franchise that began playing as the New York Gothams in 1883 on a polo field in north Manhattan (hence the name Polo Grounds for a home stadium built farther uptown in 1891). One of their stars, catcher William "Buck" Ewing, the only nineteenth century player to earn a salary of $5,000, stole second and third before announcing, "It's getting late. I'm going to steal home and then we can all have dinner." He made good on his boast. "Come on, my big fellows, my giants!" manager James Mutrie used to shout (hence, a new team name), and the club won world championships in 1888–89 and 1894. The Giants captured 10 pennants and three World Series in 31 years (1902–32) under the incomparable[13] John McGraw, including the 1905 World Series in which Christy Mathewson threw three shutouts in six days. The Giants added three pennants and a fifth title in the 1930s, the decade in which Carl "the Meal Ticket" Hubbell struck out Babe Ruth, Lou Gehrig, Jimmie Foxx, Al Simmons, and Joe Cronin *in order* during the 1934 All-Star Game. Bobby Thomson's "Shot Heard 'Round the World" walk-off homer won the 1951 pennant, and the Giants swept the heavily favored Indians in the 1954 Series.

The names of colorful Giants greats trip off the tongue: Orator Jim O'Rourke, Amos the "Hoosier Thunderbolt" Rusie, Joe "Iron Man" McGinnity, George "Highpockets" Kelly, Frankie the "Fordham Flash" Frisch, Master Melvin Ott, and Memphis Bill Terry. And there were unforgettable sights frozen in time, including Ott batting with his right foot kicked high in the air; Casey Stengel scoring an inside-the-park homer with one loose shoe; and Willie Mays making his celebrated over-the-shoulder catch to save Game 1 of the 1954 Series. No team had a better conduit to the Caribbean Basin than the Giants, who had been the first team to visit Cuba in 1890 and got more talent than anyone from the region after farm director Jack Schwarz hired Alex Pompez, whose New York Cubans shared the Polo Grounds with the Giants from 1943–50, as a scout and later as the club's director of international scouting.

In fact, the Giants were landing excellent athletes from every possible background. "Hubbell was director of the New York/San Francisco Giants farm system in the late fifties and early sixties," Bill James wrote in his *Historical Baseball Abstract*, "at a time when the farm system was producing ballplayers like McDonald's produces hamburgers—McCovey, Marichal, Cepeda, the Alou brothers, Leon Wagner, Jim Davenport, Bill White, Mike McCormick, Jose Cardenal, Jim Ray Hart, Gaylord Perry, and many others. It may have been the most productive farm system in the history of baseball."

But the team's Latinos were having a tough time with baseball. In addition to overcoming cultural and linguistic difficulties ("All I knew to order was apple pie and *chile con carne*," Cepeda has said), they suffered every kind of indignity from Anglos—more indignities than black Americans endured, Hall of Fame right fielder Roberto Clemente insisted. He told *The Sporting News*, "We lead different lives in America. The language barrier is great at first, and we have trouble ordering food in restaurants. Even segregation baffles us."

A reporter in the Pirates' Bradenton, Florida, minor league camp described the stylish Clemente as a "hot dog." By contrast, film director John Sayles said of individual behavior, "Most of what I know about style I learned from Roberto Clemente," and former commissioner Bowie Kuhn said of him, "He has about him a touch of royalty."

Clemente grew incensed when reporters quoted him in pidgin English when he was actually articulate. Writers constantly quoted Latino players saying, "theese" instead of "this" or "Chee-cago" instead of "Chicago." With any kind of inquiry, American journalists would have learned that there's no soft "i" or "sh" sound in Spanish. "The subjective process in deciding whether to clean up a quote raises questions about power, privilege, and difference," Adrian Burgos Jr. wrote in *Playing America's Game: Baseball, Latinos, and the Color Line.* "Native English speakers such as politicians, corporate leaders, and even major league officials regularly benefit from their quotes being cleaned up. Cases in which non-native English speakers such as a Latino ballplayer like [Sammy] Sosa do not benefit from the practice prompt concerns about the role of the media in the creation of public images. Latino journalists at the 2003 National Hispanic Journalists Conference decried the manner in which verbatim quotes of Latino players affect popular perceptions, leading many to see Latinos as unintelligent regardless of their individual speaking ability." (Author's note: I have edited some quotes in this book for clarity.)

Clemente also made comments that were lost in translation. When he said, "For me I am the best," reporters scoffed that he was calling himself better than Mickey Mantle, Willie Mays, or Hank Aaron. Actually, Clemente was directly translating the Spanish expression "*Por mí yo soy el mejor,*" which means idiomatically, "I feel I am as good as I'm capable of being."

* * *

While Mays was preoccupied with being a New York product the Bay Area never embraced, he needed years to befriend most of his Hispanic teammates. Marichal may not have been among them. In 1969, Marichal said Mays should quit. Speaking to a Dominican newspaper reporter, Marichal said that Mays' attitude "damages the spirit and enthusiasm of the rest of the players" and that Mays begged off facing some of the league's toughest pitchers. Though Marichal denied the quotes and the reporter stood by them (Marichal later withdrew them), Juan had a point. After going 0-for-4 against the Cardinals' Bob Gibson in 1969, Mays didn't play the next two games in which Gibson faced the Giants. Mays faced three other leading pitchers—Tom Seaver of the Mets, Don Wilson of the Astros and Ferguson Jenkins of the Cubs—just once apiece while slumping to a .283 average in only 117 games. That said, Mays' talents were still way above average.

The San Francisco scene dimmed considerably when Alvin Dark took over as manager in 1961. A brilliant strategist[14] who had been an All-American football star at Louisiana State University, Dark would have been more comfortable handling tackles and ends than shortstops and catchers. His my-way-or-the-highway style perfectly fit the corporate structure of baseball in the 1950s and early '60s. Unfortunately, his behavior clashed with that of the fiercely proud men from Latin America.

In one game Felipe Alou struck out four times, which Hispanics call taking the "golden sombrero." When he returned to the dugout, teammates teased him in Spanish. Though they were not putting him down so much as telling him to move on and getting him to laugh—Latino players simultaneously embrace having fun on the diamond and playing seriously—the uncomprehending Dark banned the Spanish language from being spoken anywhere in the clubhouse or dugout and reportedly posted a spring-training sign reading, "Speak English. You're In America." He also banned music in the clubhouse, which the Latinos took personally.

The edict succeeded in infuriating the club's 11 Latinos who comprised more than half the starting lineup. What's more, they encompassed the heart and soul of the team. *Sports Illustrated*'s Ron Fimrite, a prime San Francisco Giants historian, described Cepeda in a 1991 article, "He was 'the Baby Bull,' 'Cha-Cha' the dancing master, and he made San Francisco his personal playground in the Giants' first year in town. It was Orlando Cepeda, the new kid, the rookie, and not the established star, Willie Mays, who first won the hearts of San Franciscans in 1958 after the Giants had come west from the Polo Grounds and Manhattan. In that first season, at least, Mays was still regarded as a New Yorker, and because he was such a private man, he didn't get around town as much as San Franciscans would have preferred; in San Francisco, they like their heroes visible.

"Cepeda was all over the place, earning his nickname Cha-Cha as he danced and pounded the conga drums at the Copacabana or swayed to the sounds of Dave Brubeck at the Blackhawk. Cepeda was an exciting young presence, a Latin charmer, and the city embraced this 20-year-old Puerto Rican as if he were a native son."

Though his statistics trailed Mays', Cepeda was voted Most Valuable Giant in a newspaper survey. The son of legendary Puerto Rican star Pedro Cepeda, who was called both the obscure Spanish nickname *Perucho* and *Toro* (Bull), San Francisco's Orlando Cepeda was a proud man, the most outspoken player in the clubhouse, and not a Giant to be trifled with. "Listen," Cepeda told Dark after he barreled into the manager's office to protest the English-only edict. "I'm Puerto Rican, and I'm proud of my language. I would feel foolish if I talked to [José] Pagan in English. First of all, we won't be able to communicate because we don't speak [English] that well, and secondly, I'm Puerto Rican, and I'm going to speak my language."

The Latinos didn't speak Spanish to offend their teammates, Felipe Alou added. "They feel that the moment we begin speaking Spanish we are talking about them. That is not so."

Cepeda said the Latinos generally ignored Dark's policy and that Dark withdrew it and apologized to several of them in recent years. When Hispanic players struggled to express themselves accurately in English, they sometimes left the wrong impression on teammates, coaches, and writers. Cepeda, for one, felt Dark was attacking his position as a teammate and clubhouse leader. "Dark thought I was trying not to play," he was quoted as saying in *Viva Baseball! Latin Major Leaguers and Their Special Hunger* by Samuel Regalado. "He treated me like a child. I am a human being, whether I am black or white or green. Dark did not respect our differences."

Nor did Dark respect the literal hunger Hispanics have for baseball. After returning to the clubhouse following a loss, Dark overturned the table piled high with a postgame buffet. Disrespecting food is a sacrilege in Latin America, where many people are lucky to get one good meal a day. Felipe Alou took action. Staring directly into his manager's eyes, Alou knelt down, picked up food with his hands and stuffed it into his mouth. Alou was traded after the 1963 season and went on to lead the National League in hits twice. "I thought that was the biggest mistake the Giants ever made," Marichal said.

The straw that broke Dark's back was a 1964 interview he gave to Stan Isaacs of *Newsday*. Isaac quoted Dark as saying the team's "trouble" was having "so many Spanish-speaking and Negro players" who "just are not able to perform up to the white ball players when it comes to mental alertness."

Mental alertness? Was there ever a more mentally alert ballplayer than Willie Mays, a former high school quarterback on offense and safety on defense who transferred those skills to baseball? "I could visualize the whole field," Mays said. Tallulah Bankhead had it right when she said, "There have been only two geniuses in the world—Willie Mays and Willie Shakespeare."

But Dark wasn't finished with his ethnic characterizations. He also told Isaacs that minorities lacked the pride white players had and didn't "subordinate themselves to the best interest of the team." The club's Hispanic and black players threatened an open rebellion that was only prevented by Willie Mays' intervention.

When most of the team's black and Hispanic players met with Mays in his Pittsburgh hotel room, he said, "Shut up. Just shut up."

"You don't tell me to shut up," Cepeda said. "I'm not going to play another game for that son of a bitch."

"Oh, yes you are," Mays said. "And let me tell you why."

According to Charles Einstein's *Willie's Time,* Mays went on, "I tell you for a fact he is not going to be back next year. Don't let the rednecks make a hero out of him." Mays said that whatever Dark's views, he had fielded a lineup that was majority minority and wanted to win for the money if nothing else. Dark had helped Mays and others, and replacing Dark with the Giants two games out could cost them the pennant, Mays asserted. The rebellion subsided.

Though Dark said he was misquoted (the interview wasn't tape-recorded), subsequent revelations have vindicated Isaacs. In part because of his ethnic views, in part because Dark, a fundamentalist Christian, had been carrying on an adulterous relationship with an airline stewardess, Dark was fired at season's end. "Alvin managed percentages, not people," Willie McCovey said in *The Sporting News* the following year.

During the Dark era, Cepeda said, "There were three groups: whites, blacks, and Latinos." And they were not friendly. Billy Hoeft, a white pitcher of some distinction with the Tigers who later played for the Giants in 1963 and 1966, commented in a recent interview, "There were some foreigners on the team, and Dark was saying he wished he could take them and put them in a corner." He continued, "On the road they would get together in their own clique. You never knew what they were talking about. They had their own way.

If there was work to do, they'd do it if they wanted to. If Dark wanted them to steal or hit and run, they'd say, 'Let us do it our way.' I still feel that this game is ours. If you're going to play our game, play it our way."

When Hoeft's quotes were presented to Cepeda, he said, "He's a racist, because it's not true. I thought he was a friend of the Latin Americans. He was friendly toward us and told us jokes. He doesn't know what he's talking about. It's sad, that's what it is."

How did the clubhouse turbulence affect Marichal? Not that much. As one who played only every fourth day, he could divorce himself from the daily tension that plagued others. He had also learned to cope with American society. "We were in Houston, and Orlando wanted to go see the movie *Cleopatra*," Marichal recalled. "I said that was not a good idea. Forty-five minutes later, he came back, and he was crying [from being denied admission]. I was laughing."

"The only thing that mattered to me was baseball," Marichal said. "I wanted to prove to my mother that I could play baseball." Resolutely optimistic, he remembers kindnesses where others held grudges. When Juan was lovesick at spring training in 1962 and worried about the safety of his fiancée, whose family had been close to the Trujillos (dictator Rafael Trujillo was assassinated in 1961), Dark sent him home so he could marry Alma Rosa Carvajal in a San Bosco church. (Dark first checked to see if they could marry "by wire," as Marichal puts it. But it was impossible, and at 17, Alma Rosa was underage.) "He took care of me. When I was skinny, he brought me milkshakes. Even today, I give him a hug," Marichal said.

The Dark years didn't hurt Marichal's pitching, either. After his 6–2 rookie season, with a 2.66 ERA and six complete games in 11 starts, Marichal came to camp overweight, ran off 10 pounds during spring training in Phoenix and went 13–10 (3.89) in 1961. Back troubles cost him seven starts, and he nearly suffered a torn Achilles' tendon when the Dodgers' Duke Snider spiked him in the right heel on a 3–1 play September 9 that ended his season. Nonetheless, Marichal had a strong second half, one-hit the Dodgers on August 2, and kept the Giants in the race. In the outing that gave him most satisfaction, on August 23, Marichal outdueled 18-game winner Joey Jay of the pennant-bound Reds, leading 2–0 in the ninth before the Giants blew it open with 12 runs and won 14–0. Marichal struck out only one batter but kept the Reds swinging so futilely that they had just three hits. The game culminated in a 24-game stretch in which the Giants won 18 times and Marichal stretched his own winning streak to seven, with three on shutouts. He was effectively throwing fastballs at two different speeds, curves at two different speeds, a change-up, a slider and a screwball, with the latter two more often than in the past. Unfortunately, the spiking injury cost Juan the last three weeks of the season while the Giants limped to a third-place finish at eight games out.

In 1962, Marichal went 18–11 with a 3.36 ERA as the Giants captured their first pennant in eight years. General manager Chub Feeney, who took much heat for later moves, struck gold by acquiring veteran Harvey Kuenn, a master of bat control to play third and outfield, pulling back Billy O'Dell from the expansion draft (he won 19 games in 1962), trading for right-hander Jack Sanford, and getting useful pitchers Don Larsen and Billy Pierce for four little-known players. Sanford, who went 24–7 after Dark convinced him to throw more breaking balls, was the staff ace. A hard-scrabble Army veteran who once chauffeured for Milwaukee owner Lou Perini, Sanford spent seven years in the minors and didn't become a winner until he learned to control his pitches and his temper. Not that he was Little Mary Sunshine. On days he started, he marched morosely around the clubhouse like a prisoner on death row, as *Sport*'s Bill Libby described it. Sanford actually believed that Candlestick Park was a "bandbox" set up for hitters. But he pitched well there. In the words of a *San Francisco Chronicle* writer, "He was a bulky guy, who would be a small-size right tackle on the football team. He wasn't delicate. He was out there to throw the baseball, and he did it well. He wasn't afraid to brush back a hitter. He was an old-school pitcher. He wasn't a Cadillac, but he was a damn good Buick."

Still, the Giants wouldn't have reached the postseason without Marichal. He struck out Aaron three times and three-hit Spahn and the Braves 6–0 on Opening Day (Mays homered on the first pitch Spahn threw him), struck out 13 Dodgers in a 12–3 romp on July 6, and was the winning pitcher in the first of two All-Star Games played that year—a regular *fiesta* in which Roberto Clemente had three hits. The Giants made Marichal pitch twice on the road with the mumps, to the horror of the doctor he saw in San Francisco. The doctor wanted him rested; he wasn't. Marichal won 18 games through September 5, then missed 16 days again when he turned that ailing right ankle picking up a grounder and beating the Dodgers' Willie Davis to first base. As Marichal put it, "I felt something like concrete in my right foot." X-rays showed no fracture, though the foot had a rise on the instep and Marichal felt there was a break.

Still hurting upon his return, he pitched ineffectively in two losses, the latter a Dark-mandated start on the next-to-last day of the season that visibly annoyed Marichal's Hispanic teammates. Marichal was forced to watch the conclusion of the 162-game regular season from the bench.

On what could have been the final day with the Giants one game back, Mays hit a 500-foot, eighth-inning homer to beat Houston 2–1. The Giants stayed in the clubhouse to watch the first-place Dodgers lose on television, Cepeda and Marichal celebrating by slapping palms. That set up a best-of-three pennant playoff. The Dodgers and Giants split the first two games as Mays hit two homers to help win Game 1. In the third game, Marichal hobbled onto the field and allowed three earned runs in seven innings before leaving with the Giants trailing 4–2. Then their ninth-inning magic resurfaced exactly 11 years after Bobby Thomson's Shot Heard 'Round the World, and they kayoed the Dodgers in another pennant playoff. Matty Alou singled off Ed Roebuck, Kuenn forced him at second, and both McCovey and Felipe Alou walked to load the bases. Mays singled with a whippet smash off Roebuck's glove, leg, or hand (accounts vary) to make it 4–3. Stan Williams came in—one of several decisions second guessers tossed back at Dodgers manager Walter Alston—and immediately gave up a sacrifice fly to Cepeda to tie the score. A wild pitch advanced Mays to second, and Bailey was intentionally walked to load the bases. Davenport walked for the go-ahead run, closer Ron Perranoski come in to put out the fire, and Pagan reached on second baseman Larry Burright's error to score Mays and make it 6–4. Pierce retired the shell-shocked Dodgers in order to preserve the win. The Giants had overcome a four-game deficit with seven games left on the schedule. "It was God's will," Marichal said.

Certainly, a lot of Giants played as if inspired. Later a poster boy for ineffective Mets squads—he was called Iron Hands for his poor fielding— second baseman Chuck Hiller had a career year. So did shortstop Pagan, third baseman Davenport, and pitcher Sanford. When 50,000 fans greeted the returning Giants, swamping the airport and forcing the team to land on an auxiliary runway, a club official called it "the greatest day in the history of San Francisco sports."

The 1962 World Series against the Yankees should have been Marichal's coming-out party to the nation. Like Spahn, he would compete in the Series after only his second full season. Injured or not, he was going to pitch. "You feel so happy you forget the whole thing," he said of his injury.

His opportunity came with the Yankees leading the Series two games to one. After shutting out New York for four innings of two-hit wizardry, striking out three and leading 2–0, Marichal was given the suicide squeeze signal by an over-managing Dark with a two-strike count, men on first and third, and no outs in the fifth against a struggling Whitey Ford. You have to wonder why. A missed bunt would have trapped Pagan running home and resulted in a double play. "I never understood why [Dark ordered the squeeze]," Marichal said, and he wasn't the only one.

The result was disastrous, at least for Marichal. "The pitch was going to hit my ankle, but I had to go for it because a runner was coming in," he said. When he reached down quickly, Ford's pitch hit the index finger of Juan's right hand, leaving a blood blister that cost him the nail. Before leaving the game, Marichal argued futilely that the pitch hit his finger before the bat and he should be awarded first base. Umpire Jim Honochick ruled that Marichal had fouled off the pitch for strike three. Marichal threw his helmet in disgust and was booed by the crowd at Yankee Stadium. The Giants held on to win 7–3 on Hiller's grand slam, the first ever in a Series by a National Leaguer.

There was no way Marichal could pitch again, but Dark complicated things by saying, "He won't pitch again in this Series even if it rains for a week." Technically, Dark meant no offense to Marichal, who couldn't have pitched if it rained for two weeks. Besides, the last two games were scheduled for Candlestick Park, where the Giants' Pierce ("Without Billy Pierce, we probably wouldn't have been in the World Series," Davenport said.) hadn't lost all year and Sanford had shut out the Yankees in Game 2. But the media read Dark's remark as disrespectful, and you can imagine Marichal's dismay. "It was not a nice thing to say," Marichal said. "I was pitching the best game of my life, I was helping the team. I was giving 100 percent. I didn't feel good after that comment."

So shaken as he was, so wan with care, Marichal now could only watch his teammates until McCovey lined out to second baseman Bobby Richardson with runners on second and third to end the seventh game as bare-knuckle losers 1–0. Juan Marichal had played in his first and last World Series.

* * *

Nonetheless, Marichal picked up where he left off the next season. Four days after blanking L.A. 3–0 at Dodger Stadium, he prepared to face Houston at

Under the Radar

There have been some superb pitching duels between nonprofessionals, and we would be remiss in failing to mention one in particular.

Back in May 1981, future major leaguers Ron Darling of Yale and Frank Viola of St. John's hooked up in a classic duel that was also remarkable for who was watching and who was recording the event. Facing off in the second game of an NCAA northeast regional doubleheader as the two leading pitchers in the region, Darling had gone into the game with a 9–3 record and a 2.42 ERA, while Viola was 9–0 with a 1.00 ERA. In the stands sat some 50 scouts; Yale president A. Bartlett Giamatti (who would later become National League president and commissioner of baseball); former Yale coach Smoky Joe Wood, who was 34–5 and won three Series games for the World Champion Red Sox in 1912; and Roger Angell of *The New Yorker*. As Darling and Viola scratched zeroes across the scoreboard for the first nine innings, Angell quizzed Wood about Tris Speaker, Walter Johnson, and other memories of the dead-ball era. Wood's write-up, titled "The Web of the Game," was published in the July 20, 1981, edition of *The New Yorker*.

"Our afternoon slid by in a distraction of baseball and memory," Angell wrote, "and I almost felt myself at some dreamlike doubleheader involving the then and the now—the semi-anonymous strong young men waging their close, marvelous game on the sunlit green field before us while bygone players and heroes of baseball history—long gone now, most of them—replayed their vivid, famous innings for me in the words and recollections of my companion."

Wood called Walter Johnson, whom he beat in a 1912 classic 1–0 en route to tying Johnson's record of 16 straight wins, "a prince of men," prompting Angell to write that he had never before heard the term used in "non-satiric fashion." "Ty Cobb was the greatest bat-handler you ever saw," Wood told

Candlestick Park on June 15, 1963. Marichal was always prepared to adjust to circumstances. The following conversation, captured by journalist Al Stump, ensued between Marichal and McCovey, who was playing left field that day:

Marichal: "I think I'll do something different today. I change my windup and use the No. 2 motion. What do you think, Stretch?"

McCovey: "I think you're crazy. You just won five in a row and shut out Los Angeles four days ago. So why would you mess around with changes?"

Marichal: "Yes, but Houston hit me pretty hard the last few times and I was throwing good stuff, too. Looks like they begin to figure me out. So now time has come to give them something else." He urged McCovey to play deeper than he normally did.

Angell. "He used to go out to the ballpark early in the morning with a pitcher and work on hitting the ball to all fields, over and over. He batted that strange way, with his fists apart, you know, but he could have hit just as well no matter how he held it. He just knew what to do with a bat in hand. And base running—why I saw him get on base and steal second, steal third, and then steal home. *The* best. A lot of fellows in my time shortened up on the bat when they had to—that's what the St. John's boys should do against this good pitcher."

And so Angell's eyes, and ours, returned to the field. Darling, "never deviating from the purity of his stylish body-lean and his riding, down-thrusting delivery," carried a no-hitter through 11 innings for a tournament record [that still stands], while Viola, through "the constant variety of speeds and locations on his pitches," kept the Elis scoreless. St. John's Steve Scafa led off the 12th with a looped single, and when the announcer informed one and all of Darling's record, everyone, including the St. John's players, rose to cheer him. Alas, Scafa stole second and then third, a Cobbsian feat if there ever was one. Another player reached first on an error, putting runners on first and third with one out. Darling struck out his 15th batter. A pinch runner replaced the man on first. On the next pitch he took off and stopped between first and second: "an inserted crisis," Angell wrote. With Scafa 10' off third, the second baseman ran the pinch runner backward and threw to first. Scafa broke for home, and the first baseman hesitated briefly before throwing home too late. A St. John's reliever blanked Yale in the bottom of the 12th to clinch the 1–0 win.

In the double-elimination regional, neither St. John's nor Yale reached the College World Series. But their game will forever stand in the grateful memory of those who witnessed it. Wood told Angell, "I never saw a better-played game anyplace—college or big-league. That's a swell ballgame."

After consulting his notes on opponents, Marichal had concluded that Houston players were getting a preview of the coming pitch by reading his grip. Abandoning his high leg kick, he hid the ball, brought his hands together belt-high and pivoted quickly. Then he began to set down one Houston batter after another before 18,869 charmed fans at Candlestick Park. The innings piled up in a scoreless duel with Dick Drott, while visiting batters failed to hit safely. Carl Hubbell, who had thrown the last Giant no-hitter, beating the Pirates 11–0 on May 8, 1929, told a sportswriter how much more pressure Marichal was under, since one mistake could cost him the game and he had to pace himself for possible extra innings. The first time the Colt 45s came close to hitting safely, the deep-situated McCovey ran down a seventh-inning drive near the left-field screen. "Man, you're pitching a no-hitter," a teammate told Marichal after the seventh, violating a baseball code against using the term while a no-hitter was in progress. In the eighth, Davenport made a nice stop of John Bateman's smash down the third-base line and threw him out. In the bottom of the inning, Marichal's teammates finally gave him some breathing room when Davenport doubled and scored on Hiller's double to put the Giants ahead 1–0.

Marichal took the mound in the ninth with the crowd on its feet and got Johnny Temple on a foul pop to first and struck out Pete Runnels. With a 2–2 count on Brock Davis, catcher Ed Bailey came to the mound. "I think another screwball," he told Marichal. "What do you think?"

"I think a fastball," Marichal replied. "What do you think?"

"I think a fastball, too."

Throwing what he later called "maybe the fastest pitch I have ever thrown in my life," Marichal whipped it by Davis for strike three and a no-hitter.

Seventeen days later, Marichal would pitch an even more memorable game.

~ Chapter 6 ~

SOMETHING IN RESERVE?

No Gods, but only Trojans and Akhaians,
were left now in the great field on the plain.
It swayed this way and that between the rivers,
with leveled spears moving on one another.

—The Iliad

On July 2, 1963, there were plenty of support troops on the field, but as the game moved into the seventh inning, everyone's attention was on the two men who stood like minor deities 15" higher than anyone else—the height of the mound. They were conducting a clinic for the ages: Marichal stylish and blazing, Spahn as Shakespeare said, "firm as rocky mountains."

"I don't pitch the hitter the same way from season to season," said Spahn, who could remember pitches he'd thrown 15 years prior. "Why? Well, I think hard about hitters and try to think the way they think. So there's always the possibility that the hitter may have given considerable thought to the way I pitched him in the previous year, and he might be looking forward to those pitches next year."

Spahn may not have been much of a student in school, but he learned early in his baseball career that "study is like the heaven's glorious sun." (Shakespeare) There was no excuse for not studying hitters in Warren Spahn's world. If a hitter bent his back leg, Spahn told author Martin Quigley, he knew he was a low-ball hitter. If he had his weight on the front foot, he was looking for a high ball. Sometimes Spahn would pitch to a batter's strength to mix him up.

Sometimes his strategy defied logic—until it worked. "He's the only pitcher ever to walk a batter to get to me," Stan Musial wrote in *The Man's Own Story*, co-authored by Bob Broeg. "Back in 1957, when the Cardinals were threatening Milwaukee's league lead, Fred Haney brought Spahn in from the bullpen in the ninth inning to protect a one-run lead. He walked the batter in front of me to set up an inning-ending double play. I obliged."

Because of his many release points, Marichal had a greater variety of pitches than Spahn. Hank Aaron, who would go hitless in the 1963 game, once described the problem of batting against Marichal. "The foot's up in your face, and that's bad. Then he comes through like a fullback chargin'. He lunges off the hill. Sometimes he even stumbles from the force of his delivery. With all that confusion of motion, it's a problem seeing the ball. But his control is a bigger thing. He can throw all day within a 2-inch space, in, out, up, or down. I've never seen anyone as good as that."

"If you put up a 6" target 60' away, Juan would hit it nine out of 10 times," Giants pitching coach Larry Jansen told *Time*. Like Spahn, Marichal had an extensive mental book on hitters' weaknesses. "This is a guessing game," he said. "I'm always trying to guess what the hitters are guessing. I haven't gotten any better, only smarter." But who could guess the pitch, the direction, and the speed all at once? Or the type of pitch? Marichal's overhand curve dropped, while his sidearm curve broke away from right-handed batters.

As the game progressed, Marichal was throwing more fastballs, which were believed to be the most arm-saving of pitches, although recent studies have questioned that conclusion. The Braves blew a chance to break the scoreless tie in the seventh when Crandall singled and was thrown out at second after McMillan swung and missed on a hit-and-run. If he'd stayed put, Crandall might have scored when Spahn himself doubled off the top of the fence in right field for the only extra-base hit Marichal yielded all game. Juan got out of the inning when Maye grounded back to him. "Did you see him hit that ball?" Marichal said when asked about Spahn's drive after the game. "It was going out of the park, and then that wind caught it. What a break that was!"

Well, maybe, but the wind also might have helped the blow. In the Giants' half of the seventh, Orlando Cepeda and Ed Bailey hit two-out singles. With a hard-earned chance to score, manager Alvin Dark summoned Jim Davenport to bat for shortstop José "Lightning" Pagan, whose speed and fielding would keep him in the majors for 15 years despite a .298 on-base percentage. (Fielding was more respected back then, although the recent emphasis on run prevention is a good sign.)

Davenport was every bit the hometown hero for Giants fans that Larker was the *bête noire* for Milwaukeeans. Playing his entire 13-year career with the Giants, mostly at third, Davenport once went 97 games and 209 chances without an error. A college quarterback at Southern Mississippi who was discovered playing semipro baseball one summer, Davenport liked working under Alvin Dark (an All-American football star himself), gobbled up grounders like snaps from center, and won a Gold Glove while making the All-Star team in the 1962 pennant season. "When it comes to holding down the hot corner spot with dexterity and steadiness, nobody did it better than the Giants' Jim Davenport," Herb Fagen wrote in *Baseball Digest*.

Davenport bonded with Cepeda in the minors and didn't complain even when he had a broken collarbone or bleeding ulcers. The beat writers said he was so quiet you could forget he was around. "Baseball's been good to me, and I've given it 100 percent," he said in a rare moment of loquaciousness. Who couldn't love him? Unfortunately, this archetypal gloveman now had to hit against one of the best. Davenport hadn't started a game since June 24. What's more, he came in cold—no batting under the stands against pitching machines or off tees as players do today. Davenport flied out to center.

In the Milwaukee eighth, Ernie Bowman, finishing a three-year career as a utility man, replaced Davenport at shortstop. After Bolling fouled to third and Aaron walked, Bowman made a great stop deep in the hole to throw out Menke. Another scrub had stepped up, contributing to history. Aaron moved to second on the play but was left there when Larker flied to McCovey.

Down the left-field line, the Giant's 19-year-old left-hander Al Stanek, the youngest player on either roster, sat on a long bench with his fellow Giants relievers, all of them wearing San Francisco 49ers football windbreakers and huddled in a spot that felt like a wind tunnel. "It was damn cold," Don Larsen said, "especially when the fog came in." The others stationed in this ballpark purgatory, as Stanek remembers, were catchers Tom Haller and Jimmie Coker and pitchers Jack Fisher, Billy Pierce, and Billy Hoeft. Between innings, some of them would rise and play catch to stay warm and loose. Dark had stationed the bullpen where he could see it from the first-base dugout. If the pen had been in right field, players could duck into the clubhouse.

Not that anyone was tempted to leave this game. Stanek, who had survived the silent rookie treatment that was the norm then ("Rookies are treated like gods today," he told me when we met for lunch near his Holyoke, Massachusetts, home) to make the team and earn some respect, discussed the events with his mates. They were thinking extra innings by this point and wondering how long the starters would go before the wait staffs were summoned. "The feeling was that we'll be here a long time," Stanek said.

Though he would lead the Pacific Coast League in strikeouts, Stanek's career was cut short when he hurt his shoulder on the parallel bars in basic training. Like so many players who barely even had a cup of coffee in the majors—it was 1963 and out for Stanek—he relishes his every moment in The Show. All during the game, Stanek marveled at the high kickers on the mound. "There's no deception these days with the no-windup style," he said. "They think less will go wrong with a compact motion. I call these pitchers dart throwers and short-armers. If you wind up, you make the hitter wait longer, and they won't pick up the ball as well. I'd double pump or step off the mound. I followed Spahn's style—up and down, over the top, follow-through facing the batters—before they got me to turn and drive a little bit. You want to say to the hitters, 'I control the game, not you.'"

In their half of the eighth, the Giants went down 1-2-3, and the Braves surrendered in order in the ninth. With the scoreboard still running up zeroes, it was Spahn's turn for a close call. He had to face McCovey, perhaps the most popular player in San Francisco history, with one out in the home ninth. Once a frightened, tongue-tied kid from Mobile, Alabama, Stretch was developing into a featured speaker on the banquet circuit. Inviting Stanek and another rookie to play golf with him, he embodied what one academic called the "warm strength" so prized by San Franciscans. To listen to him speak was to hang on his gentle words. "Among his good qualities is a penchant for thinking before speaking," Ron Fimrite wrote in *Sports Illustrated*. "And his speech itself is distinctive; though there can be no questioning his impressive masculinity, he has the vocal mannerisms of an elderly Southern black woman. Speaking softly, employing homespun phrases, he is reminiscent of Ethel Waters in *The Member of the Wedding*."

Further endearing himself to the sophisticates by the Bay, McCovey loved jazz. After hitting the smoking line drive to Bobby Richardson that ended the 1962 World Series, McCovey repaired to a local club where Duke Ellington himself was performing. Renaming one of his own tunes in honor of the revered spectator, Duke played a favorite he called, "You hit it good, and that ain't bad."

McCovey had studied his idol Ted Williams and would finish his career with the same number of homers: 521. If anything, McCovey was an even more imposing sight at the plate than the Splendid Splinter. McCovey took his signature stance with left shoulder dipped, legs spread wide, all 6'4", 198 pounds of him threatening a mighty swing and a manifest outcome. Now Spahn eyed him in the ninth, a left-handed power hitter in a left-handed hitter's park. When Warren threw, Willie launched one of his patented moon shots; the ball flew somewhere past the right-field foul pole, clear out of the stadium, looking for all the world like a walk-off homer ending a nifty pitching duel. It was called fair by the Giants, fair by the fans, fair by most of the swells on press row, but foul by first base umpire Chris Pelekoudas. The Giants protested bitterly and futilely.

"I followed the ball all the way, but apparently the umpire didn't," McCovey said at the time. "It's a shame to hit a ball like that and lose what it means. It made me mad because I couldn't do anything about it. As hard as I hit the ball, it didn't have a chance to curve foul." Even Braves manager Bobby Bragan had a gripe. "The way to avoid that is to spend a little money and build a taller foul marker," he said after the game. "In Los Angeles there wouldn't have been any question whether it was fair or foul. If they made a marker like that here, the game might have ended."

Marichal felt the ball actually curved around the pole, passing it in fair territory. "It was so high and far that after it passed the fair pole you could see it curve into foul territory. It was hit so far it landed in the parking lot."

When the uproar subsided, McCovey grounded to first, Alou singled, and Cepeda grounded to third. Through nine innings, Marichal had a six-hitter with three walks and three strikeouts. Two Braves had stolen bases. Spahn had a five-hitter with one strikeout and one walk. The Giants had stolen one base in two attempts. If Spahn had the edge, the Giants figured Marichal had the lasting power. "Spahn had to get tired," said Giants pitcher Bobby Bolin, who was watching the game from the dugout. "We figured we could get a run off him—just like we did when he threw the no-hitter against us!"

How long could Spahn and Marichal go? Sometimes you can predict the future by looking into the past.

* * *

Let's pick up with Spahn back in Boston, the year after the Braves went to the 1948 World Series. As a team, they slipped in the standings amid dissension, contract disputes (Spahn reportedly threatened to demand a trade), and injury in 1949, finished four wins under .500, and began the decline that led to their departure from Boston, finishing fourth three straight seasons from 1949–51. Already annoyed by the signing of rookie Johnny Antonelli for $52,000 in 1948, some players balked at Billy Southworth's two-a-day workouts totaling six hours at spring training. Drinking heavily, his nerves in tatters over the tragic death of his only son as well as the player revolt, Southworth had to take a leave of absence two-thirds of the way through the season. Unsatisfied, the players voted him a half-share of their fourth-place Series money. Then the club further infuriated its players by trading the elite double-play combination of Alvin Dark and Eddie Stanky for four Giants on December 14, 1949. While the reconstituted Giants would win pennants in 1951 and 1954, the Braves only got their money's worth from outfielder Sid Gordon.

But not even his own salary dispute affected Spahn's concentration. He was up to 172 pounds. Using his long arms, thick wrists, and well-developed chest muscles to maximum effect in his delivery, he went 21–14, 21–17, and 22–14 with mediocre clubs in 1949–51, leading or tying for the National League in strikeouts all three years and leading in wins twice. And he proved he could go long in 1951, pitching 16 innings against the Dodgers before losing 2–1 when Carl Furillo doubled on the first screwball Spahn ever threw in a game. He struck out a then-league-record 18 Cubs in a 3–1 15-inning loss on June 14, 1952, the same day the Braves signed Hank Aaron. On September 20 of the same year, Spahn went 10 innings and lost the next to last game ever played at Braves Field 1–0 to the Dodgers on Jackie Robinson's single. A Braves minor leaguer named Pat Jordan, who ended up with a distinguished career as a journalist and novelist, later tried to build himself up for long innings by imitating Spahn's delivery. Jordan said he found "there were so many parts needed to produce that rhythm, and such a delicate balance between the parts" that he gave up the effort.

Spahn was more than just a star; he was a role model, as well. More than any other white teammate, Spahn befriended 1950 Rookie of the Year Sam Jethroe, the Braves' first black player.[15] They played lighthearted pepper games that Spahn always claimed he'd won. "That man Spahn," Jethroe said. "He just doesn't know how to count, so he never loses."

Spahn helped start the Jimmy Fund, the charitable arm of Boston's Dana-Farber Cancer Institute that was then called the Children's Cancer Research Foundation. It later became the Jimmy Fund, which is synonymous with the Red Sox as a favorite cause of the team since 1953. In the early 1950s, however, it was primarily a Braves charity until they left town and handed it off to the Sox. Spahn was one of the players who sang "Take Me Out to the Ballgame" with the original "Jimmy" in his hospital room. Warren did everything asked of him when the Braves assisted the Jimmy Fund and Dana-Farber in getting the program started. The first player to embark on speaking tours for the charity, Spahn tirelessly appeared at small town sales/picnics. Unlike today, when all athletes are expected to "give something back," in Spahn's time only personally motivated players reached out to the less fortunate.

What's more, Spahn was accessible. There wasn't the uncomfortable distance between players and fans that there is now. When a couple of kids from Malden approached Spahn outside his Brookline door unannounced, he took them to the ballpark and gave them a ball autographed by all the Braves. "He liked kids," Braves publicist Billy Sullivan told Spahn biographer Al Silverman. "We might be on a bus outside a ballpark, say Shibe Park in Philly. The players would be standing around waiting to go and inevitably some youngsters would come along. Some of the other players would just turn their backs on the kids and keep on talking, but not Warren. He would bring the youngster aside and ask him his name and about himself. Then he would write a special little message dedicated to each kid."

What couldn't Spahn do? On June 11, 1950, he and Cubs pitcher Bob Rush each stole a base on each other, a feat that wasn't duplicated until Jason Marquis and Greg Maddux did it in 2004. Spahn's celebrity was a welcome distraction for the 1952 team, which drew only 4,694 spectators to watch the Dodgers beat him 3–2 on Opening Day. The Braves slipped back into the second division, and Spahn went 14–19 (only Murray Dickson of the Pirates lost more games with 21) despite a league-leading 183 strikeouts, only 73 walks in 290 innings, and a 2.98 ERA for the second straight season. He got just 52 run support in his 19 defeats; in 14 of them, the Braves scored three or fewer runs. Well, somebody supported him. When the Braves arrived in Chicago in mid-July, Spahn was surrounded by a squad of detectives to protect him from the crank letter writer who threatened retaliation after Spahn broke the right wrist of the Cubs' Frankie Baumholtz with a pitch in June. The coward was a no-show. That was a minor irritation, but at 31 Spahn was beginning to feel his legs and knees acting up, his fastball slowing down, and his change-up suffering, too. So he started keeping his pitches low and experimenting with a screwball.

Meanwhile, Spahn struggled for compensation to match his contributions. A paramount difference between baseball in the fifties and today was labor relations. Bound then by the odious reserve clause in their contracts, players were owned by their teams unless they were traded or released. For Spahn, contract negotiations consisted of climbing the external stairs of the administration office at Braves Field—what Johnny Sain called the "Golden Staircase"—to the club's management offices, writing a number on a slip of paper, sliding it across the table to general manager John Quinn, and getting it back with a lower number on it. Players could hold out in the spring but eventually had to sign for less than they wanted or, in many cases, deserved. While negotiating his 1953 contract, Spahn accepted a $25,000 pact but rejected an alternative deal that would have paid him a lower salary, plus 10 cents for every paid admission over 800,000. That made sense to Quinn, since the Braves had drawn just 281,278 in 1952. Spahn found another payday when he and business partner Joel Greenberg invested $50,000 to open Warren Spahn's Restaurant (Motto: "The Best in Baseball, The Best in Food") near Braves Field. Little did he know what machinations the Braves had afoot. With St. Louis Browns owner Bill Veeck threatening to relocate to Milwaukee, principal Braves owner Lou Perini felt he had to take action now or never. Even as he was telling the media that the Braves would remain in Boston, the biggest Little Steamshovel was meeting with associates to plan the move to Milwaukee, where his old buddy Frederick Miller of the Miller Brewing Company had been wooing him. It would be the first move by a major league team since the Baltimore Orioles relocated to New York in 1903 and became the Highlanders and later Yankees.

When Perini announced the move to Milwaukee at a press conference on Friday, March 13, 1953—still called Black Friday in Boston—Spahn took a double loss. The Braves drew 1,826,397 for a new National League record in their first Midwestern season in what Boston columnist Harold Kaese had called "an unproven minor league town," costing Spahn a $102,639.70 bonus. And the restaurant premiered without its primary owner (though it did make money until the owners sold out in 1958). "The restaurant opened in Boston," Spahn said. "The Braves opened in Milwaukee."

Finances weren't the only concern Spahn took west. He had to leave a city he called his "second home" and comfortable quarters in Brookline. "It was such a nice apartment," Spahn's wife LoRene told *Sport's* Al Hirshberg. "We spent three years kicking around in dumps, and then we got this. Now we have to leave it."

For all his success, his popularity with fans, and the respect of the many teammates and opponents he helped, Spahn was an insecure man who never forgot his youth in Depression-era Buffalo. After ripping cartilage in his left knee during 1953 spring training, he didn't tell anyone. "I was one of the senior men on the club, and they'd have let me go in a minute if I went on the disabled list," he later told *The Sporting News'* Dave Kindred. All he did was win the Braves' Milwaukee opener 3–2 in 10 innings before an overflow 34,357 fans, win the All-Star Game, and lead the majors in wins (23) and ERA (2.10), while the Braves improved 28 games to 92 wins and finished second. "Funny thing, but I learned to follow through more on my delivery because my knee was weak," he said, "and it helped me have my best season." Only after it was over did Spahn have surgery. Then he caught the spikes of his front foot batting against Cincinnati's Art Fowler in 1954 spring training and had more cartilage removed from his right knee after *that* season.

But as Spahn was always saying, things have a way of working out in the end. Milwaukeeans showered everything on the Braves. "It wasn't just the good-time guys such as Mathews, Bob Buhl, and Lou Burdette who never had to pay for a meal and always got a free car to drive," John Schulian wrote in *Sports Illustrated*. "It was all the Braves. And the bounty didn't end with T-bones and Dodges, which were no small consideration during an era in which the minimum player's salary was $7,500, and raises for journeymen were measured in pennies. The players got free gas from Wisco, free dry cleaning from Spic 'n' Span, free beer from every brewery in town." Lou Burdette told Schulian, "Soap powder and produce were just about the only things that weren't delivered to our door."

The city and its prized lefty were an especially felicitous match. Incorporated in 1846 by French-Canadian fur trader Solomon Juneau and among the top 20 most populated cities by 1900, Milwaukee had grown into the 10th largest industrial hub in the country, a union town, and a bowling town that had completed civic projects worth $127 million since World War II, according to

John B. Parrott's *The Promise: A Baseball Odyssey*. It reminded Spahn of home. Why, you could take this sentence from *Urban Children in America*—"By the late nineteenth century Milwaukee was a major industrial and transportation center, with tens of thousands of workers employed by the tanneries, foundries, packing plants, breweries, and other world famous manufacturers, such as Allis Chalmers, Allen-Bradley, Harley-Davidson, and Miller Brewing"—and just about substitute Buffalo. Like Buffalo, Milwaukee was a roll-out-the-barrel town with distinct ethnic neighborhoods and a baseball legacy dating back to the nineteenth century, when the first baseman was expected to be Irish and the third baseman German! After playing in Buffalo, Connie Mack managed in Milwaukee in 1900, two seasons before the team was relocated to become the St. Louis Browns. When news of the Braves' move was announced, the *Milwaukee Sentinel's* Lloyd Larson proclaimed, "Milwaukee is now truly a major segment of the land of the free and the home of the Braves."

A blue-collar, beer-swilling city where 50 percent of the work force labored in factories in 1953, Milwaukee took quickly to a pitcher who worked long, worked hard, and enjoyed beer after games. Then there was the park. A $5 million, publicly funded structure built for baseball, County Stadium seated 36,011 (with another 7,080 added in 1954) and had symmetrical dimensions—320' down each baseline to go with 355' in the power alleys, 397' in the deep alleys, and 404' to center when the Braves arrived. It was very much a pitcher's park. In Spahn's 12 years there, the Braves hit better on the road than at home every season and hit more homers abroad nine times. County was also a friendly place to fans known for the best bratwurst and the best tailgate parties in the majors.

Spahn kept winning—he was 21–12 with a 3.14 ERA in 1954 and 17–14 with a 3.26 ERA in '55—while the Braves finished third and second and rebuilt with players like Aaron, Johnny Logan, Joe Adcock, Del Crandall, and Billy Bruton. In all, the Braves constituted the kind of cast that could have filled a novel, play, or movie like the Mark Harris book *Bang the Drum Slowly* that became all three. Complementing the heroic, suffering superstar Aaron was the stylish, fleet center fielder Bruton, whom Milwaukee sportswriter Sam Levy called "only slightly slower than jet propulsion." After delighting fans for the minor league Milwaukee Brewers, Bruton starred in the first two Milwaukee Braves victories. Bruton considered himself blessed to be playing for the Braves. No wonder he thanked God every night for his skill.

The Braves, moreover, boasted two slugging monoliths. One of them, Adcock, a 6'4", 220-pound Louisianan, the son of a farmer/sheriff father and ex-schoolteacher mother, had four homers and 18 total bases in a single game, and he hit a major league "first"—a 485' shot over the centerfield fence at the Polo Grounds. Clean-living, milkshake-drinking, sunrise-rising, Adcock rarely blew up, but he once charged pitcher Rubén Gómez, bat in hand, after Gómez threw at him. The incident sparked a poem by Gene Fehler that was a perfect parody of Leigh Hunt's "Jenny Kissed Me":

> *Adcock missed me when he sped*
> *Toward the mound to get his licks in.*
> *Though he planned to smash my head,*
> *My dugout saved me; I leapt in.*
> *Say I'm cowardly, or*
> *Say fame's lips have never kissed me;*
> *Yet I lived to pitched again, for*
> *Adcock missed me.*

The second stanchion of swat, Eddie Mathews, a curly-haired, tight-muscled Texan who stood 6'1" and weighed 195 pounds, joined the Boston Braves in 1952 because his father saw an opening at third base (Bob Elliott was the elderly regular) and a low-pressure atmosphere if he accepted a small offer. Mathews signed for $6,000 even though the Dodgers offered $50,000, made the club at age 20 when Elliott was traded, and hit three homers in a game, a first for any rookie. Mathews was pictured on the first *Sports Illustrated* cover in 1954. With wrists like Aaron's, Matthews hit one homer 480' another 500'. He and Aaron would hit 863 homers as teammates—more than Ruth and Gehrig or any other twosome did. "More players talk about Mathews' wrists than Marilyn Monroe's legs," declared Tom Meany, the old sportswriter. Ty Cobb said, "I've seen three or four perfect swings in my time, and this lad has one of them." Mathews also had a temper and a hard right that decked opponents Frank Robinson and Jim O'Toole. "He was a great captain," pitcher Bob Sadowski said. "When I was a rookie, an umpire told me, 'Hey, pretty boy, just throw the ball.' Eddie yelled at him, 'You just call balls and strikes and shut up.' The umpire shut up."

In the end, Mathews, the only Brave to play in Boston, Milwaukee, and Atlanta, totaled 512 homers and led the league in assists three times, all the while concentrating on the inner game of baseball. "I'd take on the other third baseman.... I wanted to beat him in every department—fielding, hitting, and running the bases. I played that game all my life, and it kept me on my toes."

As was common in his time but rare among athletes today, however, Eddie didn't always take care of himself. He heard the chimes at midnight, at least when he was sentient. "Mathews had acquired a certain renown for enjoying a fermented beverage now and again," Bob Buege wrote in a bio of Braves shortstop Johnny Logan for the Society for American Baseball Research (SABR). "Logan positioned himself on the left side of the infield according to Eddie's social behavior. Johnny explained, 'I had to find out every day if he went out having a beer with Warren Spahn, Lou Burdette, and Bob Buhl. My conversation with Eddie every day was, 'Did you get your sleep?' If he said, 'Them son-of-a-guns,' that meant he went out and drank. The only guy the next day that was gonna be playing—Spahn wasn't gonna pitch, Burdette wasn't, and so on—was Eddie Mathews. After a while I got to know Eddie. Just ask him a question. If he was very cooperative, got his sleep, I played toward the middle. If he bitched a little bit, I moved toward third. That's the honest truth right there."

Milwaukee sportswriters surely sensed Mathews' problem, but they didn't write about it any more than New York writers questioned manager Casey Stengel when he said Mickey Mantle was sidelined with some injury or other when he was obviously hung over. The writers tended to identify with the athletes, who weren't that well paid and often took off-season jobs in the communities where they played. In those days, athletes could sin in relative safety unless there was a paternity suit or assault charge because beyond the complaisant sportswriters there was no YouTube, Twitter, 24/7 news channels, tabloid media, gossip websites, blogs, camera phones, ESPN, leaked sex tapes, talking heads, critical sportswriters, or all the other accoutrements of today's deer-in-the-headlights coverage of celebrities. Modern athletes may be well paid, but all their light-on-details press "opportunities," gated communities, image-manicuring agents, and bodyguards can't protect their privacy. Just ask Tiger Woods, Roger Clemens, Barry Bonds, and Kobe Bryant.

If alcoholism was one ill that went largely tolerated in Mathews' time, so was drug usage. Oh, it wasn't cocaine, steroids, or HGH, but every team seemed to have a jar of "greenies," or amphetamines, whose use the clubs, the leagues, the commissioner's office, and the media protected by not discussing.

The thinking was that players needed something to sustain them through a six-month season, and they thought greenies did the job better than caffeine.

A better recipe for sustained success was leadership. Behind almost every great pitching staff is a great catcher. Short and "almost fat," as he described his kid self back in Fullerton, California, Del Crandall became a grade school catcher because the other positions were filled, but he grew thin, dedicated himself to the game, and matured so quickly that he was a big-league catcher at 19. "If you get beaten by a foolish pitch, it eats on you," said Fred Haney, who coached and later managed the Braves. "We don't have to worry much about that kind of thing with Crandall catching."

Possibly the most popular Brave, Johnny Logan was the quintessential Brewtown shortstop: the son of foundry worker who could bunt, hit-and-run, range wide for grounders, and fight for his mates. He and Mathews were such a successful tag team in fisticuffs, taking on everyone in bars from sailors on down that news of their prowess reached former heavyweight champion Joe Louis in Las Vegas, where he was a casino greeter. The endearing Logan could also toss out a malapropism or two. Told there was a typographical error in a box score, he said, "The hell it was. It was a clean hit." Asked to name baseball's greatest all-time player, he said, "I guess I'd have to go with the immoral Babe Ruth." Upon receiving an award, Logan commented, "I will perish this trophy forever."

Bob Buhl, who did PR work for Miller beer and drank it generously, went 18–8 in 1956 once he tamed his sidearm deliveries. Buhl fit right in with fellow pitchers Burdette and Spahn. Before games, he'd play pepper with them, and the guy who booted the most balls paying for drinks later. "I was mean on the mound," Buhl said, referring to his bent for throwing inside. "And I was wild to begin with, so that helped me."

Spahn's running buddy and prankster pal, Selva Lewis "Lou" Burdette, who was picked up in a trade with the Yankees for Sain, gave the team a superb 1-2 punch. Probably the most extraordinary character on the club, Burdette fidgeted so much that manager Fred Haney said, "He's the only man who can make coffee nervous." Burdette got the batters to think more about his alleged spitballs than how to hit him. "They'd practically undress me," he said of umpires' inspections, "and then I'd tell them they missed a place." In another diversion, Burdette would release a pitch, yell, "Look out!" and then grin sheepishly when a curve caught the inside corner while the batter backed off. Burdette was actually one of the great control artists of baseball history, averaging fewer than two walks a game. He won 203 games in his career, and he and Spahn accounted for 443 wins in 1951–63—the most ever by any two righty-lefty teammates in their time together. The Braves' combination of starters and sluggers was telling in a decade when starters were expected to finish and offensive strategy consisted of waiting for the home run. (The Braves could also manufacture runs if needed.) Willie Mays led the decade with all of 179 stolen bases, and strategy wouldn't begin to change until the running, "go-go" White Sox won the 1959 American League pennant.

Burdette and Spahn made a devilish righty-lefty tandem that frustrated hitters. Burdette also provided Spahn with a fellow practical joker to pal around with. In one of their most celebrated pranks, Burdette and Spahn arrived early in spring training and told an attendant at the gate that a midget would try to pass himself off as a club executive. When Donald Davidson, who was 4' tall and the Braves' publicity director, showed up, the attendant refused him admission. Davidson sputtered for awhile and finally began kicking the man in the shins. When the blameless worker was about to retaliate, Spahn and Burdette bolted from their hiding place and saved Davidson's neck.

Spahn and Burdette started a fire in the back of the team bus to show their displeasure with manager Chuck ("A good relief pitcher is worth two starting pitchers any day") Dressen in the early 1960s. They traded gloves in the outfield and bet steak dinners on who could catch more balls in batting practice. When the photographer from Topps bubble gum arrived to take pictures of the players, Spahn and Burdette posed together, each passing himself off as the other guy. Burdette wore Spahn's left-handed glove and Spahn had Burdette's right-handed mitt on. "We always switched gloves in the outfield to catch flies. I think they caught Warren's glove, but they let mine go," Burdette said of the photo editors. Check out the 1959 set, and you'll see Burdette with a left-handed glove.

In addition to Mathews, fellow Braves Crandall, Adcock, and Spahn made *Sports Illustrated* covers in the 1950s. By 1956, everyone knew about the Braves. Relieving and starting, Burdette went 19–10. Adcock hit eight homers in nine games and the first round-tripper to clear the left-field roof in Brooklyn. But it seemed fitting that Spahn, by now "a nice dignified old baseball gentleman" in the words of one writer, would make or break the pennant chase. Healthy for a change after winter operations on both knees, he perfected his screwball and won 10 of his last 11 decisions going into the season's final weekend. With the Braves half a game behind the first-place Dodgers and needing a win on a Saturday night in St. Louis, Spahn had a 1–0 no-hitter through five, surrendered a run in the sixth, and would have won in the 9th if the Cardinals' Bobby Del Greco hadn't made two spectacular catches in the outfield. With one out in the bottom of the 12th, Stan Musial hit a soft fly to right-center that might have been caught but dropped in for a double. Ken Boyer was intentionally walked, and Rip Repulski hit a hard grounder to Mathews that looked like an inning-ending double play. Somehow it caromed off Mathews' knee into foul territory, Musial scored on the double, and Spahn lost a 2–1, five-hit, 12-inning heartbreaker. The St. Louis crowd of 25,587, which had been rooting for the Braves all night, sat stunned.

Spahn left the mound low and dejected. After manager Haney told him, "You did everything you could," Spahn actually cried and threw his glove at AP photographer Jack Horgan for taking his picture. Spahn later apologized. Calling the effort "one of the finest pitching jobs of Spahn's career," the *New York Times'* Joseph Sheehan wrote that the defeat was "heartbreaking." Leonard Koppett of the *New York Post* called it "one of the greatest pitched games in the history of baseball." When the Dodgers held on to their lead by winning on Sunday and the Braves decamped from their funereal plane home to the shocking sight of some 10,000 cheering Milwaukeeans at Billy Miller Field, a little girl in a yellow dress ran up and told Spahn, "We'll win yet, Warren. Wait 'til next year."

Just how did a little girl get close to the Braves? In the 1950s, players were all business on the field but pretty good about handshakes and autographs off it. Today's athletes genuflect to the three P's: PR, patriotism, and piety. They make a show of throwing the ball into the stands after the last out of an inning. They stand for "God Bless America," which has replaced "Take Me Out to the Ball Game" at many parks during the seventh-inning stretch. And they're constantly pointing to the heavens, as if God just hit that 450' dinger. But just try to approach a ballplayer as he leaves the clubhouse. You are no competition for his cell phone.

In 1957, the 36-year-old Spahn bounced back to capture baseball's Cy Young Award.[16] He went 21–11 with a 2.69 ERA and league-leading 18 complete games, and he won nine times in 29 days down the stretch. This time he was rewarded—the Braves won their first pennant in Milwaukee on Aaron's 11th-inning home run on September 23. Spahn was unquestionably the best pitcher in baseball, with Buhl (18 wins) and Burdette (17) a friendly supporting cast. Aaron, with a .322 average, 44 homers, and 132 RBI, won the MVP award. Mathews finished among the top five in runs (109), homers (32), total bases (309), walks (90), and even triples (9).

Future Hall of Famer Red Schoendienst, acquired at the trading deadline, cemented the lineup as second baseman, sparkplug, and uncompromising leader. "We had a bunch of hell-raising guys in the clubhouse, but when the ball club went on the field it was all business," Spahn told baseball historian Rich Westcott. "If one guy got into a fight, everybody fought. There was that kind of camaraderie.

"We had guys who came from other ball clubs, but management never had to get on their butts about hustling. The players got on them. They'd say, 'Hey, look, you might have done it that way where you played before, but this is the way we do it here.'" (Funny, you didn't hear many "We few, we happy few, we band of brothers" descriptions of the clique-ridden 1960s Giants.)

There was much back-and-forth ribbing, usually started by Spahn and Burdette. They called Wes Covington "Kingfish" for his quick mouth, and Covington ridiculed their dress, which Aaron described as "without any kind of style whatsoever." Spahn and Burdette got in the last word when they burned Covington's straw hat at home plate in Ebbets Field.

In all, some of the Braves were a throwback to the "rowdy and raucous men" Bill Veeck celebrated from baseball's past. There was a popular story about a big, rawboned youngster named Mel Famey who could throw 100-mph pitches, but no one knew what direction they'd be headed in. One time he came out of the bullpen to put out the fire but wound up throwing gasoline on it. Famey walked his first batter, his second, then his third and finally was relieved after he walked in a run. Following the game, a couple of opposing pitchers passed the Braves bullpen and noted that it was littered with beer cans. "Well," said one of the pitchers, "I guess that was the beer that made Mel Famey walk us."

Famey never existed, but the actual Braves proved not only a boon for Milwaukee fans, who set a 1950s attendance record of 2,215,404 in 1957, but for baseball in general. In part because of television, in part because of urban decay around old ballparks, fans had been deserting the game all decade. Angry and treacly writing abounded about teams deserting their cities,[17] but the Browns were right to decamp to Baltimore and the Philadelphia Athletics to Kansas City. As for the Brooklyn Dodgers and New York Giants, boys of summer and all that, Dodgers attendance dropped to 1,028,000 and Giants attendance to 654,000 (that's fewer than 9,000 a game in Manhattan) before they left for the West Coast in 1958. Whatever the merits of deserting New York, new starts in places like Los Angeles and San Francisco augured well for the game's future because they made it a national rather than a regional pastime. Baseball also benefited when the National League adopted batting helmets in 1955 and the American League in 1956. Modernization was long overdue in an industry prone to stagnation.

Though the 1957 Braves were strong all through the lineup and rotation, the Yankees were overwhelming favorites to win the World Series. Spahn lost the opener 3–1, but with the Braves down two games to one he went the distance to win Game 4 7–5 on Logan's run-scoring double and Mathews' two-run homer in the 10th inning. In this bizarre affair, Yankee slugger Elston Howard hit a three-run homer to tie the score at 4–4 in the ninth, the Yankees went ahead, 5–4 in their half of the 10th, and the Braves' rally was set up when pinch-hitter Nippy Jones convinced home-plate umpire Augie Donatelli that he'd been hit by a pitch by pointing to a black smear on the ball and saying, "See? It's the polish from my shoe!" The Yankees' Tommy Byrne always claimed the pitch must have hit the ground first then it hit Jones' shoe.

Note the absence of relief despite a mounting score. The save, invented by Jerome Holtzman of the *Chicago Sun-Times*, did not become an official statistic until 1969. There were certainly some outstanding closers in the 1950s, including Hoyt Wilhelm, Elroy Face, Ellis Kinder, Clem Labine, and 1950 National League MVP Jim Konstanty, but top starters like Spahn were expected to finish what they began. Spahn threw 126 pitches in Game 4.

This thrill-packed Series went the full seven games. Spahn fell sick with the flu, so it was perhaps with mixed feelings that he watched as Series MVP Burdette took Spahn's scheduled start in Game 7 on two days rest. Burdette beat the Yankees 5–0 for the Braves' first World Series title since 1914. The unsung hero was Mathews, who drew eight walks, hit the homer to win Game 4, scored the game-winner in Game 5, drove in two runs in the finale, and made a great stop of a bases-loaded smash before stepping on third to end the Series.

Let's underscore what the flu may have cost Spahn. In 1957, baseball was as popular in the United States as soccer was in the rest of the world. The National Hockey League had only six teams, including four in the U.S. The National Basketball Association was less than a decade old, and the Bill Russell Celtics

Two Pitchers, One No-Hitter, One Perfect Game?

There was almost a no-hitter and a perfect game on the same day. On the same field.

One participant was no surprise: Dodgers Hall of Famer Sandy Koufax. The other was, no kidding, Cubs left-hander Bob Hendley. They met at Dodger Stadium before 29,139 fans on the Thursday night of September 9, 1965. Koufax, age 29, won 26 games that year, pulled America's heartstrings by skipping the World Series opener for Yom Kippur, then won two games and the Series MVP award. On September 9, the presence of players like Ernie Banks (28 homers, 106 RBIs in '65), Billy Williams (.315, 34 HR, 108 RBIs), and Ron Santo (33 HR, 101 RBIs) scarcely bothered Koufax. Bring 'em on. And then there was the other guy. Having been traded from the Giants to the Cubs, Hendley, 26, was a once-promising prospect in his fifth of seven undistinguished major league seasons. If he had anything to look forward to on September 9, it was the absence of sluggers in the Dodgers' lineup, which generated runs by scratching out hits and filching bases.

Koufax got Don Young to pop up on his first big-league at-bat, and he struck out Glenn Beckert and Williams. Beckert did hit a loud foul by third base. Still pitching like the flamethrower he'd been as a youngster but with much better control, Koufax had a high fastball that was hard to track, much less hit. Not to be outdone, Hendley got Maury Wills on a grounder to the mound, Junior Gilliam on a fly to center, and Willie Davis on a pop to third.

In the second, Koufax retired Santo on a foul to the catcher, struck out Banks on what Dodgers radio voice Vin Scully swore was a forkball, and induced Byron Browne (another rookie in his major league debut) to line out to right. Against Hendley, Lou Johnson fouled to first and Ron Fairly and Jim Lefebvre flied out to center. Koufax got fly outs from Chris Krug and Don Kessinger before striking out Hendley in the third. Keeping the ball down and inducing grounders, Hendley tore through Wes Parker (6-3), Jeff Torborg (5-3), and Koufax (1-3). Through three innings, both pitchers not only had no-hitters but also perfect games.

Hendley lost his perfecto in the fifth when Johnson walked. On Fairly's sacrifice bunt, Hendley may have had a play at second but dropped the ball and had to go to first. Then disaster struck. When Johnson bolted for third, catcher Krug threw into left field and Johnson scored on the stolen base and error. Hendley got the next two hitters, his no-hitter still intact. Koufax had retired all 15 of his batters. At this point, it was traditional for the Associated Press to send out a general wire that a no-hitter was in progress. Sports editors must have yelled "Typo!" at the incomprehensible news of a no-hitter *and* a perfect game.

It is not unprecedented for a pitcher to allow a run without a hit. The Yankees' Bill Bevens had a 2-1 no-hitter going before Brooklyn's Cookie Lavagetto beat him with a two-run double in the 1947 World Series. And in 1964, Houston's Ken Johnson lost a game 1-0 despite holding the Reds hitless. Koufax and Hendley set 'em down in the sixth, Koufax benefiting from first baseman Parker's dig-out of a throw in the dirt to get Krug and third baseman Gilliam's quick throw to retire Kessinger on a bang-bang play. Having pitched three no-hitters, Koufax now took aim at his first perfect game. For his part, Hendley had retired 18 of his first 19 batters without allowing a hit.

In the last of the seventh, Johnson again played spoiler. He rapped a bloop double that barely reached the outfield grass before being fielded in foul ground by first baseman Banks. This miserable safety ended Hendley's no-hitter. Now he could only hold on grimly and hope for a Cubs run. But Koufax just got stronger. He pitched another perfect inning in the seventh, although he threw one pitch to the backstop. In the eighth he struck out Santo looking and Banks and Browne flailing. It was 24 up, 24 down, and 11 on strikeouts. Hendley got through his half of the inning, as if anyone was watching him.

All eyes were now on Koufax. Leading off the ninth, Krug struck out. Joey Amalfitano batted for Kessinger and took a fastball for strike one. Koufax now threw his patented hook, the most dreaded curveball in baseball and possibly in baseball history. A fast-dropping, overhand curveball is usually called Uncle Charlie. Some hitters in 1965 called the Koufax curve Lord Charles. Other hitters called it The Hammer. Amalfitano actually fouled it off. Then he swung and missed a fastball. Two out.

Harvey Kuenn, the last out of a 1963 Koufax no-hitter, stepped in for Hendley and took a fastball for strike one. Koufax missed with the next two pitches, and the crowd tensed. Now he blew a fastball by the batter. Vin Scully called it:

> "It is 9:46 PM. Two-and-two to Harvey Kuenn. One strike away. Sandy goes into his windup. Swung on and missed. A perfect game!"

Afterward, umpire Ed Vargo told Koufax that two of the pitches Kuenn swung at would have been balls, but who could blame him for being jumpy?

In the best one hour and 43 minutes of entertainment anyone at Dodger Stadium would ever get, Koufax punched out 14-of-27 batters, including the last six, while becoming the first pitcher to throw four no-hitters, including the first perfect game by a left-hander. Hendley didn't do badly himself, walking one and striking out three while yielding just one unearned run, one (cheap) hit and two base runners (well, Lou Johnson twice). "I can sympathize with Hendley," Koufax said. "It's a shame to lose a game like that."

But not such a shame to be a partner in history. Between them, Koufax and Hendley allowed the fewest batters ever to reach base in a nine-inning game. Among pitching duels that run the usual nine innings, it's hard to imagine anything better.

had barely started winning their 11 championships in 13 years to put the game on the map. The National Football League was using baseball nicknames and playing to sparse crowds; not until the epic Giants-Colts duel in the 1958 Championship Game would football begin to challenge baseball. Though Spahn was king of the hill, he missed the chance to stand on top of the world.

Spahn wasn't taking any chances. In 1958, playing more pepper to quicken his reflexes as a fielder, he perfected his slider with help from pitching coach Whitlow Wyatt. Right-handed batters had been crowding the plate in anticipation of Spahn's screwball over the outside corner; now he had something to throw inside and drive them back. When the Yankees and Braves repeated as pennant-winners, Spahn broke a tie with Hall of Famers Lefty Grove and Eddie Plank by winning 20 games for the ninth time while batting .333 and becoming one of only 14 National Leaguers to win 20 games and bat better than .300 in the same season. It scarcely seemed to matter that he barely lost the Cy Young Award to the Yankees' Bob Turley five votes to four.

The Yankees were still seething from remarks Burdette and Spahn made after the 1957 Series. "We'd like to play them again next year. I'm sure we're going to win the pennant, but I'm not sure about them," Burdette said. "The Yankees couldn't finish fifth in the National League," Spahn said.

The lads were in a more charitable mood in October 1958. Almost as loyal to their lodge brothers as their team, Spahn and Burdette showed the Yankees' Whitey Ford how to throw a "mudball" at the Series. A pitch that dips and darts sharply because the dirt on it changes its trajectory, the mudball may have been thrown by Burdette, and something wet certainly was thrown by Ford, though Spahn was never suspected. He beat the Yankees 4–3 in 10 innings to take Game 1 of the Series, contributing two hits and an RBI himself. Then, locked in a pitcher's zone ("All I can see…is a strike zone waving a bat"), Spahn two-hit the Yankees in Game 4 and won 3–0, getting 23 called strikes and retiring the last eight batters to put the Braves up three games to one. "He threw a lot of fastballs," Crandall said, "but it wasn't the speed so much as the control. In and out, up and down…. He was putting the ball right where he wanted to."

Unnecessarily assigned by manager Haney to pitch on two days' rest with the Braves ahead three games to two—Aaron later wrote that Haney stopped managing altogether at that point—Spahn trudged to the mound with a tired arm. He hadn't started on just two days' rest following a previous start since May 20, 1956. "Go get 'em, Meatnose!" called out Warren's father, Edward, who was watching in Buffalo with newsman Jack Horrigan. When Spahn singled home Covington to put the Braves ahead 2–1 in the second, the senior Spahn yelled, "Whoopee! Attaboy, Meatnose. You may not be much of a pitcher, but you're a hell of a hitter." With the game tied 2–2 in the 10th, Gil McDougald homered and Edward Spahn drew on his cigarette and coughed. When Spahn was removed and 46,367 fans rose to cheer him, Ed's eyes filled with tears.

Scoring another run and giving up one in the bottom of the 10th, the Yankees eventually beat Spahn 4–3. His exhaustion not withstanding—Spahn pitched 28⅔ innings in eight days—the Braves might have won in regulation if Bruton hadn't misplayed a fly into a single-and-error leading to a run and third base coach Billy Herman hadn't sent 37-year-old Andy Pafko to be tagged out at home on a short fly. "It is doubtful," Milwaukee sportswriter Bob Wolf insisted, "that a losing pitcher ever dominated a World Series game as Warren Spahn did." He had gone from a pitcher throwing high fastballs, curves, and change-ups to a low-baller throwing curves at different speeds, a straight change, a slider, and a screwball. Yet in the '58 Series, he was winning with a rejuvenated fastball! Some observers considered Spahn the outstanding pitcher of the Series,[18] but the Yankees won Game 7 when Burdette was also used on two days of rest and Turley beat him 6–2 to win all the big awards, including the Cy Young, Series MVP, and the Hickok Belt for the outstanding athlete of the year. Despite stellar performances, Spahn was constantly being one-upped, first by Sain in 1948, then by Burdette in 1957, and now Turley. But what hurt him most was losing the Series.

"We stopped hitting," he said without angst. "The worst part was our wives had spent the winners' portion before the Series!"

With extraordinary staying power and his weight holding steady at 175 pounds, the 38-year-old Spahn pitched a league-high 292 innings and went 21–15 for the injury-ridden 1959 Braves, who lost the pennant in a two-game playoff to the Dodgers. Appearing only as a reliever in the series against his arch-nemesis with two men on base in Game 2, Spahn faced just two batters. He allowed a long drive that Aaron converted into a circus-catch sacrifice fly followed by a single. And then Spahn was removed. Schoendienst's lingering tuberculosis, which limited him to five games, was devastating to the 1959 team. The Braves lost the first playoff game when one of seven men used in Red's place, Bobby Avila, made two misplays that were scored as hits to give L.A. a 3–2 win. Then Milwaukee dropped the finale on a 12th-inning error by

Felix Mantilla, another second baseman relocated to shortstop after Johnny Logan was injured in the seventh inning. Had Schoendienst been healthy, David Nemec wrote in *The Ultimate Baseball Book*, "the club might have been the league's strongest of the entire decade."

The Braves led the National League with 365 wins in 1956–59. In subsequent years, as they finally began to tail off and lose veterans like Adcock, Buhl, and Crandall while getting stingy in the salary department, Spahn continued to defy the odds and the gods. He threw his two no-hitters at ages 39 and 40.

Burdette, who was competitive with Spahn, had thrown a no-no 29 days before Spahn's first and playfully let him know it. "So maybe when he pitched his no-hitter, I subconsciously made up my mind to throw one myself," Spahn told sportswriter Wolf.

On the rainy Friday night of September 16, 1960, only 6,117 fans watched Spahn pitch—the smallest crowd since the Braves moved to County Stadium. If the weather didn't keep attendance down, loyalty to high school football games played the same night probably did. Spahn showed up, a marvel of reconstruction. Because of knee trouble and cancellations, he hadn't won his second game until the second month of the season, but his fastball again sprang to life and he won six in a row and eight out of 10 over a five-week stretch starting August 7. The September 16 game was a mismatch from the start, with Spahn (19–9 at game time) against John Buzhardt (4–15, worst in the league). Spahn struck out six of the first nine Phillies hitters and 11 over the first seven innings, while his teammates gave him a 4–0 lead. Only two batters reached base, both on walks. "All right, just nobody say I've got a no-hitter going," Spahn announced to a shocked Milwaukee bench (shades of the Marichal no-hitter) in violation of the silence code. In the eighth, he struck out pinch-hitters Tony Taylor and Lee Walls. That made his strike-out total 13.

Bobby Gene Smith pinch-hit to lead off the ninth and went down quickly on strikes. Bobby Del Greco became the fourth K in a row and 15th overall. Only on June 14, 1952, when he fanned 18 in that 15-inning game to tie the league single-game record, had Spahn struck out more. That brought up Bobby Malkmus, who was batting .212 at game time. On the first pitch, Malkmus lined one back at the mound for the hardest-hit ball by a Phillie all night. Instinctively, Spahn reached up and deflected it with his glove. Shortstop Logan raced in, grabbed the ball, and threw off-balance and a little off-line. As the ball and base runner converged on first, Joe Adcock split and stretched to catch the throw. The umpire's fist went up. Spahn had started a spectacular 1–6–3 play for the final out.

Spahn sat for a time after the game, musing. "I should be in the twilight of my career," he said, "and tonight I had a fastball I haven't had in 10 years."

"You couldn't pitch a no-hitter when you won 19," Crandall said, kidding Spahn. "You had to save it for 20."

Aaron approached him more seriously and shook his hand. "I don't know what there's left for you to do in baseball," he said, "but I know you'll do it."

With 288 wins, Spahn had a ready target, but first there was another milestone. Just six starts later, on April 28, 1961, he did the impossible a second time. Before 8,518 fans on another rainy night with the game-time temperature between 38–44 degrees in County Stadium, depending on who was reporting it, Spahn faced a much better team in the Giants. San Francisco would hit 183 homers that season, and they had a much better pitcher than Buzhardt in Toothpick Sam Jones, who had won 39 games over the previous two years. Spahn allowed just two walks and wiped out both base runners on 1–6–3 double plays. Jones was almost as effective, throwing a jumping fastball and sweeping curve while allowing only five hits, all of which were singles. The Braves manufactured a first-inning run when Frank Bolling singled, took second on a passed ball, and scored on Aaron's two-out single. Once again, Spahn saved maximum drama for the ninth inning. After catcher Charley Lau dropped Ed Bailey's foul pop, Spahn struck him out, then fielded Matty Alou's drag bunt and backhanded the ball to Adcock just in time. "Only two pitchers in baseball could have made that play," Alvin Dark, the Giants manager, told *Sports Illustrated's* Tex Maule. "Spahn and [Harvey] Haddix. They're the only ones who field their position that well."

Short of a strikeout, the best ending Spahn could hope for was a grounder to shortstop Roy McMillan. He was the Braves' Clark Kent. Mild-mannered, bespectacled, son of the town barber in Bonham, Texas, he left the dugout with the range of a condor and the arm strength of a leviathan. McMillan had won three Gold Gloves and set a since-broken record of 129 double plays in a season for the 1950s Reds. Despite his anemic hitting, he made two All-Star teams, received MVP votes, and made the cover of *Sports Illustrated* mainly for his reliability and leadership. According to BaseballLibrary.com, he was "universally respected by his peers."

Denis Menke marveled, "When I was a rookie, I was a guy coming up who was supposed to take his job, and he was showing me things at shortstop." McMillan led the league in sacrifice hits once and games played twice while running up 584 consecutive games from 1951–55. "Hitting a ball toward Roy is like hitting it down a sewer," St. Louis manager Eddie Stanky once said.

But this was no routine chance. Pinch-hitter Joey Amalfitano hit what looked like an easy grounder to short, but it took a bad hop that struck McMillan in the groin. He reached for the ball, missed, and in another motion picked it up and threw it to Adcock ahead of Amalfitano to preserve both the no-hitter and 1–0 win. "Don't think my knees didn't buckle," McMillan said later, chuckling between his clenched teeth. But Spahn's second no-hitter, at age 40, was no laughing matter. Only Cy Young at the time had thrown one at a later age. Nolan Ryan threw his last no-hitter in 1991 at age 44.

Milwaukee manager Chuck Dressen, who had just witnessed his sixth no-hitter, said it was "the most perfect game I ever saw. They didn't hit a hard ball off him, not a good line drive. How often do you see that, no-hitter or not?" This was no small tribute from Dressen, who was criticized for using Spahn out of turn and in relief while managing the Braves in 1960–61—he got off to slow starts both seasons before rebounding to win his usual 20—and would take verbal jabs at Spahn after being fired.

In the *New York Herald Tribune*, legendary New York sports columnist Walter "Red" Smith wrote that "6,800 burghers lifted foaming muzzles from their steins in praises of a goose-necked, stork-legged, demi-god to the cold stars." Later in the column, he playfully referred to Spahn as "a gowky [probably a typo for 'gawky'], bat-eared old warrior with the ample nose."

Spahn said he was lucky, citing the "cardinal" mistake of walking leadoff hitters twice with a one-run lead and grooving a ball to Willie Mays that he didn't hit out. "He deserved it, no matter what he says," Mays said. "He wasn't fast, but he was all pitcher and he had amazing control. He kept the hitters off balance with his changing speeds, and he never put the ball where you could get much bat on it."

Years later Spahn, who seemed to have a thoughtful take on everything, told Minnesota Twins beat writer Jim Thielman, "No-hitters aren't that much fun. Every pitch you make can blow it, and you go out there in the ninth inning and look around and all the infielders are scared because they're afraid they're going to screw it up."

Spahn finished the 1961 season leading the league with 21 wins, 21 complete games, four shutouts, and a 3.01 ERA. And there were more challenges ahead. Pitching a no-hitter is a perk, but winning a 300th game is a career. Only 12 players had reached that mark, including just four who pitched exclusively in the 20th century, and no one since Lefty Grove in 1941. With 299 victories, Spahn received 104 four-leaf clovers from fans and a telegram from Braves owner Lou Perini before his start on August 11, 1961. After sleeping late, he had a busy morning and afternoon at his house on Martha Washington Drive, receiving calls from friends and radio stations in New York and Buffalo and posing for photographers. Somehow, he found time for family, playing rummy with his son, Greg, and eating the beef stew his wife, LoRene, always cooked for him before home starts. In fact, Warren had two helpings at the 4:00 PM meal. Anticipating a raucous celebration, LoRene put aside Warren's oldest clothes for him to wear and packed new ones in a small valise she took to the game.

A crowd of 40,775 jammed County Stadium that Friday night. Winning wasn't easy. Spahn himself hit a sacrifice fly to put the Braves ahead of the Cubs 1–0 in the fifth. Andre Rodgers singled home a run to tie the score in the sixth. The Braves were struggling to hit Jack Curtis' slow curves. Finally Gino Cimoli, a little-used outfielder the Braves picked up from Pittsburgh two months earlier, ripped a Curtis pitch into the left-field bleachers to make it 2–1. "It was destiny, that homer," Cimoli said whimsically.

There was plenty of nail biting before it was over. In the ninth, Rodgers took a called strike three. Then Cubs shortstop Jerry Kindall hit a hard liner to center where Cimoli, charging, lunging, skidding to his knees, caught the ball inches above the grass. And now Spahn had to face future Hall of Famer Ernie Banks. Spahn missed twice outside, then induced what should have been a game-ending grounder to Mathews. Unfortunately, Mathews threw it over Adcock's glove and against a box-seat railing, leaving Banks on first. Spahn had had enough theatrics. He promptly got Jim McAnany on a fly to Aaron to end it.

In a joyous departure from an emotionless sport that was noted by *Sports Illustrated*, Spahn tipped his cap N-S-E-W, blew kisses to the fans, and shook hands all around. After retrieving the ball from Aaron, Spahn did an on-field interview, retired to the clubhouse for champagne (he also sent bubbly to the press room), and enjoyed a wild party with teammates at a local restaurant.

Winning number 300 was, he said, "my biggest thrill." His kid catcher, Joe Torre, whom Spahn and Burdette had coaxed along, still recalls it as one of his biggest thrills, too.

"Most of the time I ignore the upper half of the strike zone," Spahn told a reporter. "These days I throw only below the waist. Of course, if a batter has a profound weakness—say, he can't hit a high inside fastball—I'll still throw to that spot. But a batter with a profound weakness doesn't last in the major leagues." He took a deep breath and considered what he'd done. "Walter Johnson," he told *Life*'s Paul O'Neil. "Christy Mathewson. Now me. It seems almost immoral."

In 1962, Spahn slipped to 18–14 and suffered inflammation of the left elbow. By 1963, he was surely through. He was bent and twisted, nearing 42. "Don't tell me you still have a fastball," former teammate Frank Thomas, then with the Mets, told him before a spring training game. "Know how much I think of your fastball? The first time you throw it to me today, I'm gonna embarrass you. I'm gonna reach right over the plate and catch it barehanded."

But Spahn was far from done. This was a man who could go the distance. Any distance.

* * *

Going the distance had a different meaning for Marichal. Of course he could do it physically because he was young, strong, and indefatigable. His demons lay deeper. Of all the stereotypes hurled at Hispanic players, the worst ones targeted their performance as athletes. Choker. Quitter. Malingerer. When manager Alvin Dark said of his ace, "Put your club ahead by a run in the late innings, and Marichal is the greatest pitcher I ever saw," people read the comment to mean, *"Put him behind early in a game, and he'll quit on you."* Unfortunately, some writers bought into the labels, which were facilitated by Marichal's unfortunate tendency to get hurt in August or September— legitimate injuries, to be sure. Later in his career, someone actually mailed Marichal a column titled "The Questionable Ability of Juan Marichal in the Clutch."

Strikeout pitchers often get more favorable press than control pitchers like Marichal. But as he explained with admirable logic, "It takes three pitches to strike a man out but only one to get a man out with a ground ball."[19] It was further thought by people who found Marichal "soft"—another code word hurled at Hispanics—that he ran up his record against weak clubs. Research by Bill James, who rates Marichal's career above that of the more celebrated Hall of Famer Bob Gibson, disproved this jabberwocky. Marichal was 37–18 overall and 21–4 at home against the Dodgers and faced them more than any other team. When they were less than .500, he was 5–3 against them. When the Dodgers were winners, he was 32–15. Against the Braves, he was 20–11 when they were better than .500 and 1–6 when they were less than .500. Writing for *Sports Illustrated*, Keith Olbermann uncovered more evidence. During the 11 years of his tenure with the Giants when they contended, Marichal was 34–20 against the team behind or ahead of them. When the Giants finished second five years running, he was 13–4 against the pennant winners.

Though Marichal loved his manager on most counts, he chafed when Alvin Dark said he wouldn't play hurt. It was the old malingerer stereotype hurled at so many Latinos. Even as a 25-year-old, Marichal had plenty of pain on his résumé. When his back subsequently hurt so much that he said he couldn't pitch, Dark didn't believe him. Marichal won 96 games after injuring a foot that was finally diagnosed as broken. "Periodically, [Dark] seemed to think I lacked guts," Marichal wrote in his autobiography.

"Dark once even complained loudly to his bench that if Marichal continued to strike out opponents with his screwball he would soon be unable to lift his arm and thus of no use to his teammates," Peter C. Bjarkman wrote in the Winter 1998 issue of *Elysian Fields Quarterly*. "If Marichal's arm seemed to stay surprisingly healthy throughout his long career, he was indeed plagued by numerous other small injuries which [as with Clemente] quickly brought the label of a soft ballplayer who failed to look after his own health."

In truth, Marichal was carried off the field on a stretcher at least half a dozen times, caught a line drive in the groin, nearly severed his Achilles' tendon, suffered a concussion of something described as the zygomatic skull bone but more commonly called a cheekbone, pitched with that broken foot and the mumps, and had nasal allergy that made him uncomfortable around air conditioning—all that plus chronic back pain. "He often pitched in pain from a lumbar disc problem that forced him to sleep on the floor, rioting sinuses, throbbing asthma attacks, infections, weak ankles that would have benched

Fred Astaire before he was 12 years old—you name it, Marichal had it," the late Bob Stevens, who covered Marichal's entire Giants career, wrote in the *San Francisco Chronicle*. "His locker resembled an infirmary storeroom, and he was as much a part of the trainer's table as its white-sheet covering."

These were telling words from a beat writer who surely would have detected signs of hypochondria. Stevens might have added that Marichal suffered whiplash in an October 22, 1966, auto accident. Yet he still was suspected of malingering; even the admiring *Time* cover story in 1966 cited mild

Jack Took a Giant Step

It's the quintessential moment of a pitcher's imagination: score tied after nine innings in Game 7 of the World Series. Manager approaches pitcher with the intention or relieving him. Pitcher says, "Get lost!" And manager leaves him in.

That was where Jack Morris found himself on October 27, 1991. A free agent signed by the last-place Minnesota Twins during the off-season, Morris helped them to a first-place finish in the American League West Division by going 18–12. The Twins defeated Toronto in the League Championship Series, with Morris winning twice. A veteran of the Tigers' 1984 world championship team with a 6–1 record in the postseason, Morris was poised on the brink of leading his team to a worst-to-first accomplishment that had never happened in baseball history.

For the first 7⅓ innings, Morris and Atlanta's John Smoltz staged a nail-biting scoreless duel. Morris had a scare in the eighth when speedy Lonnie Smith singled and then was running on a pitch that Terry Pendleton doubled to left-center. But Smith hesitated rounding second and had to stop at third when shortstop Greg Gagne and second baseman Chuck Knoblauch pantomimed making a double play. Not that runners on second and third with no outs gave comfort to fans in the ear-splitting Minnesota Metrodome. Morris got Ron Gant on a grounder to first baseman Kent Hrbek, and the runners held. David Justice, the National League's Rookie of the Year the previous season, was walked intentionally to load the bases. That brought up Sid Bream, a noted clutch hitter.

Bream grounded to Hrbek, who threw to catcher Brian Harper for one out, and Harper's return throw beat Bream to first for a 3-2-3 double play that left Morris screaming for joy.

Smoltz had his own troubles. When Twins pinch-hitter Randy Bush singled and Knoblauch advanced pinch runner Al Newman to second with a one-out single in the eighth, manager Bobby Cox replaced Smoltz with Mike Stanton. Kirby Puckett was intentionally walked to load the bases, and Stanton got Hrbek on a liner turned into a double play.

hypochondria. Quoted in *Sport* by Al Stump for a 1968 story that Juan implied was largely fabricated, Marichal railed at fans, radio voices, and reporters who didn't understand him; at San Francisco city officials, who complained that he'd constructed a hothouse without a permit; and at the Giants front office that wouldn't pay him what he felt he was worth. Marichal also seemed to Stump like a man who was never secure about his ability and complained that he wasn't appreciated. "Juan needs love," Jesus Alou, who roomed with him on the road, told Stump. "You see, we Dominicans do not just play for money but

Morris came off the mound after setting down the Braves in the ninth, and manager Tom Kelly told him, "Great game, Jack, couldn't have asked for more. I'm going to bring in Rick Aguilera in the 10th."

Morris refused all handshakes, walked down to one end of the dugout, and threw down his glove in disgust. "I'm fucking all right!" he shouted. Kelly, who was standing at the other end of the dugout with his arms folded over his chest, thought for a few seconds and said, "Oh, what the hell, it's just a game" and gave in.

The Twins went down in the ninth when Alejandro Peña replaced Stanton with two on and no outs and induced yet another double play. Morris justified Kelly's confidence in him and retired the side 1-2-3 in the 10th. In the Twins' half of the 10th, Dan Gladden led off by hustling a broken-bat blooper to left-center into a double. He advanced to third on a Knoblauch sacrifice, and Peña intentionally walked Puckett and Hrbek to load the bases. Then pinch-hitter Gene Larkin singled over the head of the drawn-in left fielder to score Gladden, ending the first Game 7 in 67 years to go into extra innings.

ESPN called it the greatest World Series ever at the time; it was one in which three games went into extra innings, four were decided in the final at-bat, and five were won by one run. At 69 innings, it was also the longest seven-game Series. After it was over, however, no one was speaking about Larkin, whose brief career had just peaked. All attention focused on Smoltz and Morris. The only pitcher to win 200-plus games while saving 150-plus, Smoltz is considered a lock for the Hall of Fame. Because the electors seem obsessed with 300 wins as a standard for most starting pitchers, 1991 Series MVP Morris (2-0, 1.17 ERA) and his 254 victories may have to wait awhile. As the winningest pitcher of the 1980s, a five-time All-Star, and one of the best clutch performers of his time, he shouldn't have to.

for appreciation." Stump wrote—and Marichal denied—that he was obsessed with inequality. "Eight years ago I thought the big league was the whole world," Stump quoted him as saying. "But happiness is not baseball. When someday I am just a plain farmer, *then* I'll be happy."

"He writes it like I am not happy now," Marichal protested to the *Chronicle*. "I didn't say anything about being happy when someday I am plain farmer, anyway, I did not say anything like that. I am happy as a baseball player. I owe all I have to the game and to Mr. Stoneham [owner Horace Stoneham]. I am very happy with the Giants."

Life wasn't always *cariño y abrazos* back in the Dominican Republic, either. One winter a Dominican politician pinned a "citizen supreme" medal on Marichal's chest before 40,000 worshipers in the capital city's Quisqueya Stadium. But another winter, between the 1963 and 1964 seasons, cherry bombs went off 10 times in one Dominican game when Marichal was in his pitching motion, leading to 10 balks that mercifully weren't called. When an exhausted Marichal shut down his arm after 60 innings in the Dominican leagues,[20] he was assaulted by fists and bottles at the ballpark and had to leave with a police escort. Later, he was attacked by a mob and had to fight his way out of a Santo Domingo nightclub and got arrested for "street brawling" (and was later released) when he was trying to protect himself and his wife from toughs. In the end Marichal was exiled and spent a non-playing winter with Orlando Cepeda in Puerto Rico. He passed the entirety of another off-season in San Francisco to avoid complaints about why he wasn't pitching back home. Some Dominicans accused him of being what he called a "swellhead." Representing the Dominican team in Venezuela on another occasion, he was surrounded by guards after a plot was uncovered in which thugs would kidnap him, demand ransom, and remove his toenails.

This is not to say that Marichal dreaded the off-season. He constantly sent money home and was rewarded when his mother enlarged the family farm. An expert skin diver, spear fisherman, and photographer, Marichal could swim a mile and then dive 60' deep. To the chagrin of his Giants superiors, he hunted barracuda and took pictures of sharks. As evocative in English as Spanish, Marichal once explained these underwater forays to Stump:

"Down there the rocks are shaped like the clouds I see in the sky when we fly over them in jet planes...one night not long ago the team flew into St. Louis at sunset, and the colors I see remind me of what I see when I go skin diving—all very beautiful. Sometimes I swim 6-7 miles off shore, and Felipe Alou and I look for big fish to spear. He once got one weighed 290, but my biggest so far is smaller. Sharks? We don't fear them, but the barracuda can scare you. One time Felipe got caught by a big swell and it pulled him through jagged rocks, cutting his legs very badly. He had a big fish on his spear and wouldn't let go. This has happened to me, too, but we patch up the cuts and think nothing of it—for down there, we are men without trouble, surrounded by everything gorgeous."

Marichal was such an expert on skin diving that he wrote a *Sport* article detailing its four basic rules, "1. Be a good swimmer to begin with; 2. Never dive alone; 3. Use good equipment; 4. Know your limitations and never go beyond them." One day in the 1960s, he violated the fourth rule by going out in rough water where he swam too hard and too fast, got a cramp, and began sinking. Fortunately, he also followed the second rule, and diving partner Felipe Alou pulled him out.

"I felt like I was born that day," Marichal said with a smile.

~ Chapter 7 ~

DENOUEMENT

"If the heart of baseball is the contest of wills and talent between the pitcher and the hitter, you need both good pitching and good hitting to make a good ball game. And if you do have the best of both, the pitchers should dominate because they have the inherent advantage of surprise. Even as a kid growing up in San Francisco, I preferred the great pitching duels.... Twenty-five hits in a game does not signal good hitting as much as it signals bad pitching. It makes for a lot of excitement and runners tearing around the bases, but I still don't call it a great baseball game."

—Keith Hernandez, *Pure Baseball*

The July 2, 1963, matchup wasn't just another great pitching duel. The zeroes roped across the scoreboard, the tension mounted, the sense spread that everything could change in a trice, and the pitchers took signs from their catchers rather than the dugout. Spahn was defying age, reason, and mortality. Marichal was performing as the hottest baseball *wunderkind* on the planet. So on to extra innings. It was not unusual in that era for pitchers to work overtime, and it was downright commonplace for Spahn and Marichal. Between 1947 and 1962, Spahn started 565 games (including the World Series). Fifty-two of those games went into extra innings; Spahn completed 23 of them and pitched into the 10th inning without getting a decision three other times. He also pitched in what might be called extra-extra innings, losing the aforementioned 15-inning game in 1952 and 16-inning game in 1951; in the latter, he threw 184 pitches. Granted, Spahn wore a younger man's clothes in those days, but he had gone 11 innings as recently as 1960 and 10 innings four times in 1961. For his part,

Marichal lost that 17-inning game in 1959 while pitching for Springfield and had gone 10 innings twice as a Giant.

If both men had been denied moments of greatness, this night at Candlestick would be moving and historical and other good things generally. It's never too late to be recognized, even if you aren't around to enjoy the accolades. Why, according to some accounts, Vincent van Gogh sold only one painting during his lifetime!

While Greg Spahn and 15,920 other fans sat shivering in the stands, the pitchers heated up:

Braves 10th: Spahn struck out; Maye grounded out to first, unassisted; Bolling grounded to short.

Giants 10th: Bailey grounded out to second; Bowman reached on a bunt single; Hiller forced Bowman (first to shortstop); Marichal forced Hiller (shortstop to second).

Braves 11th: Aaron struck out; Menke flied out to left; Larker grounded out to second.

Giants 11th: Kuenn grounded out to short; Mays flied out to left; McCovey grounded out, pitcher to first.

Braves 12th: Jones struck out; Crandall flied out to right; McMillan grounded out to third.

Giants 12th: F. Alou flied out to center; Cepeda grounded out to short; Bailey grounded out to first, unassisted.

Obviously, neither pitcher was visibly tiring. Marichal allowed a two-out single to Bolling in the 13th to end a streak of 16 batters retired in a row. Then Marichal got Aaron on a foul to first. In the Giants' 13th, Bowman singled, then wandered too far off first. Spahn threw behind him, and Bowman was retired in the ensuing rundown from pitcher to first to shortstop. Vengeance for the Cepeda steal! Spahn promptly retired Hiller on a grounder to second and Marichal on a fly to center.

Neither pitcher even considered surrendering to a pinch-hitter. Manager Alvin Dark visited the mound in the ninth, 10th, 11th, 13th, and 14th innings without removing Marichal. "I begged Mr. Dark to let me stay a few more innings, and he did," Marichal told the *New York Times*. "In the 12th or 13th, he wanted to take me out, and I said, 'Please, please, let me stay.'"

Marichal said catcher Bailey was telling him, "Don't let him take you out. Win or lose, this is great."

During the 14th, Marichal said he told Dark, "Alvin, do you see that man pitching on the other side? He's 42 and I'm 25, and you can't take me out until that man is not pitching."

"When Juan said that, it was a great tribute to Spahn—and to Marichal," Giants pitcher Gaylord Perry said.

Looking back over the years, Dark said, "Larry Jansen, who won 23 games for the Giants in 1951 and then hurt his arm, was our pitching coach, so we were very conscious about pitchers working too long and injuring themselves. We had just started keeping pitch counts. 'I don't want this kid to get hurt,' I was thinking. I kept going to the mound the last three or four innings asking Juan, 'Are you all right?' And he always said he was."

Dark admits that Marichal passed any conceivable pitch count, but he wasn't worried. "If a guy gets wild or starts getting his pitches up, you know his arm might be tired, but that wasn't the case with Juan."

Did you notice what Dark said? In 1963, pitchers weren't removed because of pitch count, a measure that on its own says nothing about whether they're tired or ineffective. Managers were more sophisticated than that. Rather than relying on magic numbers, they looked for physical signs like dropping the arm and getting pitches up. In one of many multi-pitch classics, Luis Tiant threw 163 pitches while winning Game 4 of the 1975 World Series. It's not just a matter of going long but often. Nailing down the 1950 pennant for the Phillies, Robin Roberts started three times in five days and pitched 22 innings. What's more, there was no residual damage. He totaled more than 300 innings in each of the next five seasons.

The very notion of babying a pitcher's arm has always been suspect. "We threw every single day," said Wilbur Wood, a White Sox knuckleballer who worked under Johnny Sain, every bit the legend as a pitching coach that he'd been as a pitcher in the 1970s. "Johnny just wanted you on the mound for five or ten minutes. You wouldn't be throwing a hundred miles an hour or trying to snap off a hard breaking ball, but you'd be out there getting accustomed to the mound and throwing to keep your rhythm. I thought he was one of the best coaches I ever had."

"The pitch count—for what reason?" Spahn protested in an interview at the Hall of Fame with former commissioner Fay Vincent. "Everything is predicated on avoiding sore arms, but you're getting more. Baseball has made cripples of pitchers. Second basemen and shortstops throw every day but [they] don't get sore arms."

"I think a pitcher needs to throw every other day for rhythm's sake," Spahn told Peter Barrouquere of the *New Orleans Times-Picayune* in 1984. "I can't conceive how these guys who are pitching today throw every other day in a five-man rotation. There's something missing."[21]

If managers think a five-man rotation keeps pitchers rested, it also may introduce an unfit starter every fifth day. Why not a least throw your best pitcher every fourth day and give marginal pitchers spot starts?

"I think that probably the medical profession has hurt our game," Spahn added. "Every pitcher's aware of the ulnar nerve and the rotator cuff before he even starts. That's enough to scare you right there.

"We didn't even know what those things were. There were two things that happened to a pitcher…stiffness and soreness. Soreness you couldn't throw with. Stiffness you were able to work out. There is not yet a machine that can do what your own body will do for you."

Of late, managers operate like metronomes, eying the "yank" button every time the pitch count approaches 100. The issue came to a head during the 2009 season. The Mets' Johan Santana, at the time the hottest pitcher in the National League, was jerked from a shutout he was throwing after 103 pitches. Santana felt fine and didn't ask to be taken out. That was manager Jerry Manuel's decision. The relief imploded, and the Mets lost. One month and three days after he brilliantly let 37-year-old Pedro Martinez throw 130 pitches, Philadelphia manager Charlie Manuel jerked him after 87 in a National League Championship Series playoff game against the Dodgers with the Phils leading 1–0. They went on to lose 2–1. And California manager Mike Scioscia pulled John Lackey after 104 pitches of shutout ball against the Yankees in the ALCS. You can guess what happened. You wonder if lesser managers even know when their pitchers are running down. They just check how many pitches they've thrown.

"Pitching coaches love The Count because it gives them something to do with their thumbs beside husking sunflower seeds and clicking a stopwatch to time a pitcher's stretch move to the plate," Bill Conlin wrote in the *Philadelphia Daily News*. "And it is a lot easier to tell a pitcher endangering the outfield customers, 'Sorry, Ace, you're at a hundred,' than the classic Tommy Lasorda World Series rejoinder upon being told by pleading left-hander Doug Rau that the next hitter is left-handed: 'I don't give a [bleep], Dougie, you just gave up three straight [bleeping] hits to three [bleeping] left-handers.'"

How did we reach the state of what Milton called "vain wisdom and false philosophy"? Blame it on specialization. In 1973, the American League introduced the designated hitter who bats all game in place of the pitcher and otherwise takes a seat on the bench. Wannabe DHs are growing up without any interest in maintaining decent gloves—no "glove story" for them. In 1974, Oakland's inventive and eccentric owner Charles O. Finley introduced a designated runner, track star Herb Washington, who pinch ran without ever taking his place in the field or batter's box. In a moment of true justice, the Dodgers' Mike Marshall picked him off first base in the 1974 World Series.

By the mid-1980s, pitchers, too, were specializing as never before. This trend owed in part to overwork. Billy Martin's A's had 60 complete games out of 109 in a strike-shortened season when they finished first in 1981. The following season, obviously exhausted, they slumped to 42 complete games (out of 162) and a fifth-place finish. Before long, we had starters who could go six or seven innings, followed by a middle reliever, a set-up man, and a closer used for all of four outs. Pretty soon we were hearing about "quality starts," which were defined as six innings with no more than three earned runs allowed. That's a 4.50 ERA.

"Not exactly the high standard to which we held ourselves back when I was playing, but the bar of expectations has been lowered over the years," the broadcaster and former pitcher Ron Darling wrote in his book, *The Complete Game: Reflections on Baseball, Pitching, and Life on the Mound*, co-authored by Daniel Paisner. "Here again, the game has changed—and I think today's big-money, long-term contracts are to blame. Clubs have so much money tied up in their top-tier pitchers that they don't think that they can afford to let them pitch beyond a certain pitch count, so it's a club-imposed cap on a starting pitcher's workload that lowers the bar. Do the math: if you're limiting a pitcher to 80, 90, 100 pitches, it follows that he won't make it much past the sixth inning, and so the sixth inning has become a kind of bare-minimum marker." Darling makes an even tougher accusation—that pitchers "tend to pitch down to the low expectations managers and coaches and front-office personnel have lately set for them."

The man given credit for popularizing the short-stay closer and generously using set-up men, Cardinals manager Tony La Russa (and his pitching coach Dave Duncan), appears to be a certain Hall of Famer and is an acknowledged baseball genius. What's more, his system makes sense for the majority of starters who can't go the distance. But what about those who can?

Far too much was made of Mets pitcher David Cone's brief slump after he threw 166 pitches in beating the Giants 1–0 on July 17, 1992. Pitch counts began rearing their ugly heads as never before. The result is a kind of self-fulfilling prophecy. Too many good pitchers can't go nine because they aren't trained to go nine. Once they approach 100 pitches, their managers prepare to remove them even in the peak of performance. And replacing a starter with a middle reliever is fraught with peril. Darling said middle men are at the "bottom of the bullpen."

Minor leaguers aren't being stretched out, either. Because their arms are babied rather than worked into tip-top condition—let's say, 70 pitches in A ball, 80 in Double A, and 90 in Triple A—they may be more likely to break down. You know, The Count is an adorable creature on *Sesame Street*. As textbook strategy in baseball, however, the words just sit on the page...an empty philosophy, cereal-box religion.

Hall of Famer Nolan Ryan, rarely taken out of a game for throwing too many pitches (one season he accumulated 5,684 in 333 innings and averaged 135 for 41 starts), has such contempt for this thinking that an epic word should be coined to describe his wrath. Actually, one has. The invention of an 18th-century student at England's Eton College, it is "floccinaucinihilipilification," which means the tendency to view or describe something as worthless.

After being appointed president of the Texas Rangers the year before, in 2009 Ryan banned the use of pitch count as any kind of measure for deciding whether to leave a starter in. Instead, Ryan ordered Rangers pitchers to improve their mechanics by running extra wind sprints, playing more toss and catch from up to 300', and throwing batting practice. "I haven't been pleased with the direction baseball's taken pitching in the last 15 or 20 years," he told the *New York Times*'s Tyler Kepner, "and I felt like we needed to regain some of what we had lost. I felt like we had a lot of pitchers that have been on pitch limits ever since Little League, and we don't know what their genetic potential is as far as the number of pitches and workload they can handle."

As a result, Ranger starters stayed in games until they wilted, instead of being removed when they were going strong.

After a team ERA of 5.37 in 2008, the Texas ERA was 4.38 in 2009—the biggest dropoff in the majors—and the staff tied for second in the league with 11 shutouts. By no coincidence, the Rangers had a winning record for the first time in five years and competed seriously for the wild-card spot in the playoffs until team hitting collapsed in mid-September. Their altered pitching philosophy was shared in some outposts. Detroit's able manager, Jim Leyland, allowed his ace, Justin Verlander, to throw 120 or more pitches 11 times, and Verlander led the American League with 3,940 pitches for the season.

Using this same philosophy in 2010, the Rangers won their division with a 3.93 team ERA and finally won a playoff series 3–2 over Tampa Bay. Then they beat the Yankees 4–2 and entered the promised land of their first World Series.

It wouldn't be fair to deny the other side its position, and Steve Wulf, the distinguished ESPN writer and the editor of ESPN Books, outlined the pro-pitch count position. "I don't buy the old-school argument," he said. "I hear it every Saturday morning when [broadcaster] Warner Wolf launches into his usual tirade about pampered pitchers. But the modern pitcher isn't built for 125+ pitches or 300+ innings, just as the pitcher of the '60s and '70s wasn't built for the 400+ innings that Iron Man McGinnity threw.

"There's also much more science involved in pitch counts than simple game totals. A 10-pitch inning followed by a 40-pitch inning is much more damaging than two 25-pitch innings.

"I say this as the father of a pitcher who led Westchester County high schools in innings pitched one year, and then had to shut down his pitching career because of overuse. But he still has pride in that one year, and his arm has recovered."

Okay, but *why* isn't the modern pitcher equipped to go 125+ pitches or 300+ innings?

"Because we're more humane," Wulf said. "Read the chapter on the '65 World Series in Jane Leavy's book [on Sandy Koufax], and your arm will start hurting."

Hall of Famer Tom Seaver said his arm began to weaken in the 125–130 range. Starters should be allowed to find their fatigue point. Good pitchers can often be hit on their fourth time through the batting order, though there's no guarantee that relievers will do any better. Workhorses like Nolan Ryan may be genetic freaks, and there's a genuine danger of ruining young arms through overwork. But there's protection against that practice. The Red Sox developed a sophisticated system for measuring shoulder strength. The team insisted that Daisuke "Dice-K" Matsuzaka broke down in 2009, not because he pitched all those innings in the preseason World Baseball Classic, but because he didn't follow Boston's shoulder-strengthening program. (Later, news came out that he also hid a groin injury.) In 2010, the Brewers, Red Sox, and Giants began running their pitchers through motion-analysis exercises, strapping their arms with electrodes in a use of biomechanics to determine if they were putting their arms and shoulders through injury-producing stress. Again, there was no mention of pitch counts.

* * *

Marichal, who would complete 244 of his 457 starts, wasn't about to leave the game in the 14th inning. He struck out Menke, walked Larker, struck out pinch-hitter Don Dillard, and got Crandall on a grounder to the mound.

Fortunately, the late Milwaukee manager Bobby Bragan was on the same wavelength as Dark. Speaking from Fort Worth, "where people love God and hate Dallas," Bragan (who died in 2010) insisted he never even went to the mound to talk to Spahn (other accounts say he wanted to remove Spahn and Spahn refused). "I was a member of the Phillies [1940–42], and I can remember hearing that Connie Mack of the Philadelphia A's would take three pitchers to Detroit for a weekend series—Grove, Earnshaw, Walberg," Bragan said. "In those glory days of baseball, when you handed the ball to the pitcher of that day, he was expected to go all the way: there was no such thing as a 'quality outing,' counting the pitches, etc."

Not only could Spahn and Marichal pitch any length of complete game, Spahn's old manager insisted, they could throw a fastball, curve, or change-up on any count. Bragan could still see Spahn in absolute concentration. "When he was pitching, he would walk by his brother."

"There was no way I was going to come out," Spahn told the *San Francisco Chronicle's* Dave Bush years later. "You didn't make any money sitting on the bench. I felt like it was my game to win or lose. And I could always get a second wind. I would get tired, and then after awhile I'd feel okay again. That's just the way I was."

People have always wondered what it was like on the bench as the game moved from memorable to historical. Did players turn to teammates and say, "I'm going to tell my grandchildren about this one?" In truth, some of them were just trying to get through the night. "I'm completely blank about the game," said Frank Bolling, who played all 16 innings at second for the Braves, going 2-for-7 at the plate and handling seven chances without an error. "When you're in a game like that, you don't think of anything until it's over. You just want someone to score." Larsen said, "It was a long time ago—I'm very vague about it." Del Crandall also blanks on the night. But others were pumped up. "You couldn't help but get into the game," Orlando Cepeda said, adding, "We knew that this was something special." Giants reliever Al Stanek, remembered thinking, "Holy cow! Two guys out there, one of them over 40!"

As the game progressed, Spahn was drinking very little water because it gave him a stomachache. Actually, water consumption was not popular among athletes at the time. Jack Mortland, a 20-km racewalker in the 1964 Olympics, reported there were no watering stations at the trials and can't recall if water was offered on the Tokyo Olympic course. For the most part, water consisted of sponges racers squeezed over their heads and necks. "In the 1960s, we were still in the era of football coaches, for example, thinking that drinking water during practice or a game was a sign of weakness," he said.

What Spahn did use between innings was unusual, to say the least. When he and Burdette were teammates, the guy pitching would come off the field and find his friend waiting in the runway behind the dugout holding a lit, filterless Camel for him. "There was no rule against smoking when people can't see you," Burdette said. On July 2, 1963, Burdette was a Cardinal, so Spahn probably lit up on his own, getting his strength from nicotine like a character in Faulkner's *Absalom, Absalom.*

"Nothing bothered him," teammate Denis Menke said. "He knew he could help himself with his bat [so he wouldn't be pinch-hit for as often as other pitchers], and he wanted to go the distance. He worked fast and threw strikes, which kept you in the game."

For his part, Marichal sat on the bench in a warm-up jacket, hands buried in a towel to keep his grip flexible in the cold, chewing Bazooka gum and studying his rival. "It was a great thrill pitching against one of the best," Marichal said.

"I used to learn so much from watching that man: in and out, up and down, fastball and breaking ball, going with your best pitch or pitches, changing in the late innings if you need to." The mounting innings would exhaust Marichal, but he insists he had seen worse. "I lost 8½ pounds in Philadelphia, nine in Atlanta. I didn't feel so bad in San Francisco because of the weather. You don't lose salt so much."

Both pitchers were left alone on the bench, as opposed to today's hurlers who have the manager or catcher or pitching coach offering advice or sharing insights from computerized data and videotapes. Marichal was running to and from to the mound, the better to stay warm. Spahn was trudging out, shoulders hunched. And what of the fans, sitting in the stands or listening to the game on the radio (it was not televised)? The broadcasts weren't prey to the noxious filler we endure today. "We didn't have the drop-ins they have now: 'The starting lineups are brought to you by…,'" said Lon Simmons, who broadcast the Giant games on KSFO-radio and received a Frick Award from the Hall of Fame for "major contributions to the game of baseball." "The commercials were between innings. The only thing we had was a home run contest. When Mays hits his 600th homer, somebody won something."

Fans in the stands weren't distracted, either, Simmons adds. "We didn't have the music and stuff that drive you crazy. Everything is a basketball game now. It's a show, and forget about the game. They have to blare music. Maybe that's what the public wants. But the crowd knows when something exciting is happening, and people don't need hands clapping on the scoreboard. The [natural] sounds of a baseball game are great. That's how baseball is supposed to be played. Ads and television have controlled the game."

Back in 1963, fans hardy enough to attend night games at Candlestick Park were getting much more than they paid for, $2.50 for grandstand or an outrageous $3.50 for box seats, as Simmons recalled. Teams hadn't yet made the cold-blooded decision that they could charge outrageous prices and still make a profit from advertisements on walls, fences, and scoreboards; companies buying enclosed luxury boxes; rich people in field-level box seats; childless couples; single men out with their buddies; and ordinary families attending the one game all year that they could afford. (The average total cost for a family of four in 2010 was $194.98 according to Team Marketing Report.) In Candlestick that July evening, people weren't texting or tweeting or cell-phoning or taking goofy pictures of each other with their iPhones or disturbing the view with the

Wave. They were watching the game, although some were also listening to it on transistor radios. Drawn to Candlestick not by some corporate promotion or giveaway, they were spellbound by Marichal and the Giants' version of Murderers Row, as well as Spahn and teammates like Hank Aaron and Eddie Mathews. Immersed as they were, the fans reflected Paul Gallico's description of baseball onlookers. "The crowd as a whole plays the role of Greek chorus to the actors on the field below. It reflects every action, every movement, every changing phase of the game. It keens. It rejoices, it moans."

Baseball commissioner Bud Selig, then an auto dealer and the largest public stockholder in the Braves, was on hand. "It was one of my first road trips," he said, "and I was in my summer clothes. [Braves G.M.] John McHale got me a hat and a jacket. We knew we were seeing a classic—the durability of two great pitchers, all those Hall of Famers playing. You're lucky to see a game like that once in your life."

As the game progressed, plenty of people listening in wished they were there. The *Chronicle*'s Bush, then a student at the University of California-Berkeley, was glued to the radio. The longer the game went, he told *The New Yorker*'s Roger Angell, the more he found himself rooting for Milwaukee. Despite his Giant sympathies, Bush was pulling for the old man. Now it's common for hometown fans to root for a visiting pitcher en route to a possible no-hitter, but this was special and perhaps unprecedented. Fans in and outside of Candlestick Park were drawn to a codger who was staring athletic mortality in the face and laughing.

Back in Buffalo, Spahn's cousin, Ken, who was working the second shift as plant manager for Carton Craft, a manufacturer of kids' books, had the game on the radio. Since Buffalo is fewer than 500 miles from Milwaukee, he probably got the Milwaukee station in the uncluttered early-morning airwaves. "I was on the second shift," he said in explanation of his post-midnight hours, "working on a paper cutter alone or with a couple of guys. I was amazed both of them were still pitching. It was a great experience."

Spahn finally began weakening. In the 14th, Kuenn doubled to lead off, and Spahn intentionally passed the dangerous Mays, ending his consecutive walkless streak at 31⅔ innings. McCovey fouled to the catcher, and Alou flied to center, but Cepeda loaded the bases when Menke made an error. Bases loaded, two outs. Bailey lined to Don Dillard, who had replaced Mack Jones in center. Whew!

Meanwhile, Marichal was cruising. After retiring the side in the 15th, he later told *The Sporting News*' Matt Grossman, "I said, 'Alvin, that's it. I don't want to pitch anymore.' They called the bullpen and told the pitcher to be ready for the next inning.

"When Warren got out of the 15th [also retiring the side in order], I grabbed my hat and glove and ran to the mound," Marichal said. "For a while I thought there were going to be two pitchers on the mound because the guy from the bullpen was coming in. They had to call him back."

The 16th inning started around 12:20 AM. Under the curfew in effect, no inning could start after 12:50 AM. Hardly anyone had left the park. Marichal got through the top half, surrendering only a two-out single to Menke. Bolling flied out to right and Aaron flied out to center before Menke singled and Larker grounded out, pitcher to first, for the third out.

"After I pitched the 16th inning, I walked off slow, waiting for some of the players to come in from the outfield," Marichal told the *Oakland Tribune*. "I was waiting for Willie Mays. I said, 'Willie, this is going to be the last inning for me.'" (Marichal told *The Sporting News* that he said, "'Chico'—we used to call everyone Chico—'Alvin is mad at me because I told him I was going to get out of the game.'") He said, 'Don't worry, I'm going to win this game for you.'"

In the bottom of the 16th, Spahn threw one screwball after another to the right-handed Kuenn, getting him at last on a fly to center. Spahn had thrown 200 pitches!

As Mays stood in the on-deck circle, Marichal called to him, "Hit one now." His teammates chuckled. "I will, Chico," Mays said. Actually, Willie was in a slump and probably hoped just to make solid contact. The previous day he had left men on base five times, heard boos in Candlestick Park, and watched his average plummet to .257. Spahn had limited him to two outfield flies, two infield grounders, a strikeout, and an intentional walk. Willie was exhausted. If it was any consolation, he figured Spahn was every bit as tired.

David Rapaport, a neighbor of Willie's, emailed Mays biographer James S. Hirsch that Mays routinely picked up four bats on the on-deck circle. "He would swing them from behind his right shoulder until he swished them through the imaginary hitting zone, and a small cloud of dirt and pebbles would rise from just beneath him. Then he would settle on one bat, and with one additional practice swing he would crack it through the air like an electric whip."

Mays stepped to the plate with no prelude like adjusting his batting helmet or knocking dirt from his spikes. In *Out of My League*, an account of pitching to All-Stars in an exhibition, George Plimpton wrote that Mays "gets set quickly at the plate, hopping eagerly into the batter's box, where he nervously jiggles and tamps his feet in the dust, twisting on his rear foot to get it solidly placed, staring down at the plate in concentration—to sense when his legs feel set—and when they do, he reaches out and taps the plate, twice, three times, with the bat before he sweeps it back over his right shoulder and cocks it. Then for the first time he looks out at the pitcher." Anything but glowering, Mays "seems to inspect the pitcher as if he were a harmless but puzzling object recently deposited on the mound by the groundskeeper," Plimpton wrote.

Mays against Spahn. Two hundred and fifty-six warm-up pitches and 427 pitches to batters had been thrown and almost as many returned from catcher to pitcher. Great fielding plays and errors, stolen bases and pickoffs, fly balls and ground balls, singles and doubles, some lucky breaks (at least to those wishing for extra innings), thousands of words over the P.A. system. And now, great man against great man for the last time in the game. The wind had died down to a soft breeze. Bathed in the strong, dueling lights that cast several shadows over each participant, Candlestick for once projected an otherworldly calm.

Swelling now, Spahn threw his first pitch to Mays: another screwball. Instantly, Spahn knew that he was in trouble. Rather than rotate away from the batter, the ball hung before Willie as juicy and tempting as a shiny apple on a tree. Mays unleashed his signature swing. Starting with his hands gripping a nearly vertical bat next to his side, he whipped it through the strike zone with ferocious speed, keeping both hands on the bat even when it stretched way ahead of him and slightly to his left. At this point, he resembled an angler getting a strike from a humungous fish and hanging on for dear life. Then Mays released his right hand and allowed the bat to swing down beside his left leg and onto the ground as he leaned forward following the flight of the ball. His right leg was extended back, his left leg bent at nearly a 90-degree angle, his right hand suspended above his left knee. That statuesque pose, everything in perfect balance, has been captured in a thousand photos and adorns the sculpture of Mays outside the Giants' AT&T Park.

The ball headed over the infield, climbing inexorably. No fly ball into even a mild breeze was guaranteed to clear the left-field fence at Candlestick, and Dark began doing mental calculations in the dugout. He knew that shots between left-center and right-center had iffy prospects. Just how close, he wondered, would this one be to the left-field line?

Relying on sound as well as sight, Dark's relievers and substitute catchers on their bench past third base were more sanguine. "When he hit it, we knew it was gone," Giants reliever Al Stanek said. "It had that sound when it hits the meat part: whacko! We all just jumped up at the crack of the bat."

Standing at third as the ball passed over his position, the Braves' Menke found his spirits plummeting as the Giants' soared. "Oh, yeah, you knew by the sound of the bat," he said. "I think Spahn had thrown enough home runs that he knew when it was out. We did the best we could, but we just couldn't get a run for him."

The ball carried, resisted whatever crosswind existed, and stayed fair by about 30'. In a *Sports Illustrated* retrospective years later, Ron Fimrite described "a high arc to left field, where, after hanging in the night sky for what seemed like an eternity, it landed beyond the fence."

Spahn started walking toward the dugout while the ball was still in flight, according to Stanek. And suddenly, *deus ex machina*, the long night's journey into history ended at 12:31 AM. It was Giants 1, Braves 0, an eight-hitter for Marichal with four walks and 10 strikeouts, and a nine-hitter for Spahn with one intentional walk, two strikeouts and a 27⅔ inning shutout string over three starts that ended with the Mays homer. Marichal allowed just two singles in the last eight innings while retiring 21-of-24 batters. In eloquent testimony to how quickly and efficiently they worked—hitters weren't endlessly stepping out of the batter's box, nor were catchers running constantly to the mound— nearly two games' worth of baseball ended after just four hours and 10 minutes. Spahn threw 201 pitches, Marichal 227. "If that happened today, they'd fire the manager and general manager—everyone but the players!" Marichal said.

During his career, Mays hit 22 extra-inning homers, the most by any player. He is also the only player to homer in every inning from the first through the 16th. Early on July 3, the crowd stood while he rounded the bases, cheered both pitchers, and applauded itself for sticking it out. Because of games like this, starting in 1983, the Giants awarded every fan enduring an extra-inning game at the Stick with the "Croix de Candlestick," a round orange badge adorned with the Latin words *"veni•vidi•vixi"*—"I came, I saw, I survived."

"We were riveted," Fimrite said. "It was the best game I ever saw." And he saw, among other classics, the sixth game of the 1975 World Series in which the Red Sox beat the Reds 7–6 on Bernie Carbo's game-tying three-run homer in the eighth, Dwight Evans' leaping catch and throw to keep the Sox alive in the 11th, and Carlton Fisk's "stay fair" homer in the 12th.

"It was the greatest game I've ever seen by two pitchers," Dark said in the clubhouse.

"It's probably the best game ever at Candlestick Park," McCovey said 36 years later. "It's the best game I've ever been involved in."

The postgame scene was almost as memorable. When Spahn entered the clubhouse, "Everyone stood up and applauded," said Bob Sadowski, an awestruck rookie pitcher who had just arrived in the Burdette deal. "He had tears in his eyes, and I think we did, too. Then we all lined up to shake his hand."

The Giants were less emotional, congratulating Marichal but figuring he pitched spectacular games all the time. The players ate their postgame spread then split. After his no-hitter, Marichal had gone to a Spanish-language movie house and watched a lousy western. After the 16-inning win, he held himself upright long enough to let hot water pound his arm in the shower—not everyone used ice in those days—then went home and collapsed into bed.

But not before both pitchers answered innumerable questions. "It didn't break at all," Spahn said of the last pitch, which left him slumping off the mound. "What made me mad is that I had just gotten through throwing some real good ones to Kuenn."

Spahn said he was a little tired. "Look, I made 10 or 12 mistakes in the game," he added. "I was inside on a lot of right-handed hitters, when I usually pitch them outside, and I got away with it. That gives me a certain amount of satisfaction. I had a good curve tonight, too, and I'm pretty proud of that. It gave me a weapon against the left-handers."

An admiring Carl Hubbell, the Hall of Fame screwball pitcher then supervising minor league scout for the Giants, marveled at Spahn's performance. "Here is a guy 42 years old who still has a fastball," he said. "He just kept busting them in on the hands of our guys and kept getting them out.... He ought to will his body to medical science."

Of Marichal, who retired 16 straight late in the game, Dark said, "He didn't throw many breaking pitches, thus tiring his arm, but just kept slipping across the fastball with a loose and fluid motion. He got stronger."

Marichal said, "In extra innings you go out there and say you're gonna pitch one more inning, so you throw as hard as you can. I said that three or four times and kept throwing hard. I didn't get very tired." Still, he added, "Oh, my back. But tonight was beautiful."

After the reporters and well-wishers left, Spahn spent several hours in the clubhouse drinking beer with his son and several teammates in attendance, everyone telling him what a splendid and even historical job he did in a gallant defeat. "I was exhausted at the end," Greg Spahn said. "I can only imagine how my dad felt."

"If ever a pitcher became a hero in defeat, it was Warren Spahn here Tuesday night," Bob Wolf wrote in the *Milwaukee Journal*.

The *San Francisco Chronicle* carried a front-page headline: JUAN BEATS SPAHN. "There were lesser Page One stories that day—something about a nuclear test ban and the FBI smashing a Soviet spy ring," Fimrite reported in *Sports Illustrated*. "But for one day at least, an epic pitching duel dominated the news. It was, I told the guys in the office, a rare exercise of sound editorial judgment."

Despite the banner headline, the game was little more—at least at the time—than a one-day story on July 3. The *Boston Globe, New York Times, St. Louis Post-Dispatch* and *Los Angeles Times* held a virtual blackout of the event over the next two days, other than the wire-service summary and box score. Only the *Post-Dispatch*, which had the advantage of an afternoon paper's late deadline, included a sidebar in its July 3 edition. Typical of morning-paper treatment was the July 4 *New York Times*, which carried a box score and briefly noted the July 2 game in its write-up of the July 3 game. For noted columnists like the *Boston Globe*'s Harold Kaese, the *New York Times*' Arthur Daley, the *Post-Dispatch*'s Bob Broeg, and the *L.A. Times*' Jim Murray, there were more pressing events like a canned column on athletes who retired too soon, yachting, Wimbledon tennis, the baseball All-Star selections, and the burning question of whether a team leading on July 4 will win its league. "There wasn't the hype then that there is today," Crandall said.

In order to understand the spotty coverage of the game, we need to consider what was happening around the world in 1963. It was 365 days of miracles and wonder, of brave heroes and cowardly villains that undoubtedly obscured many sporting achievements. Americans had never seen such style and grace as occupied the White House. President Kennedy, surrounded by aides who were termed the "best and the brightest," had a hotline installed between the White House and Moscow that would forever, it was hoped, prevent an unintended war between the superpowers. When he wasn't thrilling Germans with his "*Ich bin ein Berliner*" speech, Kennedy engineered the Limited Ban Treaty with the U.S.S.R. and Great Britain. The civil rights movement augured great triumphs. On one side was Alabama Governor George C. Wallace taking office and promising "Segregation now, segregation tomorrow, segregation forever." On the other was Martin Luther King's celebrated 6,700-word letter from a Birmingham jail and the march on Washington with King's "I Have a Dream" speech. Betty Friedan published *The Feminine Mystique,* and *The New York Review of Books* produced its first issue. Pope John XXIII released the landmark *Encyclical on Peace in Truth, Justice, Charity and Liberty.* The Warren Court issued the *Gideon v. Wainwright* decision guaranteeing defendants the right to legal counsel. West Germany and France signed a treaty that ended four centuries of strife, and the Organization of African Unity comprised 32 nations. All together, the year produced startling breakthroughs in politics, race relations, gender relations, foreign affairs, religion, and publishing. Few paid much attention to the fact that the U.S. had 15,000 advisers in Vietnam. To be sure, there were smoldering resentments producing horrific events, especially in Birmingham, including the violent hosing of and police-dog attacks on demonstrators ordered by Police Commissioner Bull Connor, the firebombing of Dr. King's brother's house, and the dynamiting and resultant burning of a Birmingham church with four doomed black girls inside. Near the end of the year, President Kennedy was assassinated on November 22. The news was enough to distract all but the most dedicated sports fans from the import of the July 2 baseball game.

The sports world was busy enough on its own. The U.S. won the Ryder Cup in golf. The Pro Football Hall of Fame opened in Canton, Ohio, and the incomparable Jim Brown set a career rushing record of 8,390 yards. John Pennel broke the 17' barrier in the pole vault. And no sport was more newsworthy than baseball, where Early Wynn won his 300th game, Roy Sievers hit his 300th homer and Duke Snider his 400th, Stan Musial capped his last season by homering on his first at bat as a grandfather while getting his then-record 1,357th extra-base hit, and Jimmy Piersall hit his 100th homer and circled the bases backward. While no ball has ever cleared Yankee Stadium in fair territory, Mickey Mantle hit a Ruthian shot that struck 3' from the top of the right-field façade.

Marichal's epic win was only one indication of the Hispanic rise in baseball. The brothers Alou—Felipe, Mateo, and Jesus—played one inning together in the Giants outfield, and the National League won 5–2 in a Hispanic American All-Star Game played at the Polo Grounds. Marichal struck out six batters in four innings, and Vic Power was honored pregame as the premier Latino player. The Giants and Colt 45s played baseball's first Sunday night game at Colts Stadium, where the heat and mosquitoes were bedeviling players by day. The baseball events perhaps most remembered from the season were Sandy Koufax's then-record 15-strikeout performance against the Yankees in Game 1 of the

World Series. The Dodgers went on to sweep their 8-to-5 favored opponents. Major League Baseball also celebrated its 100,000[th] game.

But not even the release of the song "I Left My Heart in San Francisco" focused attention on the 16-inning classic there. It didn't help that the game was played on the West Coast and concluded after the deadlines of East Coast and Midwest nightly news shows and morning newspapers. Amid all the news-breaking events in and outside of sports, the importance of the game was slow to sink in.

It's worth repeating that pitchers routinely went nine innings and sometimes more. On September 12, 1962, Washington's Tom Cheney had lasted the full 16 innings while striking out 21 Orioles and besting four Baltimore pitchers in a 2–1 win. But the Spahn-Marichal tilt was the ultimate extension of an admirable culture of complete-game pitching that would eventually erode. Only with the advantage of hindsight can people conclude that this was the greatest extended pitching duel of all time involving just two pitchers. A twosome never again has gone as many as 16 innings in the same game.

In victory, Marichal established his Hall of Fame greatness once and for all. In defeat, Spahn proved that experience, guile, and guts can trump the irreversible process of aging. For an analogy, try 59-year-old golfer Tom Watson tying for first before losing in a playoff at the 2009 British Open.

Imagine what *SportsCenter* and its access to historical data would have done with the Juan-and-Spahn game. It would have been instant immortality. But delayed immortality isn't bad, either, and gives us more time to contextualize the game.

For the title of the Greatest Game Ever Pitched, the Spahn-Marichal classic will forever tilt swords with the 12-inning perfect game that Pittsburgh's Harvey Haddix pitched in 1959 before losing in the 13th to the Braves' Lou Burdette. The Haddix game was about a familiar and definable goal: he would either complete the perfecto or not. Spahn and Marichal transcended numbers and leaped into a world of unique drama.

"Haddix was not a Hall of Fame pitcher," Glenn Dickey wrote in *San Francisco Giants: 40 Years*. "Both Spahn and Marichal are in the Hall of Fame, and so is Mays, who supplied the winning run. To have the complete story written by three Hall of Famers…it doesn't get any better than that."

In *The Giants Encyclopedia*, Nick Peters and Tom Schott call the game "undeniably the last great pitching duel in the history of modern baseball."

Believe it.

Hard-Luck Harvey

When people discuss "The Greatest Game Ever Pitched," they invariably cite the Harvey Haddix game of 1959. On its 50th anniversary, Albert Chen wrote an excellent story using that title in *Sports Illustrated*.

A Pittsburgh left-hander, Haddix dueled the Braves' Lou Burdette for 13 innings on May 26, 1959. Haddix was perfect for the first 12 innings. It was a muggy night at Milwaukee's County Stadium, and only 19,194 fans lined the stands. The first-place Braves were still an excellent team—they had won pennants the two previous years and a World Series in 1957—and the Pirates were just one year away from a world title of their own.

At 5'9" and listed at 170 pounds but considerably lighter according to his wife, Marcia, Haddix was small enough from the start to be nicknamed "Kitten," and he was sprayed with buckshot that left five pieces lodged in his skull during a childhood hunting accident. And four years after going 20–9 in 1953, his rookie year with the Cardinals, he was struck in the knee with a Joe Adcock line drive that left him with permanent nerve damage. He bounced around—St. Louis to Philadelphia to Cincinnati to Pittsburgh. Nonetheless, when he was traded to the Pirates in January 1959, Haddix told his mother, "This is going to be my big year," Chen reported.

On the morning of May 26, Haddix woke up with a scratchy throat and heard the forecast of wind and rain. Even so, he wanted to face Eddie Mathews, Hank Aaron, and Joe Adcock, the Braves' formidable 2-3-4 hitters. Why not? Haddix was 4–2, with a 2.67 ERA at the time. In the only major sport in which the defense holds the ball, the pitcher initiates the action. The batter can only respond. In any case, Haddix believed in going with his strengths without worrying about the hitters.

That night his strengths were the fastball and slider. In the first inning, Mathews worked him for a 3–2 count before lining to first. Haddix would never again allow three balls during the game. The Pirates quickly sensed something was up and grew silent in the dugout, passing around a strangely green peanut in a Planters jar for good luck. In another ritual, shortstop Dick Groat presented Haddix with a lit cigarette every time he entered the dugout. But the team didn't field three key players—Groat (slump), right fielder Roberto Clemente (sore shoulder), and first baseman Dick Stuart (night off)—and they struggled against Burdette. In the third inning, third baseman Don Hoak singled and right fielder Roman Mejias forced him at second. When Haddix himself reached on an infield single off Burdette's leg, Mejias, who had "the typical dump truck speed of a corner outfielder," as John Klima put it in his book *Pitched Battle: 35 of Baseball's Greatest Duels from the Mound,* tried to go to third and was thrown out. Dick Schofield hit the third single of the inning, and Haddix advanced to third. Alas, center fielder Bill Virdon flied out to end the inning.

The Pirates appeared to break through in the seventh when Bob Skinner hit a mammoth shot to right that sent Hank Aaron to the fence without much hope. Then, as if ordered by the perfect-game gods, a hard wind blew the ball back and Aaron came in a few feet to catch it. The fly had been "blown back by a tornado gale," Pittsburgh announcer Bob Prince said.

Meanwhile, Haddix persisted so successfully that the Braves couldn't hit him, even with the certain knowledge of what he was throwing. A reliever was watching catcher Smoky Burgess' signs through binoculars and relaying them to the batters: waving a towel for fastball, no towel for breaking ball. Still, the Braves did little damage other than a couple of liners to Schofield at shortstop. When Haddix struck out Burdette with two out in the ninth, Prince told his listeners, "Harvey Haddix pitches a perfect no-hit, no-run, nine-inning game!" (Burdette, meanwhile, was working on an eight-hit shutout.)

There had been only four perfect games since 1900: Cy Young (1904), Addie Joss (1908), Charlie Robertson (1922), and Don Larsen (1956). None had gone more than nine innings. And this one wasn't over. Though Haddix was tiring, he cruised through the 10th, 11th, and 12th. No one before or since has thrown 12 perfect innings. Leading off the 13th, Milwaukee's Felix Mantilla grounded to Don Hoak at third, but Hoak's throw was wide to first baseman Rocky Nelson. The perfecto was over, the no-no intact. Mathews sacrificed Mantilla to second and Aaron was intentionally walked. Adcock stepped to the plate at 10:54 PM and noticed that the center field flag was "still as a moose." Five years earlier, Adcock's liner had forced Haddix to alter his mechanics. Now he would lessen his legacy. The first player to homer into the Polo Grounds' center field stands, and the first to clear the left-field stands at Brooklyn's Ebbets Field, he was not a man to be trifled with.

Haddix threw a slider outside for a ball and then left one high and over the plate. Adcock launched an Adcockian shot to right-center that cleared one fence and landed in front of another one. Mantilla scored. Game over. Thinking it was a ground-rule double, Aaron cut across the diamond after rounding second and was passed by Adcock, who touched third before Hank could retrace his steps. As a result, Adcock was called out, his homer was reduced to a double, and the final score was 1–0. None of which mattered. Hard-luck Harvey, as Haddix came to be called, had thrown 12 perfect innings only to lose in the 13th.

These days, the effort surely would land a man endorsements and appearances. There were no ads offered, and Haddix declined requests from *The Ed Sullivan Show*, *What's My Line?*, and *To Tell the Truth*. Among the many letters he received after the game was a short one from a fraternity at Texas A&M University. It read: "Dear Harvey, Tough shit." "It made me mad," Haddix said, "until I realized they were right. That's exactly what it was." But Haddix didn't dwell over the game ("What's so historic about that? Didn't anyone ever lose a 13-inning shutout before?"), and he earned wins in Games 5 and 7 of the 1960 World Series. Second baseman Bill Mazeroski, whose homer ended the classic Game 7, said the Haddix heartbreaker was every bit as memorable.

Haddix ended his career in 1965 and spent 14 years as a pitching coach. In 1991, a major league committee changed the definition of a no-hitter to "a game in which a pitcher or pitchers complete a game of nine innings or more without allowing a hit." Since Harvey had completed the game and allowed one hit, the poor guy didn't qualify. Haddix died of emphysema on January 8, 1994. He was 68.

Was this the Greatest Game Ever Pitched? Let's consider. Though Haddix threw the unprecedented 12 perfect innings, he did lose in the 13th. Though Burdette threw 13 shutout innings without allowing a walk, he did scatter 12 hits and twice got breaks when runs should have scored. Nonetheless, he said afterward, tongue only partly in cheek as he demanded a $10,000 raise: "I'm the greatest pitcher that ever lived. The greatest game that was ever pitched in baseball wasn't good enough to beat me, so I've got to be the greatest."

Haddix's control was amazing. "I could have put a cup on either corner of the plate and hit it," he said. He may have made history, but under the circumstances Don Larsen's perfect game in the 1956 World Series has to be considered the greatest one-player, single-event feat in baseball, if not all sports.

Extra Innings

Extra brings

~ Chapter 8 ~

WINDING DOWN
WITH JUAN

"See the godlike youth advance!"

—Handel, *Judas Maccabaeus*

The day after their 16-inning marathon, Warren Spahn took Juan Marichal aside. "You hung one up there, and I should have knocked it out of the park," Spahn said, referencing his double. Then he turned more serious and told Juan how to prepare for his next game. Oh, to have been a fly on the wall when the winningest pitcher of the fifties (202) passed on his ineffable wisdom to the winningest pitcher of the sixties (191).[22]

"We met in the tunnel between the visiting clubhouse and the field," Marichal said in a recent conversation. "He said to be careful in your next start. He said, 'I know you pitch every fourth day, but try to take an extra day.' He showed me some stretching exercises and told me to do them and relax. I did some running and stretching, threw two days after the start to get the stiffness out of my shoulder and elbow, and played catch in the bullpen. It felt the same way I felt pitching other games."

"[Marichal] worked so easily and smoothly he should be able to take his next turn or, at most, require one extra day of rest," Dark said.

Indeed, Marichal pitched after an extra day off on July 7, felt the same as he had in other starts, and gave up five hits and two runs over seven innings in a 5–0 loss to the Cardinals. He hadn't lost much stuff, and he hadn't lost

143

much spirit, either—he was fined $50 for buzzing Bob Gibson. His confidence boosted, his knowledge of hitters and pitching expanded, Marichal pitched 10 of his 18 complete games and got 12 of his 25 wins after July 2. He finished at 25–8 with a 2.41 ERA, his first under 3.00 during a full season, and led the league with 321⅓ innings pitched. Equally telling, he broke into the list of top 10 control artists, finishing seventh with 61 walks in 321 innings, or 1.71 per game—the second of 11 times he appeared in the top 10. His ERA finished in the top 10 for the first of seven successive seasons. He accomplished all this in a pitching-heavy decade and against plenty of competition in the dominant league. Here are Marichal's numbers as the decade played out:

YR	IP	CG	W	PCT	SH	K	BB	H	BB/G	ERA
1962	263	18	18	.621	3	153	90	233	3.08	3.36
1963	**321**	18	**25**	.758	5	248	61	259	1.71	2.41
1964	269	**22**	21	.724	4	206	52	241	1.74	2.48
1965	295	24	22	.629	**10**	240	46	224	**1.40**	2.13
1966	307	25	25	**.806**	4	222	36	228	**1.05**	2.23
1967	202	18	14	.583	2	166	42	195	1.87	2.76
1968	**326**	**30**	**26**	.743	5	218	46	**295**	1.27	2.43
1969	300	27	21	.656	8	205	54	244	**1.62**	**2.10**

(**Boldface** indicates league leader)

Take special notice of innings pitched, hits, and walks. Most pitchers are content to average a hit per inning. Marichal had fewer hits than innings his first 10 seasons and in four of them had fewer hits *plus* walks than innings.

He even had enough left after the 1963 season to go 7–4 with a league-leading 1.36 ERA in Dominican winter play.

"Hardest thrower—[Sandy] Koufax," all-time hit leader Pete Rose said. "Toughest competitor—Bob Gibson. Most complete pitcher—Juan Marichal. In a jam, Marichal could throw any one of five pitches for a strike."

"He's the toughest right-hander I ever faced because of the screwball," former Dodger Ron Fairly told John Lowe of *Detroit Free Press* in the August 1998 edition of *Baseball Digest*. As broadcaster and ex-catcher Tim McCarver noted in *Tim McCarver's Baseball for Brain Surgeons and Other Fans*, Marichal would throw it with a 2–2 count and the bases loaded. In *Eddie Mathews and the National Pastime*, which he wrote with Bob Broeg, Mathews said, "For me personally, I'd have to say Marichal was the toughest pitcher I ever faced.... He had that big leg kick and that funny motion. You could never tell where the hell the ball was coming from because of his kick and his throwing motion, plus he had great control. Actually, he was a lot like Warren Spahn, except from the other side."

Starting in 1963, Marichal won 20 or more games in six of seven seasons, the exception being 1967, when he pitched just 13⅓ innings in two starts on August 1 and August 25 (after pulling a hamstring in his left leg on August 4) and went 14–10 for the season. Even without Juan's usual contribution, the Giants led the league with a 2.92 ERA, allowed the league's fewest runs (551), and led the majors with 64 complete games and a .234 opponent's batting average—and finished second.

Marichal's 191 wins in the sixties were an incredible 27 ahead of anyone else.[23] In a career that lasted from 1960–75, he was one of 20 pitchers in modern baseball history to win at least 100 more games than he lost. Marichal went 243–142 overall, with a sterling .631 winning percentage that placed eighth among pitchers with at least 200 wins in the twentieth century.[24] He had an equally eye-catching 2.89 ERA that was fourth among pitchers with at least 3,000 innings since 1920. He won 25 games twice and 26 once. In eight All-Star Games, Marichal had a 2–0 record, a 0.50 ERA, and one MVP award while fanning 12, walking two, and allowing hitters a microscopic .117 batting average and .145 on-base percentage in 18 innings. He had a 1.50 ERA in his two postseason games and finished 244 of his 457 starts for 53.39 percent durability. (Spahn finished 382 of 665 starts for a 57.44 percent mark that leads all pitchers whose careers started after 1940.)

Overall, Marichal finished among the top 10 in strikeouts six times, innings pitched eight times (leading the league twice), and complete games 10 times. Twice he led in shutouts, throwing 10 of them in 1965. Marichal won 10 straight games twice, made nine All-Star teams, won seven complete games by 1–0 scores, and won six times on Opening Day. His mark of 1.82 walks per nine innings was extraordinary, and his 3.25-to-1 strikeout-to-walk ratio was first all-time (minimum: 2,000 strikeouts) when he retired. He has since been nipped by Randy Johnson (3.26) and Dennis Eckersley (3.253-3.248) and been bested by Curt Schilling (4.38), Mike Mussina (3.58), and Greg Maddux (3.37). Active players whose strikeout-to-walk ratios through 2009 exceeded Marichal's were Pedro Martinez (4.15) and Javier Vazquez (3.48). (Spahn's numbers were

2.46 walks a game and 1.80-to-1 strikeouts to walks, respectively.) Marichal had 244 complete games, one more than the total of his wins. No wonder Seaver told broadcaster and former catcher Fran Healy that Marichal is one of the most underrated pitchers in Cooperstown.

"I think the slider was my best pitch against right-handers," Marichal told author Rich Westcott. "Against left-handers my best pitch was my screwball. Candlestick Park was a left-handed hitters' park, and I always faced left-handed lineups, so I had to come up with that pitch. I became aware of it in 1958, when I saw Ruben Gomez throwing it for the Giants on TV. He threw one of the best screwballs I ever saw. He was from Puerto Rico, and I knew him from the games he'd pitched in the Dominican Republic. I learned from him how to throw the pitch, and by 1962 I had a pretty good one."

"I tell you something people don't understand about control," Marichal said to *Sport's* Al Stump. "It's not just the arm. The fingers, they are even more important." Marichal used a typewriter to keep them loose, squeezed a rubber ball, and trimmed his nails twice a week for just the right feel.

Though he won 27 more games than anyone in the sixties, someone else was always chosen for the Cy Young Award because someone else was always judged to have had a better year:

1963
Marichal: 25–8, 2.41 ERA
Sandy Koufax: 25–5, 1.88 ERA

1964
Marichal: 21–8, 2.48 ERA
Dean Chance: 20–9, 1.65 ERA

1965
Marichal: 22–13, 2.13 ERA
Koufax: 26–8, 2.04 ERA

1966
Marichal: 25–6, 2.23 ERA
Koufax: 27–9, 1.73 ERA

1968
Marichal: 26–9, 2.43 ERA
Bob Gibson: 22–9, 1.12 ERA

1969
Marichal: 21–11, 2.10 ERA
Tom Seaver: 25–7, 2.21 ERA

There was only one Cy Young winner in the majors before both leagues began awarding them in 1967, but Marichal didn't receive a single vote until 1971. He never complained about missing the award. To the contrary, he praised the winners. "The greatest fastball I ever saw, the greatest curve I ever saw, and the greatest gentleman I ever pitched against was Sandy Koufax," Marichal said.

Marichal was named to *The Sporting News*'s National League All-Star team in 1963, 1965–66, and 1968, but he always seemed to finish third behind Koufax and Gibson in debates about the National League's best pitcher of the sixties. The Ken Burns 1994 film series *Baseball* gushed over Koufax and Gibson while ignoring Marichal. Burns basically disregarded Latinos altogether until producing an addendum called *The Tenth Inning* in 2010. To be sure, Koufax and Gibson had tremendous success in the World Series, Koufax threw four no-hitters and Gibson had that 1.12 ERA in 1968. "Left out [of that equation] is that Marichal was the greatest gate attraction in baseball for eight or nine years," Allen Barra wrote in his 2002 book *Clearing the Bases*.

Well, some critics might maunder, Marichal played for steady winners and feasted off his home field, didn't he? While he was 122–58 with a 2.67 ERA at Candlestick Park, Marichal was also 119–84 with a 3.03 ERA on the road. That's a significant difference, but to put the numbers in perspective, most pitchers are happy to break even away from home.

"He didn't have all the tools," Bob Stevens, the late San Francisco sportswriter, wrote in a retrospective of Marichal's career. "He simply had a lot of them—a curve that crackled, a screwball that bewildered, a slider that bored through the black corners of the plate, and a change-up that danced sensually up to the batter, then scooped the money off the bureau top and fled the room before the hitter had a chance to turn on the lights."

Meanwhile, Marichal's prowess notwithstanding, the Giants were foundering. Picked to finish first in 1963, they stumbled to third when Jack

Sanford and Billy Pierce, two mainstays of the 1962 rotation, won eight and 13 fewer games, respectively. After a doubleheader loss at Wrigley Field, Dark made the team work out for two hours. The only player who took some satisfaction in the standings was Al Stanek, their 19-year-old reliever. "I started at $5,000 and went to $7,500 after making the team," he said. "We got $1,153 for finishing third, and I could use it!"

In 1964, another strong year for Marichal, the Giants participated in the five-way free-for-all pennant race and placed fourth, three games behind first-place St. Louis. Marichal had an untimely injury. Taking batting practice grounders on July 30, he couldn't straighten up after his back went out, and he missed nearly four weeks. If the Giants had anything to show for the season, they did import the majors' first Japanese player, left-hander Masanori Murakami. Subsequently, the Giants seemed to have a hold on second place, where they finished five times in a row from 1965–9.

Before the wondrous events of 2010, when a ragtag, cobbled-together group of Giants who called themselves "misfits" won the World Series, the failure of the orange and black to win a Fall Classic since 1954, with none in San Francisco, was every bit as mysterious and as inexplicable as the Cubs' dry spell since 1908. If Dark had the same deft touch with players that he had with strategy, and if owner Horace Stoneham hadn't kept trading Latinos (at least he hung onto Marichal through 1973), things might have been different in the '60s. But the team's continued drought went beyond mindset and math and into metaphysics. The Giants led the National League with 902 wins in 1960–69, 18 ahead of the Cardinals and 24 ahead of the Dodgers. Yet San Francisco won one pennant and St. Louis and L.A. three apiece. The Giants were forever left outside, listening to the "music from a farther room."

Somehow, the Giants always jinxed themselves. They won 103 games but failed to reach the postseason in 1993 and blew a 3–2 advantage in the 2002 World Series and their 5–0 lead in Game 6, as well. Cynics might say it would take an earthquake before they won a championship, but when they won the pennant in 1989, the Oakland A's shut them out in the earthquake interrupted World Series. Giants failures rankled good citizens and bad. In *Men at Work*, George Will wrote, "When Richard T. Cooper, a murderer, was on the threshold of California's death chamber, his final remarks included, 'I'm very unhappy about the Giants.'"

"In the sixties, teams didn't have to spend that much to get players," Marichal said. "Willie Mays had the top salary, $160,000 [less than half the minimum salary for today's rookies]. To have the right team, you have to have the right people working for you." Without mentioning names like Stoneham, general manager Chub Feeney, or managers Dark, Herman Franks, Clyde King, and Charlie Fox, Marichal listed some of the moves the Giants made in his time that may have affected their success:

- On December 3, 1963, they traded outfielder Felipe Alou, catcher Ed Bailey, pitcher Billy Hoeft, and a player to be named later (infielder Ernie Bowman) to the Braves for catcher Del Crandall and pitchers Bob Shaw and Bob Hendley. The Giants were desperate for pitching, but they didn't get enough. Shaw had one good year, Hendley was 10–11 then got hurt, and Crandall was nearing the end of his career. By contrast, when Alou batted .327, hit 31 homers, and led the league with 122 runs and 218 hits for the 1966 Braves, teammate Hank Aaron said, "I've never seen anyone hit so consistently all season long. We all thought Felipe should have been the MVP."

- On December 2, 1965, the Giants traded young catcher Randy Hundley and pitcher Bill Hands to the Cubs for pitcher Lindy McDaniel and outfielder Don Landrum. Hundley had caught only eight games, but the Cubs sensed what a defensive wizard he'd be. "If we could have had Hundley for 10 years, we would have won three or four times," Marichal said. Hands also blossomed in Chicago (including 20 wins in 1969), while McDaniel gave the Giants one good season and Landrum tanked.

- On May 8, 1966—Mother's Day, no less—the Giants traded first baseman–outfielder Orlando Cepeda to the Cardinals for pitcher Ray Sadecki in one of their most infamous deals. Calling Cepeda "one of baseball's most misunderstood players," the *Biographical Dictionary of American Sports* said Cepeda's Giants managers Dark and Franks "regarded him as lazy and indifferent." So lazy and so indifferent that after contributing 17 homers and 58 RBI in 123 games with the Cardinals during the 1966 season, he was the National League's Most Valuable Player in 1967. Tormented by being traded for such a popular star, Sadecki went 3–7, 12–6, 12–18, and 5–8, despite turning in ERAs less than 3.00 the middle two years. While conceding that Cepeda and Willie McCovey were both considered first basemen and one had to go, Marichal said, "At least you could have had three top prospects for him."

- On November 29, 1971, the Giants traded pitcher Gaylord Perry and shortstop Frank Duffy for left-hander Sam McDowell. Perry became a Hall of Famer, while the alcoholic McDowell got smashed on the plane to San Francisco and flamed out after a mediocre 10–8 season with a 4.33 ERA. (The character of Sam "Mayday" Malone, the recovering-alcoholic ex-Red Sox pitcher played by Ted Danson on television's *Cheers*, was loosely based on the life of McDowell.) "We knew he couldn't help the team," Marichal said. "I tried to do my best, but Gaylord and I were 1–2 [on the Giants staff],[25] and he became a Cy Young winner in both leagues." Marichal and Perry had won 286 games during the sixties, second only to the 295 won by Koufax and Drysdale.

To be fair, the Giants did make a brilliant trade for Mike McCormick, who won the Cy Young Award in 1967 with a 22–10 record and a 2.85 ERA. But the team's failures boiled down to one word that indicted the whole organization: execution. "Those were good teams, or else we wouldn't have been winning so many games," said Franks, the manager in 1965–68. "But the main reason we didn't win a couple of pennants was our double-play combination. I can still remember several games we blew because we couldn't turn the double play."

When fans voted on the "dream team" covering the Giants' first 25 years in San Francisco, they elected the immortal Johnnie LeMaster as their shortstop. Another middle infielder, Hal Lanier, said, "We just weren't fundamentally sound. The Giants always waited for the home run. We could hit the long ball with anyone and we had some pretty good pitching, but we never seemed to do the little things we needed to do in the close games."

That was a significant problem at the time. "Back then, you worked on something until you got it right," said Denis Menke, a Brave in 1963. "Fundamentals aren't as pronounced now, when you'll spend maybe one day on cutoffs and relays." Menke underscores that point by comparing the work ethics of the old build-from-within and the current free-agent/trade eras. "Because of big contracts, you might protect yourself by saying, 'Today, I'm not up to it.' In my day, they'd call guys up from the minors if you weren't ready."

There were more problems with Marichal's teams. McCormick, who played for the Giants in 1956–62 and 1967–70, appeared on a player panel at the 1998 Society for American Baseball Research (SABR) convention in San Mateo. When an astute researcher named Duke Goldman asked why the Giants hadn't won more than one pennant with five Hall of Famers on the team—three of them (Mays, McCovey, and Marichal) made Bill James's 13-man All-Star team of 1960–69 for the highest representation from any club—McCormick surprised an audience used to encomiums from former players. He explained that Giants ownership wasn't especially interested in winning pennants as long as attendance stayed high and salaries low.[26] McCormick described the managing as generally bad and Franks, one of owner Stoneham's favored drinking buddies, as an especially terrible manager. Franks managed as if it were still the 1950s, favoring station-to-station, wait-for-the-homer offense.

"When we lost the '62 Series, we weren't that concerned," McCovey recalled. "We thought we'd be back every year. But down the stretch, when we needed one more pitcher, Horace would never get one. We always had the one-two punch, but we needed the three-four-five. Our starters were working every fourth day and finishing games. By late August and September, they were tired."

Well, at least San Franciscans had Marichal, whom everyone assumed would win 300 games. In 1968, he went nine or more innings in 19 consecutive starts. After that pitching-rich season, the mound was lowered 5 inches, from 15 to 10, and the strike zone was reduced from between the bottom of the knees and the top of the shoulders down to between the top of the knees and the armpits. Even so, Marichal had a 21–11 record with his best ERA of 2.10 in 1969. People calling him a choker, a malingerer, and a quitter had a tough season. Now more of a "pitcher" than a "thrower," he was outguessing hitters more than overwhelming them. As strong as ever at 31, Marichal lost to the Mets 1–0 on Tommie Agee's homer with one out in the 14th—"When I close my eyes, I can still see the ball, floating in the air, leaving the park," Marichal said—but he went 5–2 in September to keep the Giants in a divisional race they lost by three games to the Braves.

"That was a .714 winning percentage, better than his career .683 [actually .685 through 1969]," John Devaney wrote in the 1970 book *Juan Marichal: Mister Strikeout.* "In other words, as good a pitcher as Juan was from April to September, he had proved in 1969 that he was an even better pitcher in September during the tightest race in National League history." If Devaney overstates the drama—the 1964 race was much closer—he makes a solid case for how Marichal outshone his lackluster team.

Why didn't Marichal win 300 games? You've probably figured that out—more injuries and illness. Juan caught an ear infection during the Giants' 1969–70 off-season tour of Japan and had such a severe reaction to the penicillin shots he took for it that he acquired not only more back trouble but also persistent arthritis. In constant pain, he dropped to 12–10 with a 4.11 ERA in 1970. After working out under trainer Bert Gustafson at San Francisco's Marine's Memorial Building, Marichal was back in form the next year, going 18–11 with a 2.94 ERA. "Hitters look for arm slots, but Juan had eight or nine and no favorite," said catcher Fran Healy, who joined the Giants in 1971. "He demanded total concentration. He would warm up with a coach, Ozzie Virgil, who was supposed to yell at him. Then I'd catch him, and I was supposed to yell at him. He wanted you to yell at him during the game! Afterward, you'd ice your arm and take something for your throat."

When the Giants finally landed a good shortstop, Chris Speier, they won the divisional title in 1971, but as ESPN's Chris Berman wrote, "Down the stretch it was Marichal who stood out."

"There was a must-win game late in the season," Healy said. "I looked out the window around noon, and he was playing cards. I was thinking, 'He sure looks relaxed.' He won, and we won the division." Healy was referring to the season-ending game of September 30 in San Diego. The Giants had lost 16 of their last 23 games. Nonetheless, Marichal five-hit the Padres 5–1 and the Giants won the NL West by a game over the Dodgers. He performed almost as well in the League Championship Series, losing Game 3 to Pittsburgh 2–1 despite pitching a complete-game four-hitter. Because he'd pitched at season's end, he wasn't available for a second start, and the Pirates won in four games to knock our man out of his last postseason.

"He was tough to steal on," Healy continued with considerable enthusiasm. "He had that big kick but a quick delivery, so he gave you a chance to throw the runner out at second. He also had a quick pickoff move. Against Houston, he threw over about eight times, and on the eighth time picked the guy off. I think it was [Joe] Morgan.

"I remember one series against Cincinnati. We were talking about getting Bernie Carbo out. He said, 'I can get him out with a screwball, but the bat tends to slip out of his hands and go toward the mound, so I'll get him out with a slider.' I thought that was great."

After the 1971 season, Marichal returned to the 1,700-acre spread he owned with his brothers Gonzalo and Rafael, raising rice, beans, and *plátanos*. In 1972, Marichal's pitching arm started to go south on him, he re-injured a pulled groin muscle, and he went 6–16 in his first losing season. "He had a bad year, but so did the team," Healy said. "They traded Gaylord Perry for Sam McDowell, and he showed up drunk at spring training. I think Juan would have had a better year with a better team."

Marichal had off-season surgery to correct a lumbar disc in his lower back. After going 11–15 in 1973—although he did lead the league with 1.59 walks per game and won on Opening Day for the sixth time—Marichal was sold to the Red Sox. "We now have all the pitching we need to win the pennant," Boston general manager Dick O'Connell told the *Chronicle*'s Stevens. But Marichal pitched only 11 times in 1974, was hospitalized in mid-season with back trouble, and went 5–1. He closed his career in 1975 with the archrival Dodgers, of all teams, but had just two distressing outings.

The Dodgers may have figured that keeping Marichal off another team's roster was good for them. Used more against them than any other team and racking up 15 more decisions and 10 more wins than against any other team, Marichal was 37–18 against L.A., including a 21–4 record facing them at Candlestick Park. But in 1975 he had nothing left. "After his second outing, Marichal called [general manager Al] Campanis and said he would like to come into the office to see the Dodger executive," former Dodgers official Fred Claire, then vice president of public relations, wrote in *Baseball Perspectives*. "Al asked me to come over to his office to be with him when he met with Marichal.

"As always, Marichal was very polite but very much to the point. 'Mr. Campanis, Fred, I have something I need to say,' Marichal said. 'I'm not able to pitch at the level to help your team, and I don't want to take the team's money under these circumstances. I appreciate that the Dodgers have given me an opportunity to extend my career, but I have decided to announce my retirement.'"

* * *

Marichal's April 17 retirement was disappointing but hardly humiliating. Unfortunately, an ugly episode on August 22, 1965, will always besmirch his biography. In fact, when baseball fans with any sense of history hear Marichal's name, their instinctive reaction may not be to summon his Hall of Fame stats but to cite "the Roseboro incident."

This is a difficult subject, one that we need to deal with slowly and soberly. The issue at hand initially seems innocuous: throwing inside pitches. With today's batters leaning over the plate, their front elbows encased in protective padding, pitchers must throw close to them in an effort to claim the inside part of the plate. This is known as a "brushback" pitch, and it's fair enough. For that matter, pitchers have always had the right to throw inside, because a pitch that moves a batter back may set up another pitch over the outside corner that an intimidated hitter can't reach. The problem of late is that umpires aren't calling strikes over the inside corner (and are calling them on pitches 2 inches outside). As a result, pitchers are reluctant to throw inside, and batters move closer to the plate. The day an umpire calls a strike on a pitch that strikes a hitter's padded elbow extended over the strike zone, things may change.

In throwing inside with no malice, pitchers sometimes throw too far inside and knock down batters. That too is accepted as long as the pitch isn't intentional and doesn't flirt with batters' heads. But then matters grow murky. Some pitchers deliberately floor batters with a knockdown pitch, a vicious act sometimes intended to injure that can result in a warning or expulsion by the home plate umpire. (Some of today's batters don't know the difference between a brushback and a knockdown and overreact to the former, as Hall of Famers Reggie Jackson and Bob Gibson note in a book they jointly wrote. Batters have also forgotten that the safest way to avoid a dangerous pitch is to turn away from it and fall down.) A pitch thrown at a man's head is known as a beanball; no one defends the practice because it not only threatens a player's livelihood but also his health. In 1920, the Yankees' Carl Mays killed Cleveland shortstop Ray Chapman with a pitch to his head, accounting for the only player death during a game the major leagues have ever known. Mays said he was just trying to throw inside.

Back when pitchers had to bat in both leagues, the players had some control over the situation. If the pitcher for Team A knocked down a batter, he could expect to be floored by the pitcher for Team B when it came his turn to hit. After the American League adopted the designated hitter rule in 1973, pitchers didn't bat any more except in rare circumstances. Therefore, if an AL pitcher knocked someone down, the other team would retaliate only by downing one of the pitcher's teammates, most likely his best hitter, who may understandably take offense.

Sometimes teams engage in knockdown wars that result in brawls. The threat of mere expulsion isn't much of a deterrent. In recent years, batters who were deliberately (from their perspective, at least) thrown at began rushing the mound in full fury, an act of righteous folly that not only incited riots but guaranteed suspensions. Boston's best all-around player of 2009, Kevin Youkilis, charged forth and wrestled Detroit pitcher Rick Porcello to the ground after a Porcello pitch plunked him on the back on August 11. The benches emptied and both players were ejected. Porcello and Youkilis were suspended for five games. In Youk's case, the Red Sox lost three of the five games, two by close enough margins that Youk's absence may have been pivotal. In Porcello's case, the guy had his next start delayed a day or two—hardly a disincentive to throw the next knockdown pitch.

If baseball suspended onrushing batters for 50 games instead of five, the practice would cease. Officials would also have to penalize pitchers prohibitively. Did Porcello intend to hit Youkilis? *Boston Globe* columnist Bob Ryan thought so. "While it's conceivable he simply threw a bad pitch, the far greater likelihood is that he was following up on the heated activities of the previous evening, plus a first-inning plunking of first baseman Miguel Cabrera by Red Sox rookie Junichi Tazawa (unquestionably unintentional, by the way)," Ryan wrote. "Knowing what we know about baseball, we have every right to assume that Porcello, with or without direct orders from above, nailed Youkilis—just because."

Just because what? If I walk onto the street and throw a major league hardball at someone's head, chances are I will be arrested for assault with a lethal weapon or endangerment. But in baseball, a pitcher will suffer nothing worse than ejection, possibly linked with a mild suspension and fine. The Harvard law professor and activist Alan Dershowitz, who never fails to pitch himself into a controversy, wrote in the August 19, 2009, *Boston Globe*, "The time has come for Major League Baseball to ban the beanball. The only way to do this is for baseball to adopt a zero tolerance policy and to impose draconian sanctions not only on pitchers who throw at the heads of batters but, more importantly, on the managers who instruct them to do so."

Dershowitz recommended a suspension of anywhere from a season to life for miscreant managers and pitchers, with pitchers getting a break for turning in their skippers. He also wanted to penalize players who hear managers order beanballs without turning them in. Dershowitz admitted there may be trouble proving deliberate intent "in some cases." That's an understatement. In such a juvenile and androcentric culture as baseball, it's hard to imagine anyone turning in a teammate or manager, and no one would admit to deliberately beaning someone. As John Carmichael of the *Chicago Daily News* wrote in 1958, "It is virtually impossible to legislate against death, taxes, and the beanball."

Baseball has a culture in which grown men douse each other with good champagne instead of drink it. This is a society in which players "face" teammates with shaving cream pies. This is an arena in which veterans make rookies wear women's clothes as a rite of passage. As former third baseman and manager Buddy Bell once told me, the best thing about playing baseball is that you never have to grow up. So the deadly playground fight continues, forever justified by the idiotic words, "It's part of the game."[27]

As a result, teams engage in what amounts to legal assault. No teams ever hated each other more than the Dodgers and Giants, who have shared baseball's longest rivalry, dating back to 1890. When the Dodgers played in Brooklyn and the Giants in Manhattan, they weren't on speaking terms. The animosity went coast-to-coast in 1958 when the Dodgers moved to Los Angeles and the Giants settled 325 miles away in San Francisco. What had been intracity warfare simply became intrastate combat. The weapon of choice: assault with a deadly baseball.

Now we come to the events of August 22, 1965, which were presaged by some infantile activity. First, Dodgers batter Maury Wills, perhaps deliberately, tipped Giants catcher Tom Haller's glove in the fifth inning two days earlier, earning him first base on "catcher's interference" determined by home plate umpire Al Forman. In the bottom half of the inning, the Giants' Matty Alou attempted the same feat on Dodgers catcher John Roseboro, who was visibly angered. Alou didn't get the call, and Marichal yelled from the dugout to Roseboro, "Why do you get mad? Haller doesn't get mad."

According to Marichal, Roseboro told Alou, "If Marichal doesn't shut his big mouth, he'll get a ball right behind the ear." The following day, Roseboro told teammates Jim Gilliam and Lou Johnson that Marichal better not act up when he pitched 24 hours later "because I won't take any guff from him."

Both Marichal and Roseboro already had non-baseball matters weighing on them. Reacting to a civil war in the Dominican Republic and fearing "another Cuba" imposed by Marxists in the Constitutionalist faction, President Lyndon B. Johnson in April installed 23,000 troops with the blessing of the Organization of American States (OAS). Fighting continued until the centrist provisional government of Hector García Godoy was installed on September 3. Before then, however, it was almost impossible for U.S.-based Dominicans to communicate with friends and relatives back home. Marichal went to the

Dominican consulate in San Francisco to read newspaper accounts of the fighting and worried constantly. "Some say conditions in his native Dominican Republic had changed his normally amiable disposition and moods," a San Francisco reporter wrote.

For his part, Roseboro, a quiet, competitive man known to teammates as "Gabby," was obsessed by the August 11–16 race riots in the Watts neighborhood of Los Angeles (he lived in a nearby community) where 34 people died, 4,000 were injured, and property damage was estimated at $40 million. His teammates Lou Johnson and Willie Crawford, the latter accidentally arrested as a rioter and later released, also lived close to Watts.

With the Dodgers and Giants competing as usual for the National League pennant, the Dodgers had already won two extra-inning games during a four-game set at Candlestick Park. People slept in line to get general-admission tickets to the Sunday afternoon duel between Koufax and Marichal. When play started on the hazy afternoon, Wills beat out a bunt in the first inning and subsequently scored. In the second, Wes Parker doubled and Roseboro singled him home to make the score 2–0.

When Wills batted again with two out in the second, Marichal floored him with a high inside fastball. "I didn't want him bunting again," Marichal told San Francisco newsman Harry Jupiter in a *Sport* story published the following year, "so I pitched him tight." The Giants' Cap Peterson homered in the bottom of the inning to make it 2–1.

In the third, Marichal sent Ron Fairly into the dirt. Catcher Dick Bertell told Jupiter, "It was a fastball that sailed in on him." The pitch only angered Roseboro more.

With Marichal due to lead off the Giant third, all 42,807 fans in Candlestick Park assumed he or someone else would be knocked down. They forgot that Koufax, a man of principle, was afraid he might hurt someone and didn't believe in knockdowns.[28] The best Koufax could do that day was a "courtesy pitch" he threw several feet over Mays' head that went to the backstop in the second inning. That wasn't good enough for Roseboro. "Sandy was constitutionally incapable of throwing at anyone's head," he said later. "So I decided to take matters into my own hands."

When Marichal stepped to the plate, Roseboro went to the mound and told Koufax to throw one inside. After Koufax threw a curve for a called strike, Roseboro got his inside pitch. When it arrived, he deliberately dropped it and returned the pitch close to Marichal's right ear; according to some accounts, including Marichal's, the throw actually nicked it. For maybe the first time in baseball history, a catcher had buzzed a hitter. "I meant for him to feel it," Roseboro said later. "I'd made up my mind that if he protested, I was going after him!"

Marichal turned around, bat in hand, and screamed, "Why you do that? Why do that?" The muscular Roseboro took off his mask and advanced toward him, answering "You!" according to one account and telling him what he could do to himself and his mother, according to Marichal. And suddenly, Juan Marichal lost it.

In a photographed and televised sequence sent around the world, Marichal wheeled on Roseboro and whacked him over the head with his bat,[29] opening a 2-inch gash and initiating a 14-minute brannigan in which Willie McCovey and umpire Shag Crawford were spiked and Dodgers coach Danny Ozark was floored by a punch. Some felt Roseboro, whose left eye had filled with blood, had lost the eye. Only heroic intercession by Mays prevented further damage. Mays snatched a bat from teammate Tito Fuentes' hand, grabbed the bleeding Roseboro when he was chasing Marichal ("You're hurt John, you're hurt. Stop the fighting. Your eye is out," Mays said), guided him toward the dugout, and cradled his bleeding head in his arms, reportedly saying, "Johnny, Johnny, I'm so sorry." Mays subsequently tackled Johnson, who was headed after Crawford.

In the end, Marichal was ejected, while Roseboro drew no penalty and left the game only because of his injury. Shaken by the episode after play resumed, Koufax got by two batters but then surrendered two walks and a Mays homer and lost 4–3.

Afterward, everyone had a different description of what happened. Umpire Crawford said no words were exchanged. Giants manager Herman Franks said Marichal told him Roseboro clipped his ear with the throw. Roseboro, said a Dodgers spokesman, "threw it right by his ear to give him a taste of his own medicine."

"I had the bat on my shoulder," Marichal told Jupiter. "If he didn't do that on purpose, he didn't have to give me that kind of answer. He's got the mask, the chest protector. I don't think I can fight with a guy like that. I know from the way he came toward me he was coming to fight. I only hit him one time—the first time." Marichal further said he never would have gone on the offensive if Roseboro hadn't sworn at him.

In any case, with the game still in progress, Marichal was driven to the airport by an attendant from the press box, with two cops sitting in back and a policeman on motorcycle preceding the vehicle. "All I know is that he tried to hurt me," Marichal said. "He hit me in the ear with the ball when he threw it back to the pitcher—that's all I know."

But Marichal had violated a baseball code against using anything but fists in a fight. National League president Warren Giles fined him $1,750 and suspended him eight playing dates and two likely starts (Roseboro received no suspension)—it was the most severe punishment ever assessed by a National League president (to that time) but one that satisfied few people who heard about it. "What if he had gone out on the street and clubbed somebody?" an unidentified Dodger was quoted in *Time*. "He'd have been arrested. It should be a suspension of 1,750 days." Giles called the attack "repugnant" but said he pro-rated the fine based on days out of the lineup and noted mitigating circumstances he called "underlying currents."

Most sports commentators said the penalty was too lenient, and some of them raged about Marichal's ethnicity. According to Bob Broeg of the *St. Louis Post-Dispatch*, "There is a code of conduct involved. The tendency of Latin American ballplayers to fight with weapons other than their fists must be discouraged. It's both dangerous and despicable." William Chapin of the *San Francisco Chronicle* wrote, "In a situation like that, you act first and think later. Especially if you're a fiery Dominican."

By contrast, Dick Young of the *New York Daily News* made an extraordinary distinction that went unnoticed at the time. He wrote, "I wonder if the mob would be shouting so if his name weren't Juan Marichal. What would the mob shout, I wonder, if his name were a nice Nordic name like Frank Thomas, which it just happened to be a couple of months ago. I seem to recall that Thomas hit Richie Allen on the side of the head with a bat and the only penalty he got was being sent to Houston, which is pretty drastic, I'll grant you."

Young was referencing a July incident in which Allen and fellow Phillie Thomas clashed and Thomas swung a bat at Allen, hitting him on the shoulder, not the side of his head. Another Phillie, Johnny Callison, said, "Thomas got himself fired when he swung that bat at Richie. In baseball you don't swing a bat at another player—ever." A fourth Phillie, Pat Corrales, confirmed the slugging and added that Thomas was a "bully" infamous for racially divisive remarks. Apparently, Giles thought it was enough that the Phillies sold Thomas to the

Astros, and Giles didn't impose a penalty. He could not take such a hands-off position when the two most embattled rivals and perhaps the two leading pitchers in baseball staged their bloody fracas.

Young's *Daily News* colleague Phil Pepe got it right when he wrote that regardless of the fine and suspension, "There is the humiliation. Juan is a decent and sensitive man, who must know by now that he performed a dastardly act. And if he does not know it, he will hear about it, you can be sure. He will face public scorn, and in the jungle that is baseball, opponents will not let him forget what he did.

"The damage it will do to Marichal, psychologically if not physically, is immeasurable. Life could be miserable for him from now on, and that is the real punishment."

The Giants issued the following statement with Marichal's name on it:

"First of all, I want to apologize for hitting Roseboro with my bat. I am sorry I did that. But he was coming toward me, with his mask in his hand, and I was afraid he was going to hit me with his mask, so I swung my bat. If he had only said something, I would not have swung. I hit him once, and I am sorry.

I think the anger started on Friday night. On his last time at bat in that game, Maury Wills was awarded first base for catcher's interference. Our team thought Wills deliberately stepped back, forcing Tom Haller to tip Wills' bat with his glove. So when Matty Alou came to bat in the next inning, he did the same thing, but the plate umpire, Doug Harvey [Note: the plate umpire that game was actually Al Forman], did not award him first base. Then, Roseboro yelled over at our dugout, 'If this stuff keeps up we're going to get one of you guys and get him good—right in the ear.' The umpire must have heard this. And later, Roseboro repeated it to Orlando Cepeda. That is why I want him present when I meet Warren Giles.

When I came to bat on Sunday, the first pitch was a perfect strike. The second one was a little inside. Johnny Roseboro deliberately dropped the ball so he could get behind me. Then he threw the ball back to Koufax real hard—nobody ever throws the ball back to the pitcher that hard—and it ticked my ear. I might expect Koufax to throw at me, but I did not look for someone to throw at me from behind me. Then I turn around and I say, 'Why did you do that?' He did not say a word. He just took off his mask and came toward me. I was afraid he was going to hit me with his mask, so I hit him with my bat. I am sorry but many times our players on the Giants are hit by pitches and sometimes hurt, and nobody says anything then."

The Giants never explained to Marichal why the statement in his name claimed that Roseboro didn't speak to him before the fight. Marichal subsequently decided against taking his case to Giles, who didn't change the penalty. The Giants went 3–6–1 during Marichal's suspension, which amounted to 10 days and 10 games because of days off, doubleheaders, and a rainout. At the end of that period, however, the Giants were the same game-and-a-half behind the Dodgers that they'd been at the beginning of the August 22 game. Giles also prevented Marichal from playing in a September 6–7 series in Los Angeles in which Mays got a standing ovation and the Giants won both games. Once a clubhouse prankster who reportedly stole teammates' car keys, lit firecrackers under them, and released stink bombs in the team plane, Marichal grew deathly quiet around his teammates.

He finally pitched against Philadelphia on September 2 and lost, beat the Cubs on two days' rest (since he couldn't be used in the following series against the Dodgers), went 3–4 the remainder of the season, and infuriated Mays by failing to throw inside to noted hitters like Ernie Banks. But the Giants were hardly undone by Marichal's lapses. From the time he returned to the end of the season—they finished second, two games behind the Dodgers—San Francisco was 23–10. Marichal was 3–0 during the team's 14-game winning streak. He lost his last three decisions 9–1, 7–1, and 3–2, but only three times in his nine post-suspension appearances did he yield as many as four earned runs. His ERA climbed from 1.78 to 2.13. General manager Chub Feeney, a smart, educated, charming man who could be blunt, blamed the Roseboro episode for the team's second-place finish. Other commentators said that slugger Orlando Cepeda's injury-shortened 33-game season played a greater role. Marichal himself felt that the pitching collapsed. However, it took a total team effort to blow a four-game lead with 12 games left.

Roseboro later admitted that he provoked the brawl by throwing close to Marichal's ear. No matter what Roseboro did to incite his wrath, though, there was no excuse for Marichal to hit a man over the head with a baseball bat. Next to Carl Mays' killing of Chapman in 1920, it was probably the most notorious incident of ballpark violence in modern baseball history,[30] the Thomas-Allen incident being forgotten almost as soon as it happened. And for those of us who admire many Latino players, it was a kick in the stomach. The Dominican Dandy, Laughing Boy, Manito—all the friendly affection directed toward an eminently decent man had conflated into a walking stereotype. In the public mind, he was just another hot-headed Dominican from a violent culture.

Are Latino ballplayers especially prone to violent or aberrant behavior? To answer that question, we'd have to define what constitutes a violent incident, catalogue every one of them, and determine if the number of Latinos involved was greater than their percentage of the baseball population. Further, we'd have to explore the effect of poverty and prejudice on Latino players and wonder how Anglos would behave if they were from the same background.

In the twenty-first century, the matter of culture has become a subject Anglos are reluctant to discuss for fear they'll be accused of bigotry. One exception, interestingly, was Warren Spahn. When he attended a Legends of County Stadium press conference in September 2000, he was asked why there's more fighting today than in his time. Latinos, Spahn told a shocked audience. "When the Latins came to the game, they also brought their habits with them, so that now, we have people fighting with bats and charging the mound. The cultures are a lot different."

When asked if Spahn's claim had any basis, Marichal said, "No. We play hard, we play to win, but you don't often see a guy charging the mound. You see that from American players. When Pedro Martinez was pitching a perfect game a few years ago and he threw close to a Cincinnati player, he charged the mound. Do you think a guy trying to pitch a perfect game would try to hit a guy? Let me tell you, if a manager wants to get 100 percent out of a Dominican, he just has to treat him right, because they'll die for you. They give everything that they have to play for you. So I don't know why we get that trademark that we have a temper. I see a lot of Americans in the heat of the game doing things that surprise me."

From covering the game as a beat reporter in the seventies and eighties and studying it ever since, I've concluded that most Latino ballplayers are mature individuals like Felipe Alou who must be embarrassed by serially irresponsible players like Pedro Guerrero and Joaquin Andujar and roll their eyes at Manny Ramírez throwing his own team's traveling secretary to the clubhouse floor,

Roberto Alomar spitting in an umpire's face, Mario Soto shoving an umpire, and minor league José Offerman whacking another player with a bat and throwing a punch at an umpire. Unfortunately, some of the most visible and infamous incidents have involved Latinos, who, it is generally agreed, are more emotive than Anglos (a term commonly used to describe anyone who isn't Hispanic, Asian, or Indian).

But Spahn was wrong in his characterization. There's more violence in baseball because there are more games, more teams, and more opportunity for it. These are violent times, and baseball reflects the larger society. What's more, baseball violence is an equal-opportunity destroyer. When a Jewish player like Kevin Youkilis charges the mound, all bets are off on ethnic stereotyping.

If Marichal was guilty of anything on a semi-regular basis, it was speaking his mind or showing his emotions without considering how they'd look in headlines or photos. When McCovey made an outfield error early in Juan's career, Marichal stood on the mound glaring at him, hands on hips—a breach of etiquette team captain Mays was sure to remind him about. When the Cardinals' Bob Gibson broke Jim Ray Hart's collarbone with a pitch, Marichal threw one close to Gibson's head and was immediately fined $50 by home plate umpire Al Barlick. "He'll get it again!" Marichal screamed; he remained in the game only because his catcher and manager intervened. On another occasion Marichal had to be restrained from charging Cincinnati pitcher Joe Nuxhall after he decked a Giants batter.

Many a pitcher never would have recovered from the public disgrace Marichal endured late in the 1965 season. You'd never have known it from his activities back home. In January 1966, a time of maximum political tension in the Dominican Republic based on the presidential elections that occurred that month, Marichal threw out the first ball for a Santo Domingo doubleheader, signed a dozen baseballs, and did calisthenics and running between games to show an enthralled 5,000 kids how he prepared for spring training. His connection to Joaquin Balaguer—"the Juan Marichal of the presidential palace" was written on many a capital wall, and Balaguer ran on a ticket with Juan's cousin, also named Juan Marichal—may have decided the close presidential race.

Meanwhile, Marichal took note of the joint 32-day revolutionary holdout by Dodgers pitchers Sandy Koufax and Don Drysdale—they settled for $130,000 and $105,000, respectively—and demanded a $20,000 raise from his own $60,000 salary. When Giants management balked, Juan said $75,000 or retirement. "I have bought a large farm, and I can earn a lot of money growing crops on my farm," he said. "In the United States, there are those who think that Latin Americans are peasants. [In the Dominican Republic perhaps 30–40 percent lived on farms at the time.] We are not. I will do very well here without playing baseball for the Giants." The Giants acquiesced in March, and Marichal pitched all of 13 innings in Arizona.

Holdout or not, Juan's image quickly rebounded despite endless hate mail and booing, courtesy of the Roseboro incident, and despite some public incredulity over his assertion in the *Sport* article that he was more the victim than the aggressor. His pinpoint control returned once his old manager Tom Sheehan told him, "Use the whole plate[31]," he began the 1966 season 9–0 with an ethereal 0.59 ERA in his first 10 starts. Along the way, he beat Cooperstown-bound Jim Bunning and the Phillies 1–0 in 14 innings. The national news media, which by and large hadn't noticed Marichal until the Roseboro incident, suddenly took stock of his pitching. "The Best Right Arm in Baseball," *Time* touted him on a June cover that included nine sequential oil studies of his pitching motion.

But once again, Old Man Injury and the insinuations about malingering surfaced. In July, Juan's friend Manny Mota, then with the Pirates, accidentally slammed a car door on Marichal's pitching hand, and a couple of weeks later Juan turned an ankle. On August 23, the Reds' Tommy Helms smashed a liner off Marichal's right instep. After hanging in to finish the game and win 7–3, Marichal submitted to x-rays. The doctors told him there was no new fracture but discovered an old one. "I know," Marichal said. "It happened four years ago."

"You won 90 games on a broken foot?" an incredulous doctor asked him. Actually, Marichal won 96. When the old fracture didn't require surgery, Marichal finished the 1966 season with a 25–6 record and a 2.23 ERA. While becoming the only pitcher to beat every team in the league in each of the previous five seasons, he led the NL in winning percentage (.806), opponent's average (.202), and opponent's on-base percentage (.230) while batting .524 with men in scoring position. Marichal won 12 of his last 14 decisions, concluding with three wins in nine days, while the Giants contended to the last day of the season. When they beat the Pirates 7–3 on a McCovey homer, the Giants needed the front-running Dodgers to lose a doubleheader, which would have forced a San Francisco–Cincinnati makeup game that the Giants would have had to win to create another pennant playoff. Did you get all that? It was too much to expect, however. Koufax won the second game of the twin bill, and the Giants finished 1½ out.

Though Roseboro sued Marichal and the Giants for $110,000, charging actual and punitive damages over the beating, both men showed a better side in the end by settling quietly out of court seven years later for a reported $7,500. Marichal not only apologized for the beating on the day following it but repeatedly afterward, and he eventually went to Roseboro and asked his forgiveness. In 1974, Roseboro, who was no longer a Dodger but active in the organization's community relations, welcomed Marichal to the Dodgers and asked the fans to do so, too. In 1982, the Roseboros visited the Marichals in Santo Domingo.

"My father was not a man to hold grudges," Roseboro's daughter, Morgan Fouch-Roseboro, said. "He was the easiest man to know, the easiest to love. As far as he was concerned, by then, the incident and its fallout were over. My father, my mother, and I stayed with the whole Marichal family and had a truly unforgettable time. The Dominican people are so friendly, and the Marichals made us feel right at home. We're so truly grateful for our visit with them and for the subsequent years our families shared together."

After the visit to the Dominican, Roseboro pushed for Juan's induction into the Hall of Fame. "He turned out to be a hell of a nice guy, not a fighter," said Roseboro, who was moved to tears by Marichal's kind words and support at his deathbed. Juan subsequently eulogized Roseboro at his 2002 funeral, saying that one of his happiest moments was being forgiven by Roseboro. "I wish he was my catcher," Marichal added.

So enraged at being passed over twice (while Bob Gibson was elected with some 100 more votes) that he threatened to boycott the Hall—voters probably had the Roseboro incident on their minds[32]—Marichal had to wait until his third year of eligibility to be selected. On January 12, 1983, he telephoned Roseboro. "John," Marichal said. "What, Juan?" "I'm going to Cooperstown. I'm going to be the first Dominican in the Hall." The next sound heard over the line was two men crying.

Marichal was the first Latino elected to the Hall of Fame through the regular selection process. (In a departure from the usual five-year waiting period, Roberto Clemente was installed the summer following his death on December 31, 1972, after a plane he was taking to deliver emergency supplies to earthquake victims in Nicaragua crashed a quarter-mile off Puerto

Rico. And Martín Dihigo was installed in a 1977 election by a special Negro Leagues committee.) Marcia Burick, whose father, Si, of the *Dayton (Ohio) Daily News*, was also on the platform with Marichal to receive the J. Taylor Spink Award, commented that her kids were dumbstruck by the liquid beauty of Marichal's five daughters Rosie, Elsie, Yvette, Ursula, and Charlene. *¡Qué linda!* Their little brother Juan Jr. "Juanchi" and their striking mother, Alma, joined them seated in the first row. To the delight of their parents and absent grandmother, Doña Natividad—still alive (she died in 1988) and still refusing to fly but watching the live telecast on Channel 7 in the Dominican Republic—all of the kids attended college.

Immortals like Al Lopez, Bill Terry, Bob Feller, Cool Papa Bell, Monte Irvin, Sandy Koufax, Happy Chandler, and Joe DiMaggio sat on the dais, and hundreds of Dominicans waving their country's flag were among the 10,000 fans in the stands. Dressed in a light gray suit and classy as ever with his words despite evident nervousness and heightened emotion, Marichal, 45, began his acceptance speech in English and segued into Spanish before concluding in English. It was the first time any inductee had spoken in another language. While in Cooperstown, Marichal thanked his family and his compatriots; he thanked Horacio Martínez, the family friend who signed him; he thanked Francisco Pichardo, who gave him "the best instruction...discipline and the art of pitching;" and he thanked Giants owner Horace Stoneham for "warmth and support." Marichal added more gratitude to the San Francisco Giants, his teammates, his fans, and, yes, John Roseboro for his forgiveness and support. When he arrived in the Dominican Republic after induction, Marichal told the airport crowd, "Many Latins have written beautiful pages in major league history, and I am sure that my arrival will open doors for others."

Also in 1983, Marichal's No. 27 was retired by the Giants at an impressive Candlestick Park ceremony in which he entered the Hispanic Heritage Baseball Museum Hall of Fame. Three old associates, manager Herman Franks, pitching coach Larry Jansen, and fellow pitcher Mike McCormick honored Juan, and Eastern Airlines presented a full-color 16-page booklet on his achievements for the first 40,000 fans. In 1990, Marichal watched Cincinnati pitcher José Rijo, his son-in-law at the time, stage an MVP performance at the World Series. After his retirement, Marichal returned home to his now-mechanized farm and his luxury home in Santo Domingo. Always a charmer, he used to enthrall the

Giants' elderly Booster Club at spring training in Phoenix. "He's one of the classiest men I've ever met," his former catcher Healy said. "The perception [after the Roseboro incident] was that he was out of control, but on and off the field he handled himself with class."

"Juan has always been a friend to the Spahn family," Warren's son Greg said. "His son and my daughter Vicki used to run around together at the Hall of Fame."

In 2005, Marichal received an honor that touched him as deeply as his Hall of Fame plaque. A bronze statue by William Behrends of Marichal kicking high and seemingly about to launch a pitch into McCovey Cove was unveiled in Lefty O'Doul Plaza outside the stadium, whose current corporate name is AT&T Park. On the base is a replica of Juan's Hall of Fame plaque, plus the following tributes:

"If you don't get Marichal out by the third inning, forget it. He is going to beat you." [Broadcaster] Curt Gowdy

"If Marichal doesn't get one pitch over, he has nine others to throw at you. He is the best pitcher in baseball." [Longtime Met] Ed Kranepool [Interestingly, Kranepool made that comment in 1969 while sitting next to his teammate, 25-game winner Tom Seaver.]

"He can pitch all day and hit a space no wider than two inches—in, out, up, or down. I've never seen anyone as good as that." Pete Rose

"I still think that bunting against Marichal is a good idea. The only trouble is, he won't give you anything you can bunt." Jim Wynn

"When you have to win a game, Marichal gives me confidence. Juan rises to the occasion. The tougher the situation, the better he is." Alvin Dark

"Making the Hall of Fame, that was deserved," Marichal said at the ceremony. "But this was a gift."

His statue joined those of his old teammates and fellow immortals Mays, Perry, and McCovey. All the other living Giants Hall of Famers—Mays, McCovey, Perry, and Orlando Cepeda—were present, as was the president of the Dominican Republic.

"Juan was just so delightful to watch," said club president Peter McGowan, who dropped a black canopy to present the sculpture.

"He was one of the bravest players I've ever played with," said Felipe Alou, an old teammate who had been elevated to Giants manager.

"This is a wonderful day for all Latin players," Cepeda said. "All Latin people should be proud."

Charming as ever, Marichal said, "Thank you for honoring me with this impressive statue, and thank you for honoring the great tradition of our game of baseball, for keeping the Giants where they belong [in San Francisco], and for honoring the past, the present, and the future.

"And last, but never least, I'd wish to extent my heartfelt thanks to the Giants fans for their love and support throughout my career. As the songwriter once said, 'I Left My Heart in San Francisco.'"

In an aside, Marichal turned to Barry Bonds, the Giant who would set the all-time home-run record, and produced chuckles by saying, "I think I could get you out." For their part, the Giants played that day in uniforms with the Spanish word *Gigantes* on their chests.

A Dominican observer once commented that many stars "let baseball go to their heads" and have trouble dealing with retirement. That plainly has not been the case for Marichal. Among his other post-baseball activities, he helped convince fellow Dominican pitcher Pedro Martínez to move from the Expos to the Red Sox, and he taught the A's Mike Norris the screwball that made his career. Marichal directed Latin American scouting for the Oakland A's in 1983–95, signing more than 100 players, 32 of whom, including Miguel Tejada and Luis Polonia, made the majors. Marichal also spent a dozen years running a 12-team rookie league back home in which 19 major league teams participated.

In 1996–2000, Marichal was his country's Minister of Sport. One of his most heralded accomplishments was landing the Pan-American Games for Santo Domingo, but he highlights something else. "We started a program for athletes to go to school. Athletes now become doctors, nurses. You can only be an athlete for a short time. After that you have to prepare yourself. I'm happy we started that, and the ministers of sport after me have continued it."

Juan's ministry was not without its upsets, however. In 1998, he suffered head, neck, spine, and leg injuries when a car in which he was a passenger hit a concrete wall attached to an overpass in a late-night accident 30 miles north of Santo Domingo. Marichal, who was in the back seat, got peppered with windshield glass that acted like shrapnel. "My oldest daughter used to visit me in the hospital to pick glass out of my head. The accident occurred on June

27. I told people, 'There's no way I'm going to die, because that's my magic [uniform] number!'" After shoulder surgery and several months of rehab, he recovered. "Thank God," he said.

Marichal resigned as Minister of Sport in 2000 amid allegations that he had pocketed millions of dollars intended for equipment. High-ranking officials in the Dominican Republic—and in most Latin American countries—routinely take what are called "commissions" from people whose projects they oversee. Marichal's enemies probably didn't care about his alleged transgressions because they never formally charged him with anything. "The president [Leonel Fernández Reyna] told me, 'Juan, don't pay attention. That's the opposition. They don't do that to hurt you. They do it to hurt me.'"

When Fernandez was succeeded by an opposition-party candidate, Marichal said that new president Hipólito Mejía became warm friends with him and told him, "Nobody in my party will fool around with you," and invited him to his mountain retreat to play dominoes. Meanwhile, Marichal remained active as host of the Juan Marichal Golf Tournament. Its organization says much about Juan as both a citizen and a father. The selection of the recipient charities is made by Marichal's human dynamo of a daughter, Yvette, who has a B.A. in communication arts from the University of San Francisco and a master of science in broadcast journalism from Boston University. Yvette turned *Oh!Magazine* into the most read magazine in the Dominican Republic as its editor in 2001–06 and currently hosts *Hoy en tu Casa*, a daily television program geared toward women. Married to singer-actor Héctor Anibal Estrella and the mother of a son and a daughter, Yvette somehow finds time to represent her father and serve as public relations and marketing director of FUNGOLODE (*Fundación Global Democracia y Desarollo*), a non-profit organization, "dedicated to promoting collaboration between organizations in the United States and Europe and the Dominican Republic in order to conduct research, enhance public understanding, design public policies, devise strategies, offer capacity building, and foster exchange in the areas crucial for the social, economic, and democratic development of the Dominican Republic, Caribbean, and Latin America."

Given Yvette's credentials, she spelled out some of the charities funded by the golf tournament.

• "*Heartcare Dominicana*, conducts cardiovascular surgery for indigent children with visiting teams of doctors from the U.S. attending various pathologies. In addition, our local medical team performs heart surgery twice weekly completely free.

- "*Voluntariado Jesus con los Niños*, a non-profit institution that serves and supports children with cancer and their families through activities that will help alleviate the physical, emotional, and economic impact of the disease.
- "*Fundación Aprendiendo a Vivir*, offers children with diabetes the opportunity to improve their quality of life through educational campaigns.
- "*Instituto Dominicano de Desarrollo Integral*, a non-profit institution founded in 1984 with the aim of contributing to overcoming poverty in rural and urban areas. It consists of men and women who work with communities and local organizations interested in assuming the responsibility for improving their living conditions.
- "*Aldea del Niño*, a non-profit organization whose objective is to develop actions aimed at strengthening through training assistance in the areas of education, the arts, sports, and especially spirituality in the Christian faith. Reinforcement through educational opportunities for children and adolescents is fundamental to their Project of Love.
- "*Instituto de la Diabetes*, the leading institution in providing care and service to diabetics in the Dominican Republic.
- "*Hermanas Carmelitas*, focuses primarily on serving God by the attention and assistance to the poor and needy. Dedicated to homeless, orphaned, abandoned children who require a protective and helping hand.
- "The Butterfly Foundation, dedicated to operating on low-income children who have deformities of the spine with funds donated by the international company of spine implants Medtronic and respected personalities in the Dominican Republic."

In addition, Juan runs three farms and advises young athletes on contracts. You'll see his name on billboards advertising crackers in Santo Domingo. From 1998–2010 he was a member of the Hall of Fame Veterans Committee. He does Spanish-language radio broadcasts of Dominican games and Spanish-language television of the U.S. playoffs and World Series for *ESPN Desportes*.

One way or another, he always seems to be in the news. In 2008, Marichal and Pedro Martínez were criticized for attending a cockfight. Surprised at the reaction, Martínez replied that the activity plays a respected role in Dominican culture. Marichal, who once told author Rob Ruck that cockfighting is "in my blood,"[33] agreed. There was no fallout locally. Dominicans seem to love everything Juan Marichal does and says. He is referred to fondly as *El Monstro de la Laguna* (the Monster of the Lake).

* * *

And what of the nation that produced *El Monstro de la Laguna?* The Dominican Republic shares the island of Hispaniola with Haiti. Columbus landed there, and the Spanish occupation wiped out almost all the native Taíno Indians before replacing them with African slaves. Later, Haiti occupied the country in the nineteenth century, and the United States occupied the DR and Haiti in the twentieth century. *La República Dominicana* has had its share of dictators, mostly notably Rafael Trujillo, who ruled from 1930 to 1961. Survivors of that era actually say life was comfortable as long as you didn't criticize *El Benefactor.* Or if you weren't Haitian, Trujillo ordered the execution of all Haitians in the region bordering Haiti. The Dominican Republic lapsed into civil war in the 1960s but emerged from it a constitutional democracy.

People who don't understand the country say it has two industries: sugar and baseball. Depending on which local straightens you out, the leading business is either money shipments home from overseas Dominicans (which amount to about $3 billion annually) or tourism (about $2 billion a year). There are more than 400 beaches to enjoy on the Atlantic and Caribbean coasts; the Caribbean's highest mountain, 10,417-foot *El Pico Duarte* (Duarte's Peak), to climb; and excellent opportunities for windsurfing and whale watching. Rich black earth for farming, rain forests, and even deserts abound. Take a tour around Santo Domingo, and your guide will show you a national palace he says is larger than the White House while offering you *mamajuana*, an exquisite mixture of rum, wine, honey, and 16 roots that is said to be an aphrodisiac. The DR is the region's leading producer of organic bananas and cocoa beans.

To be sure, life is tougher for most residents than it is for tourists. Unemployment was in double digits in January 2010, Haitian immigrants and refugees were flooding social services, and the gap between public and private education had families forgoing every pleasure to pay for their children's schooling.

Yet Dominicans of all backgrounds are among the happiest people anywhere. They cheerfully endure three-to-five-hour electrical blackouts.

They willingly live from paycheck to paycheck—the average family income was $350-$400 a month in 2010. People joyously wear Yankees caps (there are sizable Dominican communities in the Bronx and nearby Washington Heights), while the government generously ignored its own problems to become first responders to the 2010 Haitian earthquake. Like most Latin Americans, Dominicans often cheer for routine plane landings. The World Database of Happiness, a survey by a Dutch sociologist, rated the DR 15th among 148 nations polled when Dominican respondents scored their happiness 7.6 on a scale of 100. The New Economics Institute's "happy planet index," which merges happiness, longevity, and environmental impact, rated the DR second only to Costa Rica.

* * *

The trip on Route 3 from the beach to the Marichal home in Santo Domingo takes you past stucco houses, palm and cotton trees, and billboards in English ("Flaunt your taste") as well as Spanish. When you reach the outskirts of Santo Domingo, the heavy traffic resembles a children's book on vehicles: cars, SUVs, vans, cabs, bicycles, motorbikes, cement mixers, flatbed trucks, dump trucks, 18-wheelers, buses. You half expect to see a mouse at the wheel of a tractor. After our driver asked a dozen or so pedestrians for directions ("*La casa de Juan Marichal?*"), we disembarked at a brown, seven-bedroom, stucco-sided, tile-roofed house behind walls in the fashionable *El Millón* neighborhood. An armed guard stood in the driveway.

A servant opened the front door, and we waited in a heavily air-conditioned room of Marichal memorabilia. There are trophies, photos of family, more photos of Juan with famous ballplayers like Brooks Robinson and Orlando Cepeda and politicians like Richard Nixon and Albert Gore, statues of fighting cocks, and paintings of old No. 27 in full windup.

Under the circumstances, it was amazing that Juan agreed to meet with us. Originally, we were supposed to visit for two hours and then retire with the family to a luncheon honoring the Juan Marichal Sport and Cultural Center, a project financed by a $75 million U.S. loan that will upgrade Santo Domingo's Quisqueya Stadium (renaming it in Marichal's honor) while building a 150-room hotel, 280 apartments in six towers, a baseball museum, and shopping center. The lunch was abruptly cancelled the previous day when four prominent citizens close to the Marichals drowned on a fishing trip.

Yet Juan did not cancel his appointment. He entered the room in jeans, orange golf shirt, and navy blue loafers with no socks, adorned only by a gold watch and gold ring on his left hand. He resembled nothing so much as a man in repose and at peace. I immediately stuck out my right hand and missed his. After we completed the handshake amid chuckles, Juan plopped down in a deep, aqua-colored, overstuffed leather chair. My wife noticed something I'd missed: that he has the smooth, unlined hands of a young man.

"I'd like to pick up on the way you behaved at the Hall of Fame," I began. "You said, 'Take my hand, I'm in heaven,' and 'Nothing is impossible.' You must be one of the happiest people in the world."

"Ever since I was a boy, I wanted to be a ballplayer," he said. "Not because you could make a lot of money. I didn't know anything about that. I just knew there was a team in the Dominican Republic, and I wanted to be on it. Then I was playing for the Air Force team and playing in international tournaments. On September 16, 1957, Horacio Martínez signed me to play for *Escogido* and the Giants organization. We agreed to sign for a $500 bonus. I wanted to be a baseball player; now they offered me the goal to play in the United States. Let me tell you, since that day I considered myself the happiest man on earth."

He didn't have to discuss the well-chronicled wonders that awaited him with the Giants. Marichal agreed with my suggestion that surviving three near-death experiences (the childhood coma, the near-drowning during his baseball career, and the car crash) enriched his appreciation even more. But I sensed there was something else. "Tell me about your mother," I asked. "All I know is that she wore black and didn't remarry."

Marichal laughed. "She wore a black dress for 20 years. A family doctor told her, 'You can't wear that kind of clothes in this kind of weather.' So she went from black to gray and sometimes switched from gray to black and white! My mother was a hard-working lady. In that neighborhood a lot of people came to her for help. If anybody needed money for a prescription, they came to her."

Marichal's cell phone rang. He answered in English, switched to Spanish, hung up, then continued speaking to us in tempo, like a pitcher returning from a rain delay without losing his stuff. "There was food in my house, different people eating every day. She was that type of lady. She tied money in a bandana around her head so it would be available for people. We learned so much from her: to be responsible, disciplined. I'd tell my wife and daughter that I never heard that lady say a bad word. I'm against that. I don't like seeing people say a bad word, because I didn't hear that as a kid."

Marichal was so upbeat that he shrugged off a *New York Times* article warning tourists to the DR about muggers. "They don't do that with tourists because they know what would happen if they cut a tourist [and got caught]," he said, perhaps a bit optimistically. Marichal was slightly annoyed that he was assigned a security detail when he was Minister of Sport and is still driven around. Typically, though, he reversed course to find something positive. "I have a captain of police to drive me," he said, "and I'm going to try to make him a major so he can retire with more money." I learned later that Juan was also trying to get Dominican citizenship for two of his Haitian employees.

Juan looked back happily at the progress of Latinos, who now comprise about one-quarter of all major leaguers and own nine plaques in Cooperstown. He was also encouraged by sports academies in the Caribbean Basin that train major league prospects in useful subjects like English, nutrition, patience, discipline, and focus as well as baseball. "I've talked with Dominicans about helping U.S. kids," said Milton Jamail, a consultant for the Tampa Bay Rays and a widely published author on Latin American baseball. "I think they're better prepared [to make the transition to professional baseball]."

But because they start taking shots of vitamins and painkillers and ingest who knows what else as early as age 14—the better to build their bodies for impressive tryouts yielding valuable contracts when they turn 16—Dominicans test positive for banned substances more frequently than players from any other ethnic background. In 2009, the Dominican Summer League had baseball's highest rate of positive drug tests. The *buscónes* (independent agents) who scout players, handle them, and negotiate for them are not above exploiting players by skimming off half of their bonuses. Some of the young players are naïve enough to take drugs when *buscónes* offer them; others willingly take risks to enhance their professional prospects. The ready availability of performance-enhancing drugs across the counter in the DR only exacerbates the problem.

There are also issues of age and identity fraud among the prospects who pass themselves off as younger than they are. "You told [broadcaster] Bob Costas that Major League Baseball should get involved. Can you be more specific?" I asked Marichal.

"They should supervise more about the signings. When I was scouting for the A's, the biggest bonus I gave a kid was $25,000. Now a kid signed by the A's got $4.5 million. Some people here want kids to run fast, throw like Roberto Clemente, hit like Babe Ruth, and pitch like Sandy Koufax. That's why they make kids do those things [performance-enhancing drugs]. All of a sudden they use that stuff and they're different kinds of players, but they can get hurt."

Some American and Dominican players, in fact, have died from steroid abuse, and the early death of former National League MVP Ken Caminiti was linked to drugs. Baseball is moving toward a widened international draft that could reduce both signing contracts and the incentive to cheat. As the 2010 season began, MLB began testing for steroids and fingerprinting young players to guard against identity and age fraud. By season's end, only five of the top 40 Dominican prospects had signed with major league teams. Since a staggering 13 of them failed drug tests while only two of some 1,200 major leaguers tested positive, baseball officials say the problem will persist until Dominicans change their culture.

Before leaving, we got to see two impressive living rooms. Servants were packing away ornaments from the Christmas tree in one room, and impressive portraits of women by local artists lined another. Our time up, I executed a perfect handshake with the great man.

"I still watch games every day," Marichal said. "I'm a Giant. I want to say, like Tony Bennett, they will be my team forever. But these days, teams spend too much money on the wrong players. When the Giants lost to the Angels [in the 2002 World Series], that really hurt." But when the relatively inexpensive and immensely likable 2010 Giants won the World Series, Marichal was assuaged. Finally, he had a delicous memory to savor from his team's history. Actually, two of them.

Reviewing our conversations, I was struck by something. As much as Marichal loves talking baseball, I got the impression he loves nothing more than talking about a single game he played in. Bob Buege, the Milwaukee baseball historian, came upon Juan at a card show. "Do you remember the game in which you and Warren Spahn went 16 innings?" he asked.

"Are you kidding?" Juan said, smiling broadly. "I'm still sore!"

Juan and John

For years after he clubbed the Dodgers' John Roseboro over the head with a bat on August 22, 1965, Juan Marichal carried the shame with him. If there was a moment when he could bury the Roseboro episode for good, it came on Saturday night, December 5, 2009, at New York City's Public Theater. Marichal, his wife, Alma, and their daughter, Yvette, were in town for a special performance of *Juan and John*, a one-man show created, directed, and performed by the actor and performance artist Roger Guenveur Smith. Also in attendance were Roseboro's daughter Morgan Fouch-Roseboro, film director Spike Lee, and Dominican president Leonel Fernández Reyna, who grew up as a Yankees fan in the Bronx. (In his show, Smith fantasizes about the day young Fernández saw Marichal at Shea Stadium and asked for his autograph. Marichal: "What do you want to be when you grow up, kid?" Fernández: "President of the Dominican Republic." Marichal: "Well, first you need to get rid of that Yankees hat.")

Before the performance, Morgan, public relations director at Showtime Networks, hugged Marichal warmly and said, "I'm so happy to see you." That made sense, because the theme of the play is forgiveness and redemption. On this particular night, actor Smith begins in deference to his distinguished guests by saying, *"Yo tengo una guerra en mi cabeza,"* which he translates as, "I have a war in my head." That could refer to either principal or to Smith himself.

Sometimes playing Marichal, sometimes Roseboro ("straightforward, challenging, even a bit indignant," as the *New York Times* put it in a write-up), sometimes himself, with a movie screen projecting photographs and collages behind him, Smith progressed through the episode and its path to reconciliation, touching on his own life and subjects like the Watts riots, Lyndon Johnson's incursion into the Dominican Republic, and Vietnam. A tall, handsome, muscular, light-skinned African American, Smith uses his chiseled, pliant face to good effect in each role.

When he was a six-year-old Californian nicknamed Roger Dodger who idolized Roseboro at the time of the infamous fracas, Smith recalled that he reacted to the sight of a blood-soaked Roseboro leaving the field by torching his Marichal baseball card and chanting the familiar riot refrain, "Burn, baby burn!" As the play progresses, Smith—and Roseboro—forgive Marichal. In the Roseboro persona, Smith says, "You have to remember to forget." As the set fades to black, the audience sees a final image on the screen: a photograph of the fight signed by both Marichal and Roseboro that they used to take to memorabilia shows.

Smith spent several days in Los Angeles with the Roseboros and visited the Dominican Republic, where he interviewed Marichal and socialized with him over *Negronis*, a drink invented by Italian count Camillo Negroni that combines Campari, gin, and sweet vermouth and packs a wallop. Taking the stage after the special performance, Marichal first apologized to Smith's younger psyche saying, "All I can say is I apologize, and I hope you forgive me." He added, "I don't usually cry too often, but Roger, you made me cry tonight." Analyzing Smith's performance later, Marichal said, "I think he does me better than I do." Morgan Fouch-Roseboro said Smith "got" Roseboro as well, even though her father was "a hard man to imitate."

Commenting on the play, Dominican president Fernandez said, "It's an extraordinary story with historical background: baseball, race, the Dominican Republic, and Vietnam. And the photo we see at the end is extraordinary: an African American and a Latino who take a tragedy and come together, one to apologize and one to forgive. They had the same name, Juan in Spanish and John in English. They could just as easily have been John Marichal and Juan Roseboro."

"I discussed with Marichal his disappointment that Mays never checked on him in the Giants' clubhouse [after the fight], but he never suggested that he thought that it was because of Mays' ethnic allegiance that he tended solely to his friend Roseboro," Smith said. "Nor have I seen evidence that the incident was racially motivated, either in Roseboro's provocation or Marichal's retaliation. The enduring tragedy of the fight, in my estimation, is that it was intra-racial, waged between two men with, as the president noted, the same name, and the same pedigree. Marichal, the Alous [Manny, Felipe, Jesus], and [Orlando] Cepeda endured the same Jim Crow indignities as their black American teammates and opponents.

"It's the story of two men who embraced their conflict, and transcended it, with humor and grace. If only nations might do the same."

~ Chapter 9 ~

WINDING UP
WITH WARREN

Tom and Joe were great baseball fans. Every day they pored over the box scores. They went to 60 games a year. They even had a baseball bargain: if there's baseball in heaven, whoever dies first will return to tell his friend about it.

One night Tom passed away peacefully after watching his favorite team win a game. Days later, Joe was morosely wondering how he could enjoy baseball without his buddy when he heard a voice.

"Is that you, Tom?" he said.

"Of course it is, you shmo. And I have good news and bad news for you. Which would you like to hear first?"

"How about the good news?"

"Not only is there baseball in heaven, we get to play. All the time: day games, night games, even doubleheaders."

"Fantastic! And what's the bad news?"

"You're pitching tomorrow."

—Popular baseball joke

Warren Spahn's post July 2, 1963, life was every bit as interesting as Juan Marichal's. Spahn claimed he was never the same as a pitcher after the big game with Juan. Well, yes and no. Spahn strained a tendon in his left arm on his next start, July 7, but he finished the game and beat Houston 5–0 on five singles.

179

Then, increasingly anxious about his condition, he missed the next 17 days, including the Hall of Fame exhibition at Cooperstown.

Spahn had reason to feel insecure. In *Sandy Koufax: A Lefty's Legacy*, Jane Leavy spells out what passed for "sports medicine" at the time. Athletes were treated with Butazolidin, a dangerous drug mainly used on horses that was later taken off the market, and a balm called Capsolin that left the body almost literally on fire. They took cortisone shots to dull the pain more than treat it or Empirin with Codeine added to keep their stomachs from exploding. When they used ice at all, players stuck their arms in freezing buckets of the stuff because there were no ice packs. They had their swollen limbs drained. Arthroscopic surgery was still a decade away. Midway through the 1963 season, Warren Spahn just rested his weary arm.

Somehow he recovered. He returned on July 25, went eight innings, and lost to Lou Burdette and the Cardinals 3–1. Spahn hung on to finish the season at a jaw-dropping 23–7, completed a league-leading 22-of-33 starts, including seven in 27 days, beat the Dodgers four out of four times, and became the oldest pitcher to win 20 games in a season. He threw 200+ innings for a modern-record 17th straight season. *Time* called him, "The Grand Old Arm."

In September, Spahn was reduced to tears when 37,000 fans came to County Stadium to honor him before a Braves-Giants game. With baseball immortals Lefty Grove, Carl Hubbell, Johnny Sain, and Gabby Hartnett on hand, the Braves gave Spahn a planer and joiner for his workshop, the team gave his wife, LoRene, a silver jewel box, and they gave his son, Greg, a western saddle. "If they gave you the world with a string attached, it would be nothing [compared] to this," Spahn said.

Through 2009, only one player in the last quarter-century, Seattle's Jamie "The Ancient Mariner" Moyer in 2003, has had a 20-win season past the age of 40. None of this late-career, late-season magic surprised expert Spahn-watchers. He won 75 games after the age of 40. During his career he had a .544 April-July winning percentage, followed by a .679 percentage in August-October—a staggering .135 increase. In *Baseball Research Journal #32*, a publication of the Society for American Baseball Research (SABR), Eric Marshall White described Spahn as "the most fantastic finisher of them all."

Spahn was plenty spry off the mound, as well. "What would you throw this guy?" he'd ask younger players while they sat in the dugout, or, "Don't look up: what inning are we in and what's the score?" He practiced very tough love, indeed. "When we were on a bus or plane, Spahn popped me on the back of the head with his World Series ring," Bob Sadowski, a rookie pitcher on the 1963 team, said. "It hurt, but I didn't show it. A week later he did the same thing. I was a quiet rookie, and I think he wanted to see whether I would let people push me around. After the second time, Eddie Mathews told me, 'The next time he does that, tell him, "If you hit me again, I'm going to do what Bob Buhl did to you."'"

Mathews was referencing the time Spahn messed with Buhl, a strong, quiet guy who wanted to be left alone. Buhl stood up and advanced on Spahn, ready to pop him. Spahn left him alone after that. "So the next time he came down the aisle, I didn't wait for him to hit me," Sadowski said. "I told him, 'If you hit me again, I'm going to do what Bob Buhl did to you.' Spahn never bothered me again."

Late in August 1963 Spahn made his debut—and curtain call—as an actor when he played a Nazi sergeant on an episode of ABC-TV's *Combat* called "Glow Against the Sky." Wearing a full field pack and battered helmet and carrying a Schmietzer automatic submachine gun, he gave the command to a platoon "*Kommen sie*," and five soldiers popped over a hill. Though it took only two takes for Spahn to earn his $35 pay, the shoot ran late. Spahn left the set still wearing military uniform and makeup, arrived at Dodger Stadium to much ribbing from teammates, and beat L.A. 6–1.

* * *

Spahn was in great form during the off-season, and never so much as at the Buffalo Athletic Club's annual sports dinner in December. When Steve Weller of the *Evening News* asked him to account for his efficiency and durability, Spahn revealed as much about his pitching as he ever had:

"Maybe it's because the curve ball eluded me all my life.

"I never had a big curve. It was effective because it was quick, not because it had a big break. I can stand behind a pitcher on the mound and see the bend and drop when he throws a curve. Then I watch my own and it doesn't look like anybody else's. I had to work to make up for this.

"I've always fooled around trying to make the ball spin. This helped me come up with new pitches.

"When I started losing a little off my fastball it made my curve, which wasn't great to start with, look pretty mediocre, so I picked up the screwball because I needed a double-play pitch.

"When I first started throwing the screwball, I couldn't see any break on it at all. Now I probably throw it more than any other pitcher ever did.

"Pitching still comes down to just one thing—how hard you can throw. My best days are still those on which I can throw hardest. One pitch complements another, but everything relates to the fastball. Hitters are egotists. You throw one by them, they remember it, and they start timing everything by the good fast one.

"With experienced hitters you can't go directly to a weakness. You take a guy who doesn't like the low ball. You have to lead him to it, set him up with other pitches.

"I don't mean to sound like I figure I'm a genius, but I think you have to have something you believe in, something positive. Foresight is much better than hindsight. I'd rather look five minutes ahead at a hitter who might hurt me and figure out what I want to do, instead of looking back at what I might have done. If he hurts you anyway, then you chalk it up to experience."

Following the 1963 season, Spahn sought a $22,500 salary increase to $100,000 but settled for a pitchers' high at the time of $82,500.[34] Finally, in his 19th season, he had cleared the $1,000,000 mark in career earnings. With no plans to retire, Spahn hoped great things lay ahead. Alas, the wish was father only to the thought. Spahn suffered through a disappointing 6–13, 5.29 ERA season in 1964. He could no longer raise his right leg elegantly and straight, coming over the top like a wave crashing on the beach. Spahn had become a simulacrum of his former self. He said his timing and stride were off, and he was pitching defensively. Catcher Ed Bailey believed Spahn's knees—he would endure seven operations on them, his cartilage torn and ground from high kicks and hard landings—finally got to him. Hank Aaron said there was nothing on Spahn's pitches.

Things got ugly in Milwaukee, where Spahn was reduced to bullpen duty and informed of the change by a sportswriter. After Spahn was sold to the Mets in November, Braves manager Bobby Bragan suggested he had hung on out of stubbornness and salary and played 10–15 pounds overweight all year. "He's not thinking about the team," Bragan told the *Milwaukee Journal*'s Bob Wolf. "He's just worried about Warren Spahn—the great Spahnie."

Spahn had some choice words for Bragan and club officials in return. He couldn't understand why they traded Lou Burdette and threatened to waive Eddie Mathews. He might have added that ex-Braves were blossoming elsewhere. (Trivia question: Who was the only major league pitcher to win at least 20 games in both 1961 and 1962? Joey Jay, a former Brave now with the Reds.) Whether or not Bragan was on target, there was no question Spahn had soured.

With Spahn's career evidently ending, Branch Rickey, the Hall of Fame baseball executive, offered this valedictory: "He is the consummate artist—a student and a scholar but also a polished craftsman. No pitcher has ever made such magnificent use of his God-given equipment.... He has no equal."

But Spahn wasn't through. At 43, he felt he had something left. "Pitching isn't that demanding," he told a writer. "Pitching is more recuperating than stamina. If you can go out and pitch one strong inning, then you rest and go out and pitch another inning. It's all legs and arm. I don't have any trouble with either."

Joining the Mets in 1965, Spahn was reunited with Casey Stengel, who wanted to use him as both pitcher and pitching coach. Oh, did Spahn's presence produce quotes for the writers in spring training! Recruited to warm up Spahn, Yogi Berra said, "I don't know if we're the oldest battery, but we're certainly the ugliest." Stengel regretted his earlier putdown of Spahn. "I said 'no guts' to a kid who wound up a war hero and one of the best pitchers anybody ever saw. You can't say I don't miss 'em when I miss 'em."

On April 20, Spahn was leading the Dodgers in the ninth when Stengel asked pitching coach Spahn if he should remove pitcher Spahn. Spahn declined, survived a two-run rally, and won 3–2. "The Spahn saga soon became more than a personal drama," James A. Wechsler wrote in the *New York Post*. "Thousands of his generation, give or subtract a few years, quickly identified with him. If Warren Spahn could pitch regularly and well, every middle-aged tennis player, softball player, or activist of any sort would derive inspiration from the example."

Unfortunately, after that complete game, he quickly morphed into a competent pitcher for only four innings. Too preoccupied with his declining skills to do much coaching, Spahn began pressing, lost eight straight decisions trying to break a fifth-place tie with Kid Nichols for lifetime wins at 361, blew up at Stengel for ordering him to the bullpen, and was released in July with a

4–12 record and 4.36 ERA. "I'm afraid he's lost it," Stengel said, "because the pitchers are hitting him." Spahn was his usual witty and ironic self. "I pitched for Casey Stengel before and after he was a genius."

The Giants picked up Spahn for the $1 waiver price on July 19—why not finish at the scene of your greatest performance? Spahn and Marichal were finally together as teammates. They had so much in common: the high kick, the clownish smile, the near-death experiences, the celebrity for their combined masterpiece. They became fast friends, with Spahn inviting Juan's son, Juan Jr., to his Oklahoma ranch. (He had school obligations and had to decline.) A revered, downright gnostic presence in the clubhouse, Spahn was sought out for his wisdom and experience. Gaylord Perry called him "the leader of the pitchers."

Spahn was thrilled to see Willie Mays get his 500th homer. Greeting him in the dugout, Spahn said, "I threw you the first one, and now I've seen the 500th. Was it the same feeling?"

"Same feeling, same pitch," Mays said.

Spahn and Giants veterans constantly exchanged memories. According to Willie McCovey, "We used to kid each other about that pitch [that Willie McCovey either did or did not hit out in the ninth inning of the 1963 classic]. He'd say, 'It was 10' foul,' but he knew it wasn't."

Spahn's 3–4 record with a 3.39 ERA with the Giants wasn't bad. "He pitched well for six or seven innings in several games, and the Giants did not score many runs for him," the *San Francisco Chronicle* reported. Nonetheless, Spahn was released again at season's end and unclaimed with a combined 1965 record of 7–16. No one wanted a high-salaried 44-year-old.

Spahn's final two seasons concluded a 363–245 career—only Cy Young, Walter Johnson, Christy Mathewson, and Pete Alexander won more games— and dropped his winning percentage below .600 (.597) (as did his 1–6 record in duels with Marichal) while raising his ERA above 3.00 (3.09). Nonetheless, Spahn's career numbers are impressive, to say the least. The winningest lefty ever and the winningest pitcher of the lively-ball era, he won 20 or more games 13 times, a feat matched only by Christy Mathewson among modern-era pitchers, while leading the league in complete games nine times and wins eight times for major league records. He also led the league in strikeouts, shutouts, and innings pitched four times each, ERA three times, and winning percentage once. "No pitcher in modern times has been more consistent," Lawrence Ritter and Donald Honig wrote in *The Image of Their Greatness: An Illustrated History of Baseball from 1900 to the Present.*

Few have been more quotable, either. "The difference between winning 19 and winning 20 for a pitcher is bigger than anyone out of baseball realizes," Spahn said to Bob Ajemian in *My Greatest Day in Baseball.* "It's the same for hitters. Someone who hits .300 looks back on the guy who batted .295 and says, 'Tough luck, buddy.'"

He continued, "Twenty games is the magic figure for pitchers; .300 is the magic figure for batters. It pays off in salary and reputation. And those are the two things that keep a ballplayer in business."

Spahn was an All-Star 14 times, the most of any pitcher in the twentieth century. He and Roger Clemens took ERA titles in three different decades. For a guy without overpowering speed, Spahn won four strikeout titles from 1949 to 1952 and accumulated 2,583 altogether (third most at the time of his retirement). He had 363 hits to go with his 363 wins, homered in a pitchers' record 17 straight seasons, and finished with 35 dingers, the most of any National League pitcher. (The esteemed *Boston Globe* columnist Harold Kaese wrote that Spahn won 40 games with his bat.) He completed 57.4 percent of his starts, the highest total since 1920. He started more double plays (82) than any pitcher but Phil Niekro (83). He also had one of the greatest pickoff moves of all time.

Spahn was named outstanding pitcher of the fifties in voting by a panel of 250 U.S. sportswriters, with Willie Mays the top hitter-fielder.[35] In a recent rating, the respected historian/mathematician Bill James ranked Spahn the fifth best pitcher in baseball history. Some lesser-known scribes rank him first. Yet his name doesn't come tripping off the lips of most baseball fans. Why? To begin with, he spent most of his career away from major media in Milwaukee. In addition, Spahn was consistent more than spectacular. He wore number 21, pitched in 21 seasons, and had eight 21-win years. He had a 3.05 ERA in the World Series (in which two of his four wins went into extra innings) and 3.21 in All-Star Games. During 1947–63, he started between 32 and 39 games every season. The guy was a metronome—steady, consistent, and reliable, but too often taken for granted and filed away. His kind of performance doesn't attract the attention that stunning success or headline failure do.

Naysayers have pointed out that Spahn pitched for generally good teams, with his home games in pitchers' parks—the same charge levied against

Marichal. That, again, ignores how well he did on the road. Spahn was 196–119 with a 2.73 ERA at home, and 167–126 with a 3.49 ERA on the road. A considerable difference, to be sure, but note those +41 wins in away games. Most pitchers would die for such numbers in hostile ballparks. "The greatest of modern pitchers, Warren Spahn, should have been a hitter," the redoubtable Kaese wrote. "He would have gained more recognition."

Beyond wins, all manner of statistical machination is used to determine pitching excellence these days. I wrote a biography of Lefty Grove (300–141) in 2000 and named him baseball's greatest pitcher. In that instance, dominance was the determining criterion. Grove's nine ERA titles and five winning-percentage crowns were unmatched at the time, and his .680 career win percentage was best among all 300-game winners. If Spahn were alive to see some of the more complicated systems in use today, he'd probably shrug and say, "I may not have been the best pitcher of the lively-ball era, just the winningest."

He was certainly the most enduring. Spahn's longevity fascinates baseball historians. He was baseball's Old Man River. Between the ages of 36 and 40, he topped or shared the league lead in wins every year while throwing no-hitters at ages 39 and 40. Explaining his durability, the usually loquacious Spahn needed just one word: mechanics. "You've got to be a student of pitching," he stated. "The way I threw, I never tried to put too much strain on my left arm." At a baseball writers' dinner, he elaborated, "I kept my weight back and transferred it from the back leg to the front leg."

Certainly, his silky-smooth delivery helped. He also benefited from revolutionary training habits. In his time pitchers used spring training to get in shape and babied their arms between starts. Spahn headed south with his body in tip-top condition, having spent the winters lifting 50-pound bags of corn and 68-pound bales of hay, feeding cattle, mending fences, riding horses, hunting, and fishing. He went to work on his arms by stretching himself out while hanging from the dugout. "I see this guy around second base taking a full windup and throwing to the plate as hard as he can," Chuck Dressen, the old Braves manager, said. "I think it's some dumb rookie. I start trotting out there to give him a lecture. Then I see it's the old guy. I go back to the bench flabbergasted."

"I always threw a lot because I figured that was the best way to keep my arm strong," Spahn told a *Wall Street Journal* interviewer. "Runners run a lot, don't they? Between starts, I'd take fly balls with the outfielders in practice and make the long throw in. That was my version of distance work." Spahn told author Roger Kahn his system was "throw and throw" rather than "lift and run."

When no one bid on his services after the 1965 season, Spahn said, "I didn't retire from baseball. Baseball retired me." In 1966, the Mexico City Tigers invited Spahn to spend four weeks tutoring their pitchers, and the general manager even got him to take a turn on the mound. "I can see the headlines now," Spahn yelled when a photographer shot him and his new teammates. "Spahn broke, pitching in Mexico." He had a cattle ranch in Oklahoma, several homes in Florida, and an interest in a Holiday Inn, but it was a good line.

In his signature stroll, Spahn duckwalked to the mound, shoulders moving from one side to another, at Mexico City's Social Security Baseball Park to face the visiting Jalisco *Charros* (Mexican Cowboys). The leadoff hitter, Francisco Garcia, grounded to third on the first pitch. "Well, I didn't want to wait for Warren Spahn's screwball and look foolish," he said told *Sports Illustrated–*assigned writer Myron Cope through an interpreter. Elrod Hendricks, an import from the Virgin Islands, singled, and when Spahn bounced a pitch in the dirt, a shrill whistle from the contemptuous fans emanated from the stands. After yielding two runs in the inning, Spahn retired to a dugout filled with kids, strangers, and writers as well as ballplayers, and he tried to tell his young catcher he couldn't see the finger counts he was flashing. But the fans were kinder after Spahn got through five innings of a no-decision on the same guile he had demonstrated over 21 seasons, this time mixing sidearm and even submarine deliveries into his repertoire.

When Spahn became manager of the Tulsa Oilers and pitched three times in 1967, people got the mistaken impression that he was staging a comeback. Actually, he had demonstrated technique to the Mexican team he was coaching, and then tried to improve attendance for an American team he was managing. At that time, a player had to be fully retired from professional baseball for five years before he became eligible of the Hall of Fame. Since Spahn had pitched minor league games in 1966 and 1967, his election was delayed two years. "It will be a great honor if I'm voted in," he said, "but it's something a player should never expect will happen."

When his name appeared on the ballot for the first time in 1973, he was elected easily, with 316 of a possible 380 votes, qualifying with more than the required 75 percent of the vote (83 percent). Only five players had preceded him as first-ballot electees, not counting the five original 1936 members, the special vote for Lou Gehrig (1939), or players like Josh Gibson of the Negro Leagues who were elected once the doors opened to them. Spahn was admitted along with posthumous induction for his son Greg's favorite player, Roberto Clemente. (Both Spahn and Marichal got the necessary votes seven years after their major league careers ended and were inducted in the eighth year.)

Spahn, 52 at the time, was giving his acceptance speech on August 6, 1973, when a figure slumped over in the audience 20' away. "It's my brother-in-law!" Spahn exclaimed, referring to his sister Gertrude's husband, Lee Curran. A good soldier to the end, Spahn tried to go to Curran's aid but was dissuaded by medical personnel. Curran was taken to Mary Imogene Bassett Hospital with a heart seizure and pronounced in satisfactory condition. Spahn eventually continued his address and thanked his wife, son, and father, all of whom remained at the ceremony.

* * *

At McGill's, a popular restaurant in Tulsa, Oklahoma, Greg Spahn sits over his vodka and steak. With him are elementary school teacher LuAnn Cannon and two SABR members—Sheila Parr, a diamond broker and award-winning artist, and her husband Royse "Crash" Parr, a retired lawyer who once dreamed he was sliding into first and awoke having crashed into a nightstand.

The younger Spahn, born a day before the opening game of the 1948 World Series, looks nothing like his father. Greg is hefty and handsome, with a button nose, a dimpled face, and graying hair that's just starting to thin out. Dressed on this day in slacks and a short-sleeved red shirt despite the winter weather, he sports a 1957 World Series championship ring and a 1958 National League championship ring.

An only child, Greg speaks worshipfully of his parents. His half-Cherokee mother LoRene, a secretary to an oil executive when she met Warren, got her husband to give up the Buffalo winters and settle in Hartshorne, Oklahoma, where he grew rich running a 2,000-acre cattle ranch and leasing some of his land for gas wells. "My mother talked us into buying four beachfront properties in Florida," Greg said. "They're worth $8 million now."

LoRene's baseball sense was almost as sharp as her business acumen. Beginning as a ballpark neophyte, she sat in the press box learning from the writers to keep score and eventually gave her husband pitching and managing advice. "She was prim and proper," Greg said, "but she always sat on the edge of her seat at the park. She had hypertension, which Dad's career didn't help." LoRene had a stroke at age 56, and for the next year and five days of her life, Warren helped care for her at home, sometimes alone when the nurse didn't show up. She died in 1978. "He was with her every day—I thought I'd lose him as well as her," Greg said.

In a famous photo, a nine-year-old Greg, surrounded by reporters, looks up admiringly at his father after a World Series win. "He and I were as close as any father and son in baseball," said Greg, who loved his time as a clubhouse assistant and batboy for the Braves. "His father pushed him, and he never did that with me."

When Greg was 10, Cleon Walfoort of the *Milwaukee Journal* wrote of him, "Greg is a bright, active, and surprisingly unspoiled boy, considering that he has a famous father and, at the moment, a palomino pony, a French poodle, a hot rod car that can make 20 miles an hour since Warren assembled it in his workshop, a gasoline scooter, a .22 rifle, and fishing tackle among other things." Later when Greg, a good-hitting third baseman and outfielder who suffered three shoulder separations, elected to quit baseball at the University of Oklahoma rather than submit to an operation that would have slit him across his chest, Warren didn't object.

"He and my mom would go through the back roads and give toys they'd bought to needy children," Greg remembered. "Sometimes they'd take most of the toys that I wasn't using and give them away. I remember being mad about that."

But he got to keep the important things. A pitching rubber from Milwaukee's defunct County Stadium sits in Greg's Broken Arrow, Oklahoma, home with a painting of Babe Ruth, crossed swords that West Point sent his father, a 60-inch projection TV, hunting trophies, and a loaded electric golf cart. Greg has the air of a man who has lived long and lived well. Through his dad, Greg got to golf with famous athletes and celebrities; he and Warren were scheduled to meet President John F. Kennedy, but the president was assassinated two weeks before their date.

Not everyone was charmed by Warren. "I spent half my life being embarrassed," Greg said, smiling into his vodka. "Dad would say whatever came into his mind, and he liked to be outrageous. At one card show, he was signing something for a gorgeous blonde when he noticed an ugly guy with a scarred face standing behind her. 'Who's that guy?' he asked. 'That's my husband,' the woman said. 'You can do better than that,' my dad said."

* * *

Spahn kept making news in and out of baseball. In 1976, the United States Supreme Court voided a lower court's $10,000 damages award against a man who wrote an unauthorized biography of Spahn. As long as the book contained no reckless disregard for truth and was in the public interest, the judges ruled that the author was within his rights and that a state's right-to-privacy laws weren't violated. The ruling effectively voided similar suits by Hank Aaron, Don Drysdale, and Eddie Mathews. "The popular biography enterprise was given a big boost when writers were freed to cover their subjects without obtaining approval," David Quentin Voigt wrote in *American Baseball: From Postwar Expansion to the Electronic Age.*

Spahn's baseball life played out amid tension between his extraordinary knowledge and blunt honesty. Spahn beat out 24 other candidates and took over a poor Tulsa team in 1967, and a year later he managed it to the Pacific Coast League title, all the while offering candid assessments of his players to the media. He was nice to kids but yelled back at hecklers. When he refused a promotion to the Cardinals as pitching coach—it was big league manager or bust for him at the time—his days with the St. Louis organization were numbered. He was fired in 1971 after five seasons, one championship, and two second-place finishes at Tulsa.

Unsatisfied with his life on the ranch and at his seaside cottage on Florida's Anna Maria Island, Spahn relented and coached Cleveland pitchers for two miserable years in 1972–73. "Spahnie and I had been teammates, and we became close friends when he was managing in Tulsa and I was with Wichita," said Ken Aspromonte, the Indians manager at the time. "When I became manager of the Indians, I decided he could help a major league club."

"He was a great pitching coach, fun to be around," said Gaylord Perry, the Hall of Fame spitballer reunited with his old friend. "He didn't fool around and didn't chew you out. You knew where you stood and what the game plan was."

Alas, Spahn had trouble relating to younger players and was fired in a general housecleaning. "Superstars expect young players to be as good as they were," a chastened Aspromonte said. "He had some problems. He was an old blue-collar guy who expected other guys to be the same. He was a finesse pitcher, but the young guys couldn't adjust. He didn't have the patience."

That said, who would have been patient with the 1972–73 Indians, one of baseball's most bedraggled franchises? "They didn't keep people too long," Perry said. "They traded [Graig] Nettles and [Chris] Chambliss, and in 1975 they got rid of the whole rotation! You were an old-timer if you were there three years." The front office reportedly lent a deaf ear to Spahn's pleas to spend more money for better pitchers. Old Municipal Stadium was freezing in the spring and fall. He was better off elsewhere.

Spahn's final aspiration, managing in the majors, was not to be. Former pitchers are more suspect as skippers than everyday players because they compete only once every five games as starters and in fewer than half the games as relievers. "How can they disqualify a man as a major league manager simply on the grounds he was a pitcher?" Spahn asked UPI's Milt Richman.

"I think it's perfectly ridiculous. What about Freddie Hutchinson? Did being a pitcher detract at all from his efficiency as a manager? How about Bob Lemon? Or Ted Lyons?"

Spahn also may have been disqualified from the managing fraternity because he spoke his mind. He wasn't exactly plugged in to the late-seventies zeitgeist. In 1973–78, he worked part-time in Japan instructing professional pitchers and youth leagues. While helping the '74 Hiroshima Carp go from sixth place to a championship, he praised Japanese players ("They have to learn to win without brute strength," and, "Their players' concentration and dedication is much better.") while blasting their long-haired brethren in the U.S. He said that official scorers should be on field level and hired like umpires because their jobs aren't "a popularity contest." You'd "need binoculars" to see players on the mammoth cookie-cutter ballparks in Cincinnati, Philadelphia, and Pittsburgh. "You can't lose if you have good defense, and 95 percent of defense is in the pitching." His opinion of the designated hitter rule was succinct and devastating: "I think pitchers should be athletes."

LoRene's declining health took a big toll on Spahn that he relieved by taking a job coaching minor league pitchers for the Angels in 1979–81. "It hit me hard," Spahn told Thomas Boswell of the *Washington Post* in 1981. "I was drinking too much. I didn't give a damn about anything. Then this job with the Angels came along. Best thing that ever happened to me—working with young people." At a July stop in Buffalo with the Angels' Holyoke, Massachusetts, farm team, Spahn signed autographs for large crowds of well-wishers and offered his opinion of the ongoing players' strike.

"The player union is just like all unions," he was quoted as saying in the Buffalo *Courier-Express*. "It does a lot of good for the working guy, but it also has some evils. What we have now is a case of people wanting more and more. I feel the players are overstepping their bounds.

"When you have labor asking management to open its books and show how much money it has made, that's just going too far."

Pete Weber, former radio voice of the Buffalo Bisons, said, "He was happy to sit there and talk as long as people would listen. He was always correcting the record and wasn't afraid to make himself look bad. He called himself stupid for throwing a curve high in the zone for Willie Mays' first hit. He probably remembered every pitch he ever threw. It was just plain fun listening to him. I was glad to be part of King Warren's court."

Tired of riding "funny little airplanes," Spahn left baseball employment after the 1981 season for fund-raising and public relations at several organizations and companies, including Borden's. In 1982, he and other former All-Stars arrived in Washington, D.C., for the inaugural Cracker Jack Old-Timers Baseball Classic, a benefit game for the Association of Retired Ball Players of America. At a pregame lunch hosted by Tip O'Neill, Spahn said, "Mr. Speaker, baseball is a game of failure. Even the best batters fail about 65 percent of the time. The two Hall of Fame pitchers here today"—Spahn with 245 losses and Bob Gibson with 174—"lost more games than a team plays in an entire season. I just hope you fellows in Congress have more success than baseball players have."

As if to prove his point, Spahn gave up a 250' homer at RFK Stadium to Luke Appling and chased him around the bases, whacking him on the head with his glove to much merriment all around. The scene became such a popular tableau that it attracted more *alter kakers* to Old-Timers' Games and made the events downright fashionable. In fact, it is no exaggeration to say that there was a positive residual effect on card and memorabilia shows, speeches, celebrity golf tournaments, and other chances for ballplayers to relive their glory days. "The older they are, the better they were when they were young," said the old pitcher and author Jim Bouton.

A year later, in the second Old-Timers Classic, Spahn gave up a homer to Al Kaline. "He threw me nothing but screwballs," Kaline said, "but he tried to get a fastball by me." In the summer of 1986, Roger Angell ran into Spahn at an Old-Timers' Game in Fenway Park. The next spring, Angell wrote in *The New Yorker*, "Spahn, a leathery, wiry, infallibly cheerful man, was sitting with some of the Texas Rangers (they would play the Bosox that afternoon, once the exhibition innings were over), and in no time he had begun teaching his famous sinker-screwball delivery to another left-hander—the veteran Mickey Mahler, who was trying to stick with the Rangers as a middle-innings relief man.

"'Look, it's easy,' Spahnie said. 'You just do this.' His left thumb and forefinger were making a circle, with the three other fingers pointing up, exactly as if he were flashing the 'Okay' signal to someone nearby. The ball was tucked comfortably up against the circle, without being held by it, and the other fingers stayed up and apart, keeping only a loose grip on the pill. Thrown that way, he said, the ball departed naturally off the inside, or little-finger side, of the middle finger, and would then sink and break left as it crossed the plate. 'There's nothing to it,' he said optimistically. 'Just let her go, and remember to keep your hand up so it stays inside your elbow. Throw it like that, and you turn it over naturally—a nice, easy movement, and the arm follows through on the same track.' He made the motion a few times, still sitting down, and it certainly *looked* easy—easy but impossible.

"Spahn went off to join some other uniformed geezers, and I asked Mahler if he intended to work on the pitch now that he'd had it from the Master.

"'Oh, I don't think so,' he said. 'I'm trying to learn the screwball from our pitching coach, and this would mess me up for sure.' He seemed uncomfortable, and after a couple of minutes he told me that a little earlier he and Spahn had been standing near the stands and some kids there had asked him, Mickey Mahler, for his autograph. 'They asked me—not Warren Spahn,' he said. 'Can you *believe* that?' He was embarrassed."

In May 1987 baseball writer (*A Player for a Moment*) and Civil War novelist (*Seen the Glory*) John Hough Jr. saw Spahn at a Mets–Red Sox exhibition in Shea Stadium. "He is raw-boned and sunfried as an old wrangler," Hough wrote, "and he watches the game with a critical squint, pulling on a cigarette and blowing smoke through his crooked nose."

Spahn eyed Hough coldly, as if he were a pinch-hitter, Hough wrote. Eventually, the old guy opened up. "Your Braves repeated [as pennant winners]," Hough said.

"Yeah, and we would have won four in a row, not just two," Spahn said. "In '56 we had a one-game lead over Brooklyn going into the final weekend. We played the Cardinals three games, and they beat us two out of three. They played way over their heads. In '59 we finished in a tie with the Dodgers. We lost the playoff when Mantilla booted the ground ball."

Teams don't repeat any more, he told Hough, because they get complacent. "We were a hell of a ball club. Talk about pride. Listen, we didn't need management to get on us when we were goin' bad. We got on each other. We chewed each other out. Red Schoendienst wouldn't *let* us lose. 'Make 'em hit the ball to me,' he used to say. 'Make 'em hit it to me.' That was the attitude."

Spahn's greatest frustration was his 24–37 record against the Dodgers, who always seemed to be loaded with veterans, a right-handed hitting lineup and a home field with a short left-field porch. (He was better than .500 against every other team except the Braves; he went 0–2 against the Braves after moving on in 1965.) His favorite opponent was Stan Musial, who might easily have been mistaken for Spahn's cousin with roughly the same height, weight, and nose shape. From the first time they faced each other, on June 17, 1946, to the last, on September 13, 1963, Musial batted .314 with 17 homers in what must be considered a standoff. Actually, Musial insisted, "Most of those long balls came early in both our careers when he could really throw hard and I had quicker reflexes and he'd try to buzz one by me." "This season will be different from all others I've spent in the big leagues," Spahn said in 1964. "Stan Musial will no longer be there. He enriched the game with his incomparable skill.... Once Musial timed your fastball, your infielders were in jeopardy." Musial said of Spahn, "Facing Warren was the greatest challenge I knew because this man was a pitching scientist, an artist with imagination." On another occasion, Musial said, "I don't think Spahn will ever get into the Hall of Fame. He'll never stop pitching."

In 1989, Spahn showed Bob Oates of the *Los Angeles Times* around his spread in Hartshorne, Oklahoma. "The ranch now rolls for three and a half miles along a graveled old wagon trail—grandly renamed Savage Highway— and extends picturesquely into the distant foothills," Oates wrote. "Today, a foreman is responsible for Spahn's 500 cows.

"His rambling ranch house has every modern convenience, including an indoor swimming pool. The largest oil painting in the living room is an artist's interpretation of Milwaukee's County Stadium, where he won so many of his 363 games."

The house also had a 4½-acre pond stocked with largemouth bass, catfish, crappies, and sunfish, a 25' power boat, and a Cadillac in the garage. Asked about his longevity, Spahn told Oates that pitchers should avoid hyper-extending their elbows and relying too much on speed guns. In addition to a bent elbow, he said to keep the elbow in front of the body and above the shoulder while using the other arm's leverage to throw down on the ball, whiplike. It was like Picasso teaching a student how to paint.

If Spahn's enthusiasm and ever-inventive baseball mind wowed visitors to the Diamond Star Ranch, they were equally staggered by the business sense of this high school dropout. Spahn had incorporated the ranch, including an oil well generating $500 a month. He had other oil well investments, three rental houses in Florida, and Warren Spahn Enterprises, which enabled him to collect $2,000 for a day signing autographs and talking baseball with slack-jawed wannabees. In addition to his promotional work for Borden's, he was representing AT&T and the Equitable Assurance Co. Spahn showed up at the Dodgers' Fantasy Camp, made appearances at sporting events, and advised the commissioner on youth projects. A typical week might find him in Hawaii, all expenses paid, playing in a charity golf tournament. Son Greg, an honors graduate from Oklahoma, was his No. 1 business partner.

The world of economic opportunity had opened for former greats. "They [modern players] are entitled to it [large salaries], and I am all for it," Hall of Fame pitcher Bob Feller said. "In fact, it's a changing world for old-timers, too. I make more money now traveling around the country and appearing at card shows with hobby groups than I ever did as a player."

Many former athletes have sad lives after sports. Nothing they do will recapture the competition and camaraderie, except maybe recalling them. "There's a feeling of emptiness at first, as though you don't exist anymore," Spahn told David Lamb of the *Los Angeles Times*. "You think no one gives a damn about you. I was never divorced, but it must be something like that. You just have to go out and build a new life for yourself. Some athletes can never handle it, and that leaves them bitter. Well, I decided that I was going to be productive until I die. I know I'd be lost if I ever retired and was out of the mainstream."

He went on: "I guess the secret is making the most of wherever you're at in life. Some people look in the mirror and they're unhappy. What do I see? Well, I see someone with gray hair who's growing old, and you know what? It makes me feel good, sort of content. I like where I've been and where I'm at. Baseball and the military did that for me. They gave me everything."

In 1990, Spahn, 69, made his last pitching appearance in Buffalo, relieving Sandy Koufax and getting credit for a 3–0 win in the National Old-Timers Classic before 17,967 fans at Pilot Field. The next year he was inducted in the first class of the Buffalo Baseball Hall of Fame. "It means very much to me, being honored by my hometown," he said. It meant as much that his hometown inducted a guy who had basically put Buffalo in his rearview mirror.

"Warren would come back home every year or so and meet with his family and friends," said his cousin, Ken Spahn. "There was never any big hoopla about his visits until he came back for the old-timers baseball games with the Bisons. Warren was a hell raiser who loved to drink with his friends.

"Warren's wife LoRene took care of the money in the family, and that's probably why he never donated any back to anyplace in Buffalo."

Still, people were kind to Spahn in his retirement. In 1991, *Sports Illustrated* selected him as the designated left-handed pitcher in its all-time All-Star team. But the years weren't kind to Spahn's body, and they eventually took a toll on his spirit. His knees appeared to have been operated on by sewing machines. He fell off a gurney and broke some ribs (Greg Spahn settled a lawsuit with the hospital in 2006). He had a broken hip and an aneurysm. He also caught pneumonia.

Spahn could be aloof and ornery at annual meetings of the Boston Braves Historical Association—Warren being Warren, the organizers shrugged, happy to have him there at all. On October 16, 1994, Spahn was inducted into the Boston Braves Hall of Fame at the third annual reunion of the BBHA. For the last time together, he and fellow Braves inductee Johnny Sain visited Braves Field (now Boston University's Nickerson Field and almost unrecognizable from its former self) and the memories of 1948. Addressing a gathering of several hundred fans, Spahn remarked that with that kind of attendance, the Braves might still be playing in Boston. When the pair returned again four years later for a dinner to mark the 50th anniversary of Boston's last NL championship, an even bigger crowd came out—and Spahn drew laughs yet again with the same comment.

"[The late broadcaster] Ken Coleman and I were in a lounge with Spahn, Williams, and Feller," recalled Art Johnson, an old Braves pitcher from the forties. "A fellow asked for an autograph. 'Why don't you sit down and talk to us?' Warren said. Two and a half hours later, the man was sitting there with his mouth open."

Rich Westcott, a dogged interviewer of ex-players, was turned down by Spahn because he was out of baseball at the time and wanted to preserve his privacy. But five years later, Westcott got his chance.

"Spahn was signing autographs at a memorabilia show in Ocean City, New Jersey," Westcott wrote in a retrospective of ballplayer interviews he'd done. "Now back in baseball—and hence in the public eye—he easily agreed to an interview. The only stipulations were that I had to wait until he was finished at the show, then bring a six-pack back to his hotel room.

"I met both requests. And the interview began at about 10:00 PM. Spahn was magnificent. He answered every question thoroughly and with the utmost articulation. Reporters aren't supposed to feel this way, but I was thoroughly enchanted.

"Spahn had told me earlier that he was going to be picked up at 5:30 AM and driven to Philadelphia where he would catch a 7:00 AM flight home to Oklahoma. Then he had a 1:00 PM tee time for golf with friends.

"The interview progressed into the wee hours of the morning, Spahn meticulously answering every question, sometimes even rising to demonstrate a point he was trying to make. When I finally looked at my watch, it read 2:30 AM. 'Holly crap, Warren,' I said (or something like that). 'You have to leave in a couple of hours, and I have to drive back to Philly.' Worse yet, my dear wife, Lois, out of the goodness of her heart, had ridden to the shore with me and was still waiting in the car. She had plenty to read and some knitting to do, but her willingness to keep me company had now exceeded all bounds of marital bliss.

"So Spahn and I parted company. When I got to my car, Lois, being the devoted and exceptionally good-natured wife she is, said nary an unkind word. We drove home in good spirits, joyously saluting one of the greatest nights I ever had as a writer."

Westcott's interview appeared in his book, *Splendor on the Diamond.* When people got Spahn talking about baseball, they never forgot the experience. Tom Glavine, another lefty who won 300 games pitching mostly with the Braves, sat next to Spahn at a baseball dinner and left shaking his head in appreciation. "Just talking with him, you can feel the passion he had for pitching and how much he loved to take the ball and win a ballgame for his team," Glavine told the *Boston Globe*'s Nick Cafardo.

Every year, Spahn would arrive at Cooperstown's induction weekend on a Friday and stay until Tuesday. Fans who recognized him would invariably say one of two things: "Spahn, Sain and pray for rain," (to his dismay) or, "That was some game you and Marichal pitched!" (to his delight). With a longneck beer in hand, he would be surrounded by veterans like Aaron, Musial, Mays, and Yogi Berra, not to mention younger immortals like Johnny Bench and Ferguson Jenkins, all of them listening intently.

Neal Mackertich, a former pro tennis player and now a systems engineering fellow at Raytheon, said, "I was fortunate to have met Warren Spahn on a couple of different occasions while attending the inductions at Cooperstown, and he is one of my all-time favorites. I can still picture him with a cigarette precariously hanging from his lower lip, passionately explaining why the Braves moved from Milwaukee to Atlanta ('The fix was in!') and lamenting that his diner back in Boston had just really started to get rolling when the team left the city. I was also fortunate to chat with Juan Marichal on that same day at Cooperstown about his duel with Spahn. Marichal, ever the gentleman, was effusive in his praise of Spahn and humble about his own performance. Nearby, Harmon Killebrew and Rollie Fingers were signing autographs and couldn't wait to stop what they were doing to get in on the conversation and ask questions themselves."

Spahn had been a world-class practical joker in the majors, and his brand of humor occasionally surfaced. A story told by Crash Parr is instructive. One day a man and his son appeared at Spahn's door. "We'd like your autograph," the man said.

"I'm not Warren Spahn," Spahn said. "He lives next door."

"But they told me next door you lived here!" the man pleaded.

In 1999, the Oklahoma Sports Museum established a Warren Spahn Award to honor the majors' best left-handed pitcher. Why name it after Spahn rather than Lefty Grove, Sandy Koufax, Steve Carlton, Carl Hubbell, or Eddie Plank? Simple—Spahn won the most games.

Once, after presenting the award to Randy Johnson, Spahn asked him, "What kind of year did you have?"

Johnson replied, "Oh, I threw 270 innings and had 12 complete games."

"That's a nice year, Randy, but I did that every year," said Spahn, who averaged 269 innings and 20 complete games in his 19 full seasons.

On October 24, 1999, Koufax escorted a hobbling Spahn over the dugout steps and onto the grass of Atlanta's Turner Field, where both men were honored among the 100 players selected by an expert panel to the All-Century Team. Spahn's name was originally omitted, an oversight that so enraged Koufax he threatened to boycott the ceremony. A panel, hastily assembled, corrected the oversight. The greatest lefty ever? Unequivocally Spahn, said Koufax, because "he pitched the whole damn century."

An honored guest when the Milwaukee Brewers closed County Stadium on September 28, 2000, Spahn said, "This has been a part of my life. I came here as a young man, and I'm leaving here as an old man." Though his health was slipping away and he now resembled less a larger-than-life figure than a shriveled old timer, Spahn and Hank Aaron threw out first balls at the 2002 All-Star Game in Milwaukee. On August 8, 2003, the Braves unveiled Native American sculptor Shan Gray's 9' bronze statue of Spahn kicking high at the Osage Tribal Museum in Pawhuska, Oklahoma. Four days later it was installed outside of Turner Stadium in Atlanta. (Another one stands in the Oklahoma Sports Hall of Fame in Oklahoma City.) Ailing with a broken leg, four broken ribs from a fall, a punctured lung, internal bleeding, and fluid buildup in his lungs from the aneurysm, Spahn, 82, was wheeled in to see the work. He hadn't lost his sense of humor. "That nose is a little too big," he said. Considering the timing, he added, "The only scary thing I have is the statue is going to be here when I leave. That disserves me. Either the statue goes with me, or I'm going to stay with the statue." Viewing the whole sculpture, he added, "I took great pride in mooning people. That's the reason I developed that leg kick."

It was one of the last and best memories of Spahn: kicking and joking. He died on November 24, 2003, and his son was immediately comforted by a leading Oklahoma church figure, Mouzon Biggs Jr.

"Warren Spahn was a baseball hero of Mouzon's dad, who lives in Carthage, Texas," Crash Parr explained. "Both served in the Army in Europe during World War II. For a birthday present to his dad about 20 years ago, Mouzon went to Warren Spahn's home with three baseballs that were then autographed by Spahn for his dad and Mouzon's two sons. Greg Spahn told us that when Warren was dying, he thought of Mouzon (whose service was on TV live in Tulsa every Sunday morning at 11 AM) and his Boston Avenue United Methodist Church. Greg telephoned the church, and Mouzon arrived at the home within minutes and just before the ambulance arrived. Mouzon recalled that Spahn was dead but sitting up in a chair."

Though he was a non-member, Spahn's funeral was celebrated in style at Boston Avenue Church, an art-deco, limestone building with a terra-cotta motif and Gaudi-esque spires that make it Oklahoma's most photographed building and a designated national historic landmark. A prominent figure in the National Conference of Christians and Jews, Biggs presided. Gary Caruso, the editor of the Braves' fan magazine *Chop Talk* and the prime force raising $95,000 to finance the statue, gave the eulogy. Calling Spahn "the most majestic of all pitchers," "a warrior's warrior," and "the Rembrandt of pitching," Caruso said, "Warren Spahn was the Wyatt Earp of the National League. No one maintained law and order against the larger-than-life hitters of baseball's grandest era better or longer than the man we are here today to remember."

Encomiums poured in. "The likes of Warren Spahn will not come down this road any time soon," Commissioner Bud Selig said. "For the years I was watching him, Koufax was tops," said Johnny Podres, pitching hero of the 1955 World Series and later a pitching coach. "But for the long haul, year-after-year performance, Warren Spahn was the best I ever saw. He was just a master of his trade. I couldn't take my eyes off him. Watching him was an education." Hank Aaron, Spahn's teammate from 1954 to 1964 and one of the few Braves at the service, said, "He could be winning a game 1–0 or 2–0, and if he gave up one run you'd think he had lost the World Series. That kind of rubbed off on everybody." Of his "tremendous friend," Aaron added, "I don't know what I would've done if I hadn't been able to come up in the time I came up. Because back then, you traveled on the train and you sat in a booth and you could listen to him talk. Everything he talked about as a pitcher I listened to, and I learned an awful lot."

"He would talk, and then he would produce," Spahn's old shortstop Johnny Logan said. "Everybody said, 'Oh, we gotta listen to this guy,'" Logan went on enthusiastically, "Warren was like a professor, a specialist. Every young pitcher adored him. He advised those young kids. He told them that speed isn't everything, that it's control and knowing the weaknesses of the hitters." Spahn's granddaughter, Niki Spahn, said, "He was a hard-headed, hard-nosed, loving man. He was the strongest man I ever met."

Even so, Spahn had a much more understated sendoff than baseball would give Joe DiMaggio or Ted Williams. "Spahnie was best known for his Jimmy Durante beak and self-deprecating humor, not pinstripe charisma and a marriage to [Marilyn] Monroe," the *Washington Post*'s Thomas Boswell wrote. "Spahn was a decorated-for-bravery G.I. at the Battle of the Bulge who almost lost toes to frostbite before his career ever began. But his three seasons sacrificed to military service seldom got compared to Williams' tours as a jet pilot in two wars. Spahn also played his best years in understated Milwaukee, where a kid named Bud Selig cheered him, not in New York or Boston where the scribes from huge media markets could worship and adore."

In Buffalo, South District Council member James D. Griffin designated Warren Spahn Way to replace Cazenovia Parkway where it runs into Cazenovia Park, the site where Spahn pitched many a summer league game. On April 9, 2009, the Broken Arrow Youth Baseball facility in Spahn's longtime home was dedicated to him.

Spahn even earned a place in American culture. In one of the three *Naked Gun* movies, the three producers, all Milwaukee products, include Spahn's name in the credits, adding, "He's not in the film, but he's still our all-time favorite left-handed pitcher." And in 2009, Choc Beer Company's Spahnie 363 ale was introduced as the most recent attempt to honor—and profit from—a legendary athlete. Greg Spahn has the beer trademarked.

It would have been nice if Spahn had faded into the sunset amid happy memories. One pictures the scene late in *King Lear* in which Lear and his beloved daughter, Cordelia, who understands that true love is unconditional but not uncritical, have been captured by the French. All Lear wants is to be with Cordelia. Consoling her, he says in part:

> *So we'll live,*
> *And pray, and sing, and tell old tales, and laugh*
> *At gilded butterflies, and hear poor rogues*
> *Talk of court news; and we'll talk with them too —*
> *Who loses and who wins; who's in, who's out —*
> *And take upon us the mystery of things,*
> *As if we were God's spies; and we'll wear out*
> *In a walled prison, packs and sects of great ones*
> *That ebb and flow by the moon.*

But Spahn was sick of being rhapsodized for great performances in games he lost. "He never forgot a mistake," Selig said. Spahn couldn't let go of the bad

More Tireless Pitchers

The way things are going, baseball will never see another game in which both starting pitchers last 16 innings. There has been only one pitcher who did it since the Marichal-Spahn tilt. Gaylord Perry went 16 innings on September 1, 1967, but then he gave way to Frank Linzy, who pitched the final five innings of the Giants' 1–0 win against the Reds at Cincinnati's Crosley Field. Perry allowed 10 hits and two walks while fanning 12. The Reds used four pitchers.

Yankees Hall of Famer Catfish Hunter and California southpaw Frank Tanana faced off for 13 innings on August 27, 1976. In their scoreless duel, fastballer Tanana, 23, yielded seven hits and two walks while striking out 13. The craftier Hunter, 30, allowed 11 hits, four walks, and fanned eight. The Yankees scored five times in the 15th to win 5–0. Five days later, Tanana went nine innings and beat the Tigers 4–1 on six hits, no walks, and eight strikeouts en route to his best year: 19–10. He lasted another 17 seasons, reconstructed himself as a control pitcher after shoulder surgery in mid-career, and was 240–236 with a 3.66 ERA lifetime. In the best game of his career, Tanana, a junkballing 34-year-old for the Detroit Tigers, beat Jimmy Key and the Toronto Blue Jays 1–0 on October 4, 1987, to win the AL East title. Pitching five days after his 13-inning duel, Hunter lasted just 4⅓ innings in a loss and split his last six decisions. It's not clear if the 13-inning game contributed to his decline. Suffering from arm strain and diabetes, Hunter was a part-time pitcher for his final three seasons and went 224–166, with a 3.26 ERA overall.

On May 17, 1980, Oakland's Matt Keough pitched 14 innings for Oakland and Toronto's Dave Stieb went 12 innings when the Athletics beat the Blue Jays 4–2. Four times that year Oakland starters pitched 14 innings.

We're still waiting for another game in which both starting pitchers go as long as 13 innings. With today's emphasis on pitch counts—many managers are reluctant to allow a pitcher to exceed 100 pitches—don't hold your breath.

memories as his health declined, his activities decreased, and his spirit devolved into what Jack Kerouac called "the forlorn rags of growing old."

Those who remember him in his last, occasionally querulous years need to understand him in context. Anyone growing up during the Depression is indelibly marked by it. "He didn't buy lavish shoes or clothes," Greg Spahn said. "My dad threw away nothing—he was even a string saver. He kept all plumbing fixtures; you never know when you can use one. He kept all 363 balls from his wins, each with the opponent and score on it. I got a friend to crawl through a space in his house, and he found 31 bats."

One piece of memorabilia is pointedly missing from the Spahn estate: the last ball he threw to Willie Mays early on July 3, 1963. "That pitch probably bothered him more than any other he ever threw," Greg said. "For years he said that if he had one pitch he'd like to take back, that was it."

But the game established Spahn's greatness forever. There he was, the ageless marvel, astounding the fates and fans alike, matching wits and wisdom with the greatest young pitcher of his time. On July 2, 1963, Spahn and Marichal merged as mirrored pitchers, doppelgangers, future friends, and authors of baseball's greatest pitching duel. What a pity they'll never meet again, except in baseball heaven.

Appendix

WARREN SPAHN
(From BaseballProspectus.com)
Boldface added to show led league

YEAR	TEAM	W	L	SV	ERA	G	GS	TBF	IP
1942	BOS-N	0	0	0	5.74	4	2	79	15.7
1946	BOS-N	8	5	1	2.94	24	16	514	125.7
1947	BOS-N	21	10	3	**2.33**	40	35	1174	**289.7**
1948	BOS-N	15	12	1	3.71	36	35	1064	257.0
1949	BOS-N	21	14	0	3.07	38	**38**	1258	**302.3**
1950	BOS-N	21	17	1	3.16	41	**39**	1217	293.0
1951	BOS-N	22	14	0	2.98	39	36	1289	310.7
1952	BOS-N	14	19	3	2.98	40	35	1190	290.0
1953	MIL-N	**23**	7	3	**2.10**	35	32	1055	265.7
1954	MIL-N	21	12	3	3.14	39	34	1175	283.3
1955	MIL-N	17	14	1	3.26	39	32	1025	245.7
1956	MIL-N	20	11	3	2.78	39	35	1113	281.3
1957	MIL-N	21	11	3	2.69	39	35	1111	271.0
1958	MIL-N	22	11	1	3.07	38	36	1176	**290.0**
1959	MIL-N	21	15	0	2.96	40	36	1203	**292.0**
1960	MIL-N	21	10	2	3.50	40	33	1110	267.7
1961	MIL-N	21	13	0	**3.02**	38	34	1064	262.7
1962	MIL-N	18	14	0	3.04	34	34	1088	269.3
1963	MIL-N	23	7	0	2.60	33	33	1037	259.7
1964	MIL-N	6	13	4	5.29	38	25	759	173.7
1965	NY-N	4	12	0	4.36	20	19	543	126.0
1965	SF-N	3	4	0	3.39	16	11	303	71.7

	W	L	SV	ERA	G	GS	TBF	IP
CAREER	363	245	29	3.09	750	665	21547	5243.7

Winning percentage: .597 (led league with .667 in 1958)

H	R	ER	HR	BB	SO	HBP	IBB	WP	BK	CG	SHO
25	15	10	0	11	7	0	–	0	0	1	0
107	46	41	6	36	67	1	–	4	0	8	0
245	87	75	15	84	123	1	–	5	0	22	7
237	115	106	19	77	114	1	–	4	0	16	3
283	125	103	27	86	**151**	3	–	4	0	**25**	4
248	123	103	22	111	**191**	1	–	8	0	25	1
278	111	103	20	109	**164**	1	–	7	1	**26**	7
263	109	96	19	73	**183**	6	–	5	0	19	5
211	75	62	14	70	148	1	–	3	2	24	5
262	107	99	24	86	136	1	–	3	1	23	1
249	99	89	25	65	110	2	4	4	0	16	1
249	92	87	25	52	128	3	12	7	0	20	3
241	94	81	23	78	111	2	4	2	0	**18**	4
257	106	99	29	76	150	2	7	2	1	**23**	2
282	106	96	21	70	143	1	9	2	0	**21**	**4**
254	114	104	24	74	154	4	9	1	0	**18**	4
236	96	88	24	64	115	4	1	4	0	**21**	**4**
248	97	91	25	55	118	3	4	4	0	**22**	0
241	85	75	23	49	102	0	4	4	0	**22**	7
204	110	102	23	52	78	2	4	6	0	4	1
140	70	61	18	35	56	2	1	1	0	5	0
70	34	27	8	21	34	1	1	1	0	3	0

H	R	ER	HR	BB	SO	HBP	IBB	WP	BK	CG	SHO
4830	2016	1798	434	1434	2583	42	60	81	5	382	63

Juan Marichal
(From BaseballProspectus.com)
Boldface added to show led league

YEAR	TEAM	W	L	SV	ERA	G	GS	TBF	IP
1960	SF-N	6	2	0	2.66	11	11	328	81.3
1961	SF-N	13	10	0	3.89	29	27	769	185.0
1962	SF-N	18	11	1	3.36	37	36	1101	262.7
1963	SF-N	**25**	8	0	2.41	41	40	1270	321.3
1964	SF-N	21	8	0	2.48	33	33	1089	269.0
1965	SF-N	22	13	1	2.13	39	37	1153	295.3
1966	SF-N	25	6	0	2.23	37	36	1180	307.3
1967	SF-N	14	10	0	2.76	26	26	839	202.3
1968	SF-N	**26**	9	0	2.43	38	38	1307	**326.0**
1969	SF-N	21	11	0	**2.10**	37	36	1176	299.7
1970	SF-N	12	10	0	4.12	34	33	1035	242.7
1971	SF-N	18	11	0	2.94	37	37	1124	279.0
1972	SF-N	6	16	0	3.71	25	24	699	165.0
1973	SF-N	11	15	0	3.82	34	32	888	207.3
1974	BOS-A	5	1	0	4.87	11	9	244	57.3
1975	LA-N	0	1	0	13.50	2	2	34	6.0

CAREER	W	L	SV	ERA	G	GS	TBF	IP
	243	142	2	2.89	471	457	14236	3507.3

Winning percentage: .631 (led league with .806 in 1966)

H	R	ER	HR	BB	SO	HBP	IBB	WP	BK	CG	SHO
59	29	24	5	28	58	0	1	3	2	6	1
183	88	80	24	48	124	2	5	7	1	9	3
233	112	98	34	90	153	3	5	3	1	18	3
259	102	86	27	61	248	2	6	2	3	18	5
241	89	74	18	52	206	1	8	4	2	**22**	4
224	78	70	27	46	240	4	4	2	0	24	**10**
228	88	76	32	36	222	5	3	3	0	25	4
195	79	62	20	42	166	1	9	0	0	18	2
295	106	88	21	46	218	6	9	8	2	**30**	5
244	90	70	15	54	205	6	7	5	0	14	**8**
269	128	111	28	48	123	1	3	4	0	14	1
244	113	91	27	56	159	3	6	6	1	18	4
176	82	68	15	46	72	3	7	2	0	6	0
231	104	88	22	37	87	1	7	2	3	9	2
61	32	31	3	14	21	2	1	0	2	0	0
11	9	9	2	5	1	0	1	0	1	0	0

H	R	ER	HR	BB	SO	HBP	IBB	WP	BK	CG	SHO
3153	1329	1126	320	709	2303	40	82	51	20	244	52

Spahn vs. Marichal

(Compiled by Bill Deane)

Date	Score: SF-Mil	Marichal IP	ER	W-L	Spahn IP	ER	W-L
7/28/60	3–2	10 *	2	W	9.1 *	3	L
6/14/61	11–2	9 *	2	W	6	5	L
4/10/62	6–0	9 *	0	W	3.2	5	L
6/24/62	3–1	9 *	1	W	8 *	3	L
4/28/63	1–3	8	2	L	9 *	1	W
7/ 2/63	1–0	16 *	0	W	15.1 *	1	L
4/14/64	8–4	9 *	1*	W	7.1	6	L
	(7)	70	8	6–1	58.2	24	1–6
* Complete game		1.03 ERA			3.68 ERA		

Game Played on Tuesday, July 2, 1963 (N) at Candlestick Park

San Francisco Giants 1, Milwaukee Braves 0

(From Retrosheet.com)

	1	2	3	4	5	6	7	8	9	10	11	12	13	14	15	16	R	H	E
MIL N	0	0	0	0	0	0	0	0	0	0	0	0	0	0	0	0	0	8	1
SF N	0	0	0	0	0	0	0	0	0	0	0	0	0	0	0	1	1	9	1

BATTING

Milwaukee Braves	AB	R	H	RBI	BB	SO	PO	A
Maye lf	6	0	0	0	1	0	3	0
Bolling 2b	7	0	2	0	0	0	3	4
H. Aaron rf	6	0	0	0	1	1	3	0
Mathews 3b	2	0	0	0	0	2	0	0
Menke 3b	5	0	2	0	0	1	1	1
Larker 1b	5	0	0	0	2	0	14	4
Jones cf	5	0	1	0	0	2	7	0
Dillard ph,cf	1	0	0	0	0	1	3	0
Crandall c	6	0	2	0	0	0	5	0
McMillan ss	6	0	0	0	0	0	4	7
Spahn p	6	0	1	0	0	3	3	4
Totals	55	0	8	0	4	10	46	20

FIELDING -
E: Menke   (12).
BATTING -
2B: Spahn (3, off Marichal).
Team LOB: 11.
BASERUNNING -
SB: Maye (5,2nd base off Marichal/Bailey); Menke (1, 2nd base off Marichal/Bailey).
CS: Crandall (1, 2nd base by Marichal/Bailey).

San Francisco Giants	AB	R	H	RBI	BB	SO	PO	A
Kuenn 3b	7	0	1	0	0	0	5	2
Mays cf	6	1	1	1	1	1	3	1
McCovey lf	6	0	1	0	0	0	4	0
F. Alou rf	6	0	1	0	0	0	5	0
Cepeda 1b	6	0	2	0	0	0	15	1
Bailey c	6	0	1	0	0	0	12	1
Pagan ss	2	0	0	0	0	0	1	1
Davenport ph	1	0	0	0	0	0	0	0
Bowman ss	3	0	2	0	0	0	0	2
Hiller 2b	6	0	0	0	0	0	2	2
Marichal p	6	0	0	0	0	1	1	3
Totals	55	1	9	1	1	2	48	13

FIELDING -
E: Kuenn (5).
BATTING -
2B: Kuenn (6, off Spahn).
HR: Mays (15, 16th inning off Spahn 0 on 1 out).
IBB: Mays (2, by Spahn).
Team LOB: 9.
BASERUNNING -
SB: Cepeda (2, 2nd base off Spahn/Crandall).
PITCHING

Milwaukee Braves	IP	H	R	ER	BB	SO	HR	BFP
Spahn L (11-4)	15.1	9	1	1	1	2	1	56

IBB: Spahn (2, Mays).

San Francisco Giants	IP	H	R	ER	BB	SO	HR	BFP
Marichal W (13-3)	16	8	0	0	4	10	0	59

Umpires: HP - Ken Burkhart, 1B - Chris Pelekoudas, 2B - Frank Walsh, 3B - Jocko Conlan
Duration of Game: 4:10   **Attendance:** 15,921

Starting Lineups:

Milwaukee Braves	San Francisco Giants
1. Maye lf	Kuenn 3b
2. Bolling 2b	Mays cf
3. H. Aaron rf	McCovey lf
4. Mathews 3b	F. Alou rf
5. Larker 1b	Cepeda 1b
6. Jones cf	Bailey c
7. Crandall c	Pagan ss
8. McMillan ss	Hiller 2b
9. Spahn p	Marichal p

BRAVES 1ST: Maye popped to first; Bolling singled to left; H. Aaron popped to first in foul territory; Mathews struck out; 0 R, 1 H, 0 E, 1 LOB. Braves 0, Giants 0.

GIANTS 1ST: Kuenn popped to shortstop; Mays was called out on strikes; McCovey grounded out (first to pitcher); 0 R, 0 H, 0 E, 0 LOB. Braves 0, Giants 0.

BRAVES 2ND: Larker grounded out (third to first); Jones struck out; Crandall reached on an error by Kuenn (Crandall to second); McMillan flied out to center; 0 R, 0 H, 1 E, 1 LOB. Braves 0, Giants 0.

GIANTS 2ND: F. Alou flied out to left; Cepeda singled to center; Cepeda stole second; Bailey flied out to center (Cepeda to third); Pagan popped to catcher in foul territory; 0 R, 1 H, 0 E, 1 LOB. Braves 0, Giants 0.

BRAVES 3RD: Spahn grounded out (pitcher to first); Maye flied out to right; Bolling made an out to third; 0 R, 0 H, 0 E, 0 LOB. Braves 0, Giants 0.

GIANTS 3RD: Hiller grounded out (second to first); Marichal flied out to center; Kuenn grounded out (second to first); 0 R, 0 H, 0 E, 0 LOB. Braves 0, Giants 0.

BRAVES 4TH: H. Aaron flied out to left; Mathews struck out; Larker walked; Jones singled to left (Larker to second); Crandall singled to center [Jones to second, Larker out at home (center to catcher)]; 0 R, 2 H, 0 E, 2 LOB. Braves 0, Giants 0.

GIANTS 4TH: Menke replaced Mathews (playing 3B); Mays grounded out (shortstop to first); McCovey singled to right; F. Alou forced McCovey (shortstop to second); Cepeda popped to pitcher; 0 R, 1 H, 0 E, 1 LOB. Braves 0, Giants 0.

BRAVES 5TH: McMillan grounded out (shortstop to first); Spahn struck out; Maye walked; Maye stole second; Bolling lined to third; 0 R, 0 H, 0 E, 1 LOB. Braves 0, Giants 0.

GIANTS 5TH: Bailey grounded out (first unassisted); Pagan popped to shortstop; Hiller popped to second; 0 R, 0 H, 0 E, 0 LOB. Braves 0, Giants 0.

BRAVES 6TH: H. Aaron popped to catcher in foul territory; Menke singled to left; Menke stole second; Larker popped to second; Jones popped to third; 0 R, 1 H, 0 E, 1 LOB. Braves 0, Giants 0.

GIANTS 6TH: Marichal flied out to center; Kuenn flied out to right; Mays flied out to right; 0 R, 0 H, 0 E, 0 LOB. Braves 0, Giants 0.

BRAVES 7TH: Crandall singled; Crandall was caught stealing second (catcher to shortstop); McMillan popped to second; Spahn doubled to right; Maye grounded out (first to pitcher); 0 R, 2 H, 0 E, 1 LOB. Braves 0, Giants 0.

GIANTS 7TH: McCovey flied out to center; F. Alou grounded out (shortstop to first); Cepeda singled to left; Bailey singled to right (Cepeda to second); Davenport batted for Pagan; Davenport flied out to center; 0 R, 2 H, 0 E, 2 LOB. Braves 0, Giants 0.

BRAVES 8TH: Bowman replaced Davenport (playing SS); Bolling popped to third in foul territory; H. Aaron walked; Menke grounded out (shortstop to first) (H. Aaron to second); Larker flied out to left; 0 R, 0 H, 0 E, 1 LOB. Braves 0, Giants 0.

GIANTS 8TH: Hiller grounded out (pitcher to first); Marichal grounded out (third to first); Kuenn popped to catcher in foul territory; 0 R, 0 H, 0 E, 0 LOB. Braves 0, Giants 0.

BRAVES 9TH: Jones flied out to center; Crandall flied out to left; McMillan grounded out (second to first); 0 R, 0 H, 0 E, 0 LOB. Braves 0, Giants 0.

GIANTS 9TH: Mays grounded out (pitcher to shortstop to first); McCovey grounded out (first to pitcher); F. Alou singled; Cepeda popped to third; 0 R, 1 H, 0 E, 1 LOB. Braves 0, Giants 0.

BRAVES 10TH: Spahn struck out; Maye grounded out (first unassisted); Bolling grounded out (shortstop to first); 0 R, 0 H, 0 E, 0 LOB. Braves 0, Giants 0.

GIANTS 10TH: Bailey grounded out (second to first); On a bunt Bowman singled; Hiller forced Bowman (first to shortstop); Marichal forced Hiller (shortstop to second); 0 R, 1 H, 0 E, 1 LOB. Braves 0, Giants 0.

BRAVES 11TH: H. Aaron struck out; Menke flied out to left; Larker grounded out (second to first); 0 R, 0 H, 0 E, 0 LOB. Braves 0, Giants 0.

GIANTS 11TH: Kuenn grounded out (shortstop to first); Mays flied out to left; McCovey grounded out (pitcher to first); 0 R, 0 H, 0 E, 0 LOB. Braves 0, Giants 0.

BRAVES 12TH: Jones struck out; Crandall flied out to right; McMillan grounded out (third to first); 0 R, 0 H, 0 E, 0 LOB. Braves 0, Giants 0.

GIANTS 12TH: F. Alou flied out to center; Cepeda grounded out (shortstop to first); Bailey grounded out (first unassisted); 0 R, 0 H, 0 E, 0 LOB. Braves 0, Giants 0.

BRAVES 13TH: Spahn struck out; Maye flied out to right; Bolling singled to right; H. Aaron popped to first in foul territory; 0 R, 1 H, 0 E, 1 LOB. Braves 0, Giants 0.

GIANTS 13TH: Bowman singled; Bowman was picked off first (pitcher to first to shortstop); Hiller grounded out (second to first); Marichal flied out to center; 0 R, 1 H, 0 E, 0 LOB. Braves 0, Giants 0.

BRAVES 14TH: Menke struck out; Larker walked; Dillard batted for Jones; Dillard struck out; Crandall grounded out (pitcher to first); 0 R, 0 H, 0 E, 1 LOB. Braves 0, Giants 0.

GIANTS 14TH: Dillard stayed in game (playing CF); Kuenn doubled to center; Mays was walked intentionally; McCovey popped to catcher in foul territory; F. Alou flied out to center; Cepeda reached on an error by Menke (Mays to second, Kuenn to third); Bailey flied out to center; 0 R, 1 H, 1 E, 3 LOB. Braves 0, Giants 0.

BRAVES 15TH: McMillan popped to first in foul territory; Spahn popped to third in foul territory; Maye flied out to right; 0 R, 0 H, 0 E, 0 LOB. Braves 0, Giants 0.

GIANTS 15TH: Bowman flied out to right; Hiller flied out to left; Marichal struck out; 0 R, 0 H, 0 E, 0 LOB. Braves 0, Giants 0.

BRAVES 16TH: Bolling flied out to right; H. Aaron flied out to center; Menke singled to left; Larker grounded out (pitcher to first); 0 R, 1 H, 0 E, 1 LOB. Braves 0, Giants 0.

GIANTS 16TH: Kuenn flied out to center; Mays homered; 1 R, 1 H, 0 E, 0 LOB. Braves 0, Giants 1.

Final Totals	R	H	E	LOB
Braves	0	8	1	11
Giants	1	9	1	9

NOTES

Chapter 1: High-Kicking To Glory

1. In another version of the story, Feeney visited the site in the afternoon and asked, "Does it always blow like this?" The construction worker answered, "Only in the afternoon."

2. Alex Bowman, a former Brandeis baseball player who lives in San Francisco, said that Candlestick fog looked like "rain falling upward." Some fly balls hit into the fog just disappeared.

3. The writers called him Lew, but he preferred Lou and that spelling is on his gravestone.

4. They weren't the only ones who emphasized control. Satchel Paige said, "Just take the ball and throw it where you want to. Throw strikes. Home plate don't move."

5. Among current pitchers, only the Rockies' Ubaldo Jiménez has a repertoire reminiscent of Marichal's.

Chapter 2: Searching for Juan in Cooperstown

6. Thanks to overspending on talent, professional baseball in the DR stopped after the 1937 season and didn't resume until 1951.

Chapter 3: Searching for Spahn in Buffalo

7. In 1985, Billoni had a promotion for each home game, including Fridaynightbash, Dad's the Greatest Day, and a water-sliding race between a 350-pound bat boy called The Butcher and a seal on Niagara Falls

Aquarium Night. Among his stadium vendors were a tuxedoed dancing beer hawker called the Earl of Bud, a Conehead, and a Zorro.

8. That failure evidently ate at him for years because in 1950, Billy Meyers, who scouted and signed him for Boston, wrote South Park principal Frank P. Regan asking how Spahn could get his degree. Regan replied:

    "Dear Bill:

    "As you requested Saturday evening, I examined the record of Warren E. Spahn, and I find that he would have to pass Regents examinations in English Four Years and Business Law to be eligible for graduation. However, I am enclosing an application for a high school equivalency diploma which will be issued to him if he secures satisfactory ratings in the General Educational Development Tests. On the back of this application is a complete explanation of how he should go about securing this equivalency diploma.

    "In my opinion, he would have no difficulty in passing the GED Tests. He could fill out this application in the presence of any high school principal in New York State, and I offer as a suggestion that he take care of it some time when the Braves are playing the Giants in New York City.

    "Very truly yours,

    "Principal Frank P. Regan"

    It is not known whether Spahn ever took him up on the offer.

Chapter 4: Big League in the Bush Leagues

9. Later explaining that there was a runner on second who could see the catcher's signals, Spahn said he decided to cross him up by throwing something other than a brushback pitch when the brushback was called for.

10. Brissie is the subject of an extraordinary book, *The Corporal Was a Pitcher: The Courage of Lou Brissie* by Ira Berkow (Triumph Books, 2009).

Chapter 5: From the Sticks to the Series

11. What couldn't Mays do? Players rarely qualify for two all-decade teams, but Mays belongs on the '50s and '60s rosters. A young pitcher named Jerry Hinsley once knocked down Mays and then yielded a triple to him. "They didn't tell me what to throw him on the second pitch," Hinsley said.

12. "Satchel [Paige], Warren Spahn, Juan Marichal, and Jim Kaat were probably the greatest ever at destroying a hitter's timing."—*Bill James Baseball Abstract*, 2004

13. "There has been only one manager, and his name is John McGraw."—Hall of Fame manager Connie Mack

14. Dark was known as the "Swamp Fox" for watering the baselines at Candlestick Park to prevent the Dodgers from stealing, and as the "Mad Scientist" for his reliance on percentages and the pluses and minuses he created for players' performance late in games. His sophisticated thinking went way back. With Cleveland runners on first and second in the second game of the 1954 World Series, Dark, then the Giants shortstop, fielded Rudy Regalado's one-out grounder and aimed his throw at the center of second baseman Dave Williams' chest. Dark missed by about a foot, and Williams' relay to first was too late for a double play. Dark had nightmare visions of the next batter, Vic Wertz, homering to put the Indians up 4–3.

As it happened, Wertz was retired and the Giants won 3–1. Nonetheless, Dark remained obsessed with the play the next spring. "I gave Dave the ball on his outside shoulder instead of his chest," he told Joe King of the *New York World-Telegram*. "It made all the difference between a double play he could have made and one he didn't. His throwing rhythm was ruined. The absolutely essential part of the double play is the first throw. The play is made or lost there. The target is about the size of the glove on the chest of the pivot man. He is a machine adjusted to receive the throw there. You cannot be far off target and give him much chance on a close play. When a pivot man throws wild to first, he goes down for an error, but in most cases the error was caused by a poor first throw, which is not penalized."

Chapter 6: Something in Reserve?

15. The Braves also had the inside track on signing Willie Mays, but—*o rage, o desespoir!*—the times wouldn't permit it. James S. Hirsch writes in *Willie Mays: The Life, The Legend* that "bringing in two Negroes in one year could be seen as excessive."

16. Spahn was *The Sporting News*'s National League Pitcher of the Year in 1953, 1957–58, and 1961, and its Major League Pitcher of the Year in 1961.

17. Asked to name the three most evil figures of the 20th century, New York writers Pete Hamill and Jack Newfield both cited Hitler, Stalin, and Dodgers owner Walter O'Malley.

18. The late historian Fred Lieb wrote, "Even though he lost his third game (the sixth of the series, which the Yankees won 4–3 in 10 innings), he will

always be regarded as the standout player of the series. Warren won the first game over Whitey Ford and Ryne Duren in a fine 10-inning performance; he pitched a brilliant two-hit shutout over Ford in the fourth, and hurled almost as brilliantly in the sixth, though losing. In addition, he had four hits in the series and drove in two important runs."

19. Like Marichal, Spahn wasn't obsessed with strikeouts. "What a pushover pitching would be if every batter hit the first pitch," he told *Sport's* Al Hirshberg. "Why, you could finish a ball game with 27 pitches. But when you have to strike guys out, you have to throw an absolute minimum of three to each man, and between called balls and two-strike fouls, you can pile up a lot more." Sandy Koufax said something similar. "I became a good pitcher when I stopped trying to make them miss the ball and started trying to make them hit it." What all these men had in common was more than wisdom—they were on the side of the angels. As Crash Davis said in the movie *Bull Durham*, "Relax, all right? Don't try to strike everybody out. Strikeouts are boring! Besides that, they're fascist. Throw some ground balls—it's more democratic."

20. You'd think his overall winter ball record of 36–22 with a 1.87 ERA and 32 complete games would have been enough to satisfy his countrymen.

Chapter 7: Denouement

21. Braves right-hander Gene Conley recalled, "Spahn hated to miss a turn. He expected to pitch every fourth day no matter what. If your turn was rained out and he was due the next day, then you sat it out and he pitched. I remember one time it didn't work out that way and they started me and held Spahn back a day. He didn't like that at all. I heard he went up to the front office and got it squared away. He didn't want to miss a turn. And I'm not being critical of him; to the contrary, I think his attitude was great."

Chapter 8: Winding Down with Juan

22. The linkage of Spahn and Marichal is no accident. Since 1950, Spahn had the most wins over a selective 10-year period (205 in 1954–63) with Marichal second (202 in 1962–71). In calling Sandy Koufax the best and most dominant pitcher he faced, left-hander Jim Kaat said Koufax edged Spahn, Marichal, Bob Gibson, Tom Seaver, and Steve Carlton (*Baseball Digest*, August 2005). Another left-hander, Bill Lee, said Spahn, Marichal,

Koufax, and Gibson were the only players he'd pay to watch (*Baseball Digest*, March-April 2006).

23. Next in line were Gibson (164), Don Drysdale (158), and Jim Bunning (150).

24. Ahead of Marichal were Whitey Ford (.690), Lefty Grove (.680), Christy Mathewson (.665), Three Finger Brown (.648), Roger Clemens (.647 in the twentieth century alone), Pete Alexander (.642), and Jim Palmer (.638).

25. "I loved to follow him in the rotation because the hitters would be all screwed up after they'd come up against him," Perry said years later.

26. The Giants bid only $15,000, well under what they knew they'd need to be competitive, for Dean Chance, a future Cy Young Award winner with the Los Angeles Angels. Owner Horace Stoneham didn't have especially deep pockets, and he rarely reached into them.

27. Up to a point. Through 2009, Vicente Padilla had hit 97 batters in the 221 games he'd pitched since becoming a starter. When the Rangers' Padilla hit Mark Teixeira twice on June 2, 2009, blowing a lead and eventually losing the game, the team put him on waivers. Unsurprisingly, Padilla wasn't claimed by another club. He avoided hitting batters for eight games, then threw a gopher ball to Scott Hairston and hit Kurt Suzuki two batters later on August 5, whereupon the Rangers released him. He was "regarded as a disruptive clubhouse presence," according to *Sports Illustrated*. Acquired by the Dodgers later in the season, he went 4–0, didn't hit a batter, and was signed to a contract extension with L.A., possibly a reformed man.

28. "Koufax was not alone in this aversion to committing potential manslaughter; it was shared by other members of the pitching elite, most notably Bob Feller, Tom Seaver, and Robin Roberts."—Donald Honig, *The Greatest Pitchers of All Time*.

29. Marichal said he hit Roseboro only once. Other accounts cite three glancing blows. There was only one gash on Roseboro's head.

30. In *The Dark Side of the Diamond: Gambling, Violence, Drugs and Alcoholism in the National Pastime*, author Roger I. Abrams gives prominent mention to the Marichal-Roseboro incident and the Mays-Chapman tragedy in the chapter "Violence on the Field." Despite beanballs, fighting, and Ty Cobb's spikes-high sliding style in the twentieth century, baseball was actually more violent in the nineteenth.

31. Marichal initially was scared of throwing a pitch anywhere near a batter. When Mays was decked on Opening Day, Marichal retaliated by throwing

softly over a batter's head. Mays and Marichal were supposed to appear together on a postgame radio interview with a Giants announcer. "Fuck it," Mays said, declining to be interviewed with his teammate. "Use Marichal."

32. Another strong Latino candidate, Roberto Alomar, fell eight votes short in 2010, his first year of eligibility, perhaps for a similar reason. Alomar once spat in the face of umpire John Hirschbeck during an argument over a called strike three and was suspended five games, but Hirschbeck forgave him and campaigned for his election. Though he may have been the greatest all-around second baseman ever, Alomar undoubtedly drew the wrath of some voters.

33. When Marichal's late father heard stories of a local player named Martínez and nicknamed *El Gallo* (the Rooster), he'd shout "*¡Ese es mí gallo!*"— "That's my rooster!"

Chapter 9: Winding Up With Warren

34. In 1946, Bob Feller signed a $45,000 contract but earned $148,000 by satisfying clauses for extra pay based on wins and attendance.

35. Other winners were Jim Brown and Chuck Bednarik (football), Bob Cousy (basketball), Rocky Marciano (boxing), Maurice Richard (hockey), Arnold Palmer (golf), Don Carter (bowling), Eddie Arcaro (horse racing), Del Miller (harness racing), and Roger Ward (auto racing).

BIBLIOGRAPHY

Aaron, Hank, with Lonnie Wheeler. *If I Had a Hammer: The Hank Aaron Story.* New York: Harper Perennial, 2007.

Abrams, Roger I. *The Dark Side of the Diamond: Gambling, Violence, Drugs and Alcoholism in the National Pastime.* Burlington, MA: Rounder Books, 2007.

Allen, Thomas E. *If They Hadn't Gone: How World War II Affected Major League Baseball.* Springfield: Southwest Missouri State University, 2004.

Angell, Roger. *Once More Around the Park: A Baseball Reader.* New York: Ballantine Books, 1991.

Barra, Allen. *Clearing the Bases: The Greatest Baseball Debates of the Last Century.* New York: St. Martin's Press, 2000.

Barra, Allen. *Yogi Berra: Eternal Yankee.* New York: W.W. Norton & Company, 2009.

Bedingfield, Gary. *Baseball in World War II Europe.* Charleston, SC: Arcadia Publishing, 2000.

Berkow, Ira. *The Corporal Was a Pitcher: The Courage of Lou Brissie.* Chicago: Triumph Books, 2009.

Bjarkman, Peter C. *Warren Spahn.* New York: Chelsea House, 1995.

Brosnan, Jim. *Pennant Race.* Chicago: Ivan R. Dee, 2004.

Buckley, James Jr., and Phil Pepe. *Unhittable: Reliving the Magic and Drama of Baseball's Best-Pitched Games.* Chicago: Triumph Books, 2004.

Buege, Bob. *The Milwaukee Braves: A Baseball's Eulogy.* Milwaukee, WI: Douglas American Sports Publications, 1988.

Burgos, Adrian, Jr. *Playing America's Game: Baseball, Latinos, and the Color Line.* Berkeley: University of California Press, 2007.

Cepeda, Orlando, with Herb Fagen. *Baby Bull: From Hardball to Hard Time.* Lanham, MD: Taylor Trade Publishing, 1998.

Cohen, Richard M., and David F. Neft, *The World Series.* New York: MacMillan, 1986.

Cruz, Hector J. *Juan Marichal: La Historia de Su Vida.* Santo Domingo: Alfa & Omega, 1983.

Cutter, Robert A. *Warren Spahn.* New York: JKW Sports Publications, 1964.

Darling, Ron, with Daniel Paisner. *The Complete Game: Reflections on Baseball, Pitching, and Life on the Mound.* New York: Alfred A. Knopf, 2009.

Devaney, John. *Juan Marichal: Mister Strikeout.* New York: Putnam, 1970.

Dickey, Glenn. *The San Francisco Giants: A 40-Year Anniversary.* San Francisco: Woodland Press, 1997.

Dickson, Paul, ed. *Baseball's Greatest Quotations: From Walt Whitman to Dizzy Dean, Garrison Keillor to Woody Allen, a Treasury of Over 5,000 Quotations, plus Historical Lore, Notes, and Illustrations.* New York: Edward Burlingame Books, 1991.

Dickson, Paul, ed. *The Dickson Baseball Dictionary: 5,000 Terms Used by Players, the Press, and People Who Love the Game.* New York: Facts on File, 1989.

Echevarría, Roberto Gonzáles. *The Pride of Havana: A History of Cuban Baseball.* New York: Oxford University Press, 1999.

Einstein, Charles. *Willie's Time: Baseball's Golden Age.* Carbondale, IL: Southern Illinois University Press, 1979.

Goodman, Michael E. *San Francisco Giants/NL West.* Creative Education, 1992.

Harrison, Lawrence E. *Underdevelopment Is a State of Mind: The Latin American Case.* Cambridge, MA: The Center for International Affairs at Harvard University and University Press of America, 1985.

Hernandez, Keith, with Mike Bryan. *Pure Baseball: Pitch by Pitch for the Advanced Fan.* New York: Harper Collins, 1994.

Honig, Donald. *The Greatest Pitchers of All Time.* New York: Crown, 1988.

James, Bill. *The Bill James Historical Baseball Abstract.* New York: Villard Books, 1986.

Johnson, Richard A. *Images of America: Boston Braves.* Charleston, SC: Arcadia Publishing, 2001.

Kaese, Harold. *The Boston Braves 1871-1953.* Boston: Northeastern University Press, 2004.

Kahn, Roger. *The Head Game: Baseball Seen from the Pitcher's Mound.* New York: Harcourt, 2000.

Kalb, Elliott. *Who's Better, Who's Best in Baseball? "Mr. Stats" Sets the Record Straight on the Top 75 Players of All Time.* New York: McGraw-Hill, 2005.

Kaplan, Jim. *Baseball's Great Dynasties: The Giants.* New York: Gallery Books, 1991.

Kerrane, Kevin. *The Hurlers.* Alexandria, VA: Redefinition, 1989.

Klima, John. *Pitched Battle: 35 of Baseball's Greatest Duels from the Mound.* Jefferson, NC: McFarland, 2002.

Leavy, Jane. *Sandy Koufax: A Lefty's Legacy.* New York: HarperCollins, 2002.

Lowry, Philip J. *Green Cathedrals: The Ultimate Celebration of Major League and Negro League Ballparks.* New York: Walker & Company, 2006.

Marichal, Juan, with Charles Einstein. *A Pitcher's Story.* New York: Doubleday, 1966.

Mathews, Eddie, and Bob Broeg. *Eddie Mathews and the National Pastime.* Milwaukee, WI: Douglas American Sports Publications, 1994.

McCarver, Tim, with Danny Peary. *Tim McCarver's Baseball for Brain Surgeons and Other Fans: Understanding and Interpreting the Game So You Can Watch It Like a Pro.* New York: Villard, 1998.

Musial, Stan, as told to Bob Broeg. *Stan Musial: "The Man's" Own Story.* New York: Doubleday, 1964.

Nowlin, Bill, ed. *Spahn, Sain and Teddy Ballgame: Baseball's (Almost) Perfect Summer of 1948.* Burlington, MA: Rounder Books, 2008.

Okrent, Daniel, and Harris Lewine, eds. *The Ultimate Baseball Book.* Worthington, MA: The Hilltown Press, 1979.

Parrott, John B. *The Promise: A Baseball Odyssey.* Avoca, PA: Proteus's Compass Publishers, 2003.

Plimpton, George. *Out of My League.* New York: Harper & Row, 1961.

Porter, David L., ed. *Biographical Dictionary of American Sports: Baseball.* Westport, CT: Greenwood Press, 1987.

Regalado, Damuel O. *Viva Baseball! Latin Major Leaguers and Their Special Hunger.* Champaign, IL: University of Illinois Press, 1998.

Ritter, Lawrence, and Donald Honig. *The Image of Their Greatness: An Illustrated History of Baseball from 1900 to the Present,* third revised and updated edition. New York: Crown Trade Paperbacks, 1992.

Ruck, Rob. *The Tropic of Baseball: Baseball in the Dominican Republic.* Lincoln, NE: Bison Books, 1999.

Schlossberg, Dan. *The Baseball Catalogue. Millennium Edition.* Middle Village, NY: Jonathan David Publishers, 2000.

Schott, Tom, and Nick Peters. *The Giants Encyclopedia.* Champaign IL: Sports Publishing Inc., 2003.

Sehnert, Chris W. *San Francisco Giants.* Edina, MN: Abdo & Daughters, 1997.

Silverman, Al. *Warren Spahn: Immortal Southpaw.* New York: Bartholomew House, 1961.

Staten, Vince. *Why Is the Foul Pole Fair? Answers to 101 of the Most Perplexing Baseball Questions.* New York: Simon & Schuster, 2003.

Stein, Fred, and Nick Peters. *Giants Diary: A Century of Giants Baseball in New York and San Francisco.* Berkeley: North Atlantic Books, 1987.

Thorn, John, Pete Palmer, Michael Gershman, and David Pietrusza, eds. *Total Baseball: Fifth Edition.* New York: Viking/Penguin Books, 1997.

Valdez, Dr. Tirso. *Notas Acerca del Béisbol Domicano del Pasado y del Presente.* Ciudad Trujillo, Dominican Republic: Editorial del Caribe, 1958.

Violanti, Anthony. *Miracle in Buffalo: How the Dream of Baseball Revived a City.* New York: St. Martins, 1991.

Voigt, David Quentin. *American Baseball, Volume III: From Postwar Expansion to the Electronic Age.* State College, PA: The Pennsylvania State University Press, 1983.

Wallace, Joseph, Neil Hamilton, and Marty Appel. *Baseball: 100 Classic Moments in the History of the Game.* New York: Dorling Kindersley, 2000.

Wendel, Tim, and José Luis Villegas. *Far from Home: Latino Baseball Players in America.* Washington D.C.: National Geographic Society, 2009.

Westcott, Rich. *Splendor on the Diamond: Interviews with 35 Stars of Baseball Past.* Gainsville, FL: University of Florida Press, 2000.

Will, George. *Men at Work: The Craft of Baseball.* New York: Macmillan, 1990.

Wisnia, Saul. *The Jimmy Fund of Dana-Farber Cancer Institute.* Charleston, SC: Arcadia Publishing, 2002.

Many newspapers were consulted in the making of this book, including the *Boston Globe*, the *Springfield Union*, the *New York Times*, the *New York Daily News*, the *New York Post*, the *Buffalo Evening News*, the *Buffalo Courier-Express*, the *Milwaukee Journal*, the *Washington Post*, the *Daily Oklahoman*, the *Tulsa Daily World*, the *San Francisco Chronicle*, the *San Francisco Examiner and* the *St. Louis Post-Dispatch*.

Among the magazines used were *Life, Time, Sport, Sports Illustrated, The Sporting News, The New Yorker, The National Pastime, The Baseball Research Journal* and *Baseball Digest*.

The author also made frequent use of websites, especially retrosheet.com and baseball-reference.com—and blogs, Billy-Ball.com in particular.

INDEX

Two Giants greats—Carl Hubbell (left) and Juan Marichal—celebrate Juan's superb effort on July 2, 1963. Exactly 30 years earlier, Hubbell went 18 innings to beat the Cardinals. (Photo courtesy San Francisco History Center, San Francisco Public Library)

Warren Spahn (left) and Johnny Sain pitched the 1948 Boston Braves to a National League pennant, inspiring poetry that was shortened in the public imagination to "Spahn and Sain and pray for rain." Spahn disliked the phrase because he felt it ignored contributions by other teammates. (Photo courtesy National Baseball Hall of Fame Library, Cooperstown, N.Y.)

Despite enough turmoil in the Giants clubhouse to fill a novel, Juan Marichal kept a happy face most of the time. In fact, one of his nicknames was "Laughing Boy." (Photo courtesy National Baseball Hall of Fame Library, Cooperstown, N.Y.)

Warren Spahn (left) and Juan Marichal were linked in more ways than their 1963 marathon. With Spahn kicking high from the left side and Marichal from the right, they looked like virtual bookends. There were differences in their deliveries—Spahn came over the top, Marichal from many different angles—but they resulted in the same bewildered hitter.

Spahn presented an annual Warren Spahn Award for the best left-handed pitcher in the majors. Randy Johnson was the recipient in this case. Spahn's 363 career wins, the most by any southpaw, topped other storied pitchers like Sandy Koufax, Carl Hubbell, and Steve Carlton. (Photo courtesy National Baseball Hall of Fame Library, Cooperstown, N.Y.)

In his last uniformed trip to his hometown of Buffalo, New York—here playing in the National Old-Timers Classic—Warren Spahn acknowledged the fans' applause for his lifetime of achievement. Despite many happy childhood memories in Buffalo, Spahn moved to his wife's state of Oklahoma early in his career. (Photo courtesy Greg Spahn)

Nothing in 2010 made Juan Marichal smile more than his Giants winning their first World Series title in 56 years. Playing for the National League champion Giants in 1962, he was injured in Game 4 and watched from the dugout while his teammates lost a heartbreaking seven-game Series to the Yankees. (Photo courtesy National Baseball Hall of Fame Library, Cooperstown, N.Y.)